Managing
Incompetence

Managing Incompetence

William P. Anthony

amacom

A Division of American Management Associations

Library of Congress Cataloging in Publication Data

Anthony, William P.
    Managing incompetence.

    Bibliography: p.
    Includes index.
        1.   Organizational effectiveness.   2.   Management.
I. Title.
HD58.9.A55   658.4'09   81-66226
ISBN 0-8144-5672-3   AACR2

First Printing

Preface

Look around you. How many truly competent people do you see at work? How many competent managers, engineers, accountants, salespersons, and secretaries can you identify? Most managers work in organizations—be they business, government, educational, or civic—that have their full share of incompetent people. How do effective managers get their job done despite this fact? How can you protect yourself from the incompetence of others?

Any manager can perform well if surrounded by competent superiors, subordinates, and peer managers. Managerial work is much easier when competent engineers, salespersons, accountants, and personnel specialists are available, ready and willing to help. But how many managers face this situation? The true test of a manager is the ability to be successful *in spite of* the incompetence of the people with whom he or she must work.

Many books and articles have been written on management effectiveness. Most of them deal with how to get more out of subordinates—that is, how to get subordinates to perform well. But not much has been written on how to deal with incompetent fellow employees. It is these people on whom managers must often depend for success.

Furthermore, it seems to me that what has been said about achieving management effectiveness assumes that the manager basically has competent people to work with, that all he needs to do is to fine-tune them. I am not so sure that this is the prevailing situation today. Therefore, what is needed is a book that helps managers work with *incompetent* people. That is the purpose of this book.

I have tried to make the book lively, interesting, and concise. I have also tried not to clutter it with a lot of academic mumbo-jumbo, but I have included an annotated bibliography for those who wish to pursue in-depth analysis of the concepts.

The book is a result of many consulting experiences I've had over the past 12 years. I've noticed how difficult it is for managers to apply many of the basic management concepts, an observation that has led me to believe that we all have to deal with the barrier of incompetence, even though some of us see more of it than others. In this book I've tried to present solid, practical advice that is well grounded in sound management theory and research, but I have also presented and analyzed examples in each chapter and included cases and exercises based upon actual situations at the end of the book. I hope I have struck a happy balance between the cookbook and the ivory-tower approaches.

Many people have assisted me in the book's preparation. I'd especially like to thank Ms. Diane Dyer, who typed the entire manuscript. My father, Philip Anthony, helped me formulate the idea for the book and provided many insights. Finally, I appreciate the various concepts and case examples that have been shared with me by many managers and other professionals in organizations over the years. Of course, I've changed names and locations in the examples and cases in order to protect both the innocent and the guilty.

We'll never completely overcome the problem of incompetence in organizations, but this book is at least a step in the right direction.

William P. Anthony

Contents

1

Manage Them Before They Manage You

One simple fact of life in organizations today is this: If competent people do not manage situations, then incompetent people will. Incompetence always rises to dominate the situation. It forces competent managers to devote their time and effort to nonproductive work, with the result that competent managers become slaves to incompetent people. They allow themselves to be pulled into situations where they must work harder, faster, and with greater difficulty because of the mistakes made by incompetent people.

It should not be this way and it need not be so. Managers must manage incompetence rather than be managed by it. If they do not manage it, they *will* be managed by it. Ignoring incompetence does not make it go away, and making excuses for incompetent people does not correct the situation. Incompetence exists in all organizations to one degree or another and must be managed. Managers should approach the issue of incompetence with the same vigor and resolution they bring to bear on any other problem they face in their management roles.

In this book we review a number of actions managers should take in order to manage incompetence. We will examine some tried and true methods and also some newer, more radical methods. The theme of this book bears repeating: If managers do not manage and control incompetence, it will manage and control them and their organizations. It simply will not disappear without any action. It is an issue to be faced head-on in a no-nonsense fashion. This is true in *all* types of organizations—government, business, churches, trade associations, whatever. Unfortunately, incompetence exists in all of them—it is not just the province of government, as we often believe.

Incompetent people are great consumers of time. They make mistakes that others must correct. They work slowly and miss deadlines, which holds up other people. They can't solve problems themselves so they are constantly asking advice. They *will* manage your time if you let them.

Who Are These People, Anyway?

Incompetent people are people who simply cannot get the job done right and on time. They lack the skills, interests, aptitudes, ability, or motivation in some combination to properly perform their jobs. They exist in every organization at just about every level, from supervisor to chief executive office and board member, and in every occupation, from accountants, engineers, secretaries, lawyers, professors, teachers, maintenance workers, waiters, and doctors, to carpenters.

They exist in all sizes of organizations, from the very small to the very large, and in all industries—steel, rubber, glass, paper, plastics, shipping, autos, energy, and every other. They are in the service industries of health delivery, social work, education, legal services, consulting—in fact, it is virtually impossible to avoid them. We cannot avoid them, therefore we must manage them.

Some managers believe that we cannot do anything about these people. Consider this manager's attitude.

WHO'S INCOMPETENT?

I'm not sure you can really tell if someone is incompetent. We all have our bad days from time to time. Also, it's through no fault of their own that most managers have difficulty. Usually they work for a disorganized superior or they have weak subordinates who make the manager look bad. Budgets are cut, the economy turns sour, key people leave—all of these cause people to look bad. It's not their fault; it's the environment in which they work.

> The good Lord set definite limits on man's wisdom, but set no limits on his stupidity—and that's just not fair!
>
> *Konrad Adenauer*

Thus, blaming an individual manager for being incompetent really isn't fair. Rather, the reason for the unit's poor performance must be diagnosed and dealt with. Blaming the manager is nothing but an easy way out. The manager is a convenient scapegoat. You can call the manager incompetent and fire the person, but unless you deal with these other problems, it won't have any effect. It's like football coaches and baseball managers who are fired after a bad season, usually with little effect. It's simply a move to placate the owners, alumni, and fans. The coach is a scapegoat. This same action happens with managers every day.

No, I don't believe you can really tell whether a manager is incompetent. And if you do find one who is, I don't think you can do much about it.

Analysis

Do you agree? Is incompetence caused more by the situation the person faces than by the person? Are managers sometimes used as a scapegoat?

That attitude expresses the philosophy of environmental determinism, which states that the environment in which a manager manages determines effectiveness and that the structuring of this environment is largely beyond the manager's control. This philosophy implies that managers cannot take control of their own actions and that they are victims of the system, pushed along by events. Thus, it logically follows that a manager cannot be held personally accountable for ineffective performance.

This philosophy neglects the inherent role of managers in making and carrying out decisions. It also ignores personal accountability. While there are often factors in the work environment that make effective performance difficult, environmental determinism absolves managers of the responsibility to manage, control, and influence these factors. The central role and purpose of managers ceases to exist.

Certainly a diagnosis of the job environment is necessary when managing incompetence. But we must go beyond this and examine the manager's effectiveness in managing that environment. Managers who cannot manage it are themselves incompetent and must be developed, transferred, or terminated.

Why Are There So Many Incompetent People?

Incompetent people exist for a number of reasons. First there is the issue of *entitlement*. People today feel entitled to a whole host of privileges and opportunities, regardless of whether they are qualified for them. They demand them as a matter of right, not because they have earned them. They want their equal share whether they are entitled or not. They want to run a race and then have all the runners receive the gold medal. The idea of entitlement completely negates merit and performance as the bases for rewards in organizations. Under this philosophy people get financial raises because of years of service, not because of performance. Promotion is determined by tenure, not ability to perform. If bonuses are available, everyone should share in them equally.

The second reason why incompetent people are so numerous today is related to the question of entitlement. It is a confusion between *equality* and *equal opportunity*. People are not equal. We have differing abilities, skills, interests, and aspirations. We perform at different levels. While we all should have equal opportunity to demonstrate our skills and abilities, this does not mean our performance or output will be equal. Equal opportunity does not mean equal performance.

The third reason is the culture of *narcissism* that pervades our society today. The seventies have truly been the "Me Decade," as writer Tom Wolfe labeled it. People are more concerned about watching out for themselves than for others. Selfishness no longer seems to be considered a negative characteristic. Instead it's labeled "assertiveness" and is viewed as a desirable form of aggressiveness.

This narcissism makes people demand certain things from the organization whether they deserve them or not. It also means that they are less likely to subjugate their own desires in order to cooperate with others for the good of the organization. They want to do their own thing and expect to be allowed to do it. "What's in it for me?" "Looking out for number one." "Getting all that I can!"—these are the catch phrases of the day.

Consider this situation:

ME TOO

Oh, oh, thought Jim, here comes Fred again. I'll bet he's coming to see me. Dammit, too late to hide.

Jim was looking out the glass panel in his door, facing a hallway connecting a row of offices at Proctor, Inc., a manufacturer of precision instruments. Jim was Accounts Manager at Proctor and supervised 11 subordinates. Fred was one of them.

"Hey Jim, could I see you for a minute?" asked Fred.

"Yeah, I guess. I'm kinda busy," responded Jim. Jim knew Fred liked to come into his office frequently to shoot the breeze, and he hoped Fred would not eat up the better part of an hour this time.

"Had a great experience last night, Jim, and I thought I'd tell you about it."

"What happened?" asked Jim.

"I attended one of those FIND meetings. It was great!" exclaimed Fred.

"What's FIND?" asked Jim.

"It stands for For Individuality—FIND—get it? Anyway, we really got down. We really got into our feelings. Here we were, a roomful of strangers, and we all opened up to one another. We explored what we wanted out of life and how we could get it."

"All that in just one night?" inquired Jim.

"Sure," replied Fred. "It was a really loose group. Anyway, we . . ."

"Look, Fred. I'd like to hear more about this but I've got a stack of papers to get through and I should really get started. Don't you have work to do, Fred?" asked Jim.

"Yeah, but it can wait. I'm really turned on by FIND. I really feel good about the experience."

"Well, how about feeling good about your job, Fred? I've noticed your work has been slipping the last few weeks. You know we discussed the problems you had on that Bolger contract. You just didn't seem to put the time and effort into that one that you should have, and we almost lost it," said Jim.

"I know we had some trouble with that one, but I'll do better. I really feel good about myself. I'm going to another FIND session tonight."

"But aren't you behind on that Ramsey job? That was due yesterday. I've got to have that. Maybe you should have worked on it last night and even tonight until you get it done."

"Oh sure, I'll get it done. But I've got to have some time to myself, Jim. I've got to think about other things besides my job. I've got to think about me, too. This company isn't everything in my life."

"Of course not," said Jim. "But you do have an obligation to this company and you must fulfill that obligation. People count on you to get your work done. I count on you. You've got to think about others, not just yourself. We've got to get that Ramsey thing done. Let me know if I can help you with it," offered Jim.

"OK, I guess I'll be going. I'll let you know," said Fred as he left Jim's office.

"Oh well, he was only here for ten minutes," sighed Jim as he watched Fred walk down the hall. Suddenly Fred turned into Bill's office. "What the hell is he doing?" thought Jim. "He should be getting back to work."

Analysis

What do you think of the way Jim handled Fred, both on his lack of performance on the two contracts and in getting him to move on? Would you have done anything differently? What should Jim do right now? Are there people in your organization who like to come in and shoot the breeze? What do you do about it?

There are really three key issues in this case. First is the problem of the time waster who wastes time in a variety of ways. Here Fred is wasting his and also Jim's time in an office visit. While something positive may come of the visit (Jim tried to encourage Fred to get busy on the uncompleted Ramsey contract), that was not the main reason Fred came to Jim's office.

Second is the issue of an employee who is not getting the work out on time. His performance is suffering, and apparently this is causing others to suffer. (Jim points out to Fred that other people in the organization are depending upon Fred for his work.)

Third is the issue of narcissism. Fred seems to be more interested in finding himself than in getting his work done. This may be symptomatic of deeper psychological problems affecting Fred's work.

Jim should go immediately to Bill's office, ostensibly on another matter. While there, he should ascertain if Bill is helping Fred with the Ramsey contract or whether Fred is, instead, wasting Bill's time with idle chatter. If it is the second case, Jim should ask to see Fred back at his office and give him a specific deadline for the Ramsey contract of 8:00 A.M. tomorrow. If Fred misses this deadline, Jim should consider transferring or terminating him. Of course, termination assumes that Fred is not an outstanding performer and that his output will continue slipping.

There is a fourth reason why incompetent people exist in organizations: Competent people seem to be more tolerant than ever before of their behavior. While we've experienced the narcissistic Me Decade of the seventies, we've also been told to let people have their own life space, be mellow and not try to run other people's lives. We've been told to be compassionate and to forgive and forget. The right to a second and even a third and fourth chance is now commonplace. This tolerance often allows people to get away with actions today that would have resulted in severe reprimands in the past. ④

Still another important reason why people tolerate incompetent behavior is because they are afraid that corrective measures will bring legal action. We have become a legalistic society. The web of legal rules that govern our organization worklife has become extremely complex. Managers hesitate to use severe discipline because they do not wish to be sued. ⑤

How Do I Recognize an Incompetent?

Oddly enough, it is not always easy to spot incompetent employees. If it were easy, they would never be hired in the first place. Most are clever enough to disguise their incompetence. Sometimes they hide behind a facade of smooth talk and big words. Sometimes they hide behind a facade of expensive, fancy clothes. Often they rest on their laurels or old credentials.

It is especially difficult to determine when a superior is incompetent. Often what seems like incompetent superior behavior to a subordinate is not incompetent—the subordinate just does not have all the facts. Furthermore, sometimes a superior acts in a certain way because the superior's superior requires it. So maybe your boss is not incompetent but your boss's boss is.

Nevertheless, a general pattern eventually emerges when a superior is incompetent:decisions don't get made, there is much flip-flopping on directions, the superior does not represent subordinates well to his or her boss, and more. We'll look at incompetent superior behavior in more detail later in the book.

We all make mistakes, but this does not mean we are incompetent. What must be observed is a *pattern* of incompetent behavior. A series of mistakes, inaction, missed deadlines, lack of job knowledge, poor performance, and so on reveal incompetence. If this pattern is observed over a period of several days, you know you have an incompetent employee or boss on your hands.

Why Do These People Take Up So Much of My Time?

Because you end up doing or redoing their work for them. Your job is made more difficult because of their stupidity, lack of motivation, or sheer clumsiness. They end up managing your time by making great demands on it, and you must devote time you could better spend elsewhere untangling the problems they have created.

Futhermore, co-workers have their work disrupted, since they must cover for incompetent employees, using their own valuable time. Subordinates who often cover for an incompetent superior don't get their job done. What starts out as a minor problem usually blossoms into a major one when it involves an incompetent employee or manager.

Managers will not delegate to incompetent subordinates because they know the job will not be completed properly and on time, so they end up doing work which rightfully should be done by subordinates. Many managers end up working 70- and 80-hour workweeks because they do not only their own job but also the jobs of two or three incompetent subordinates.

It need not be this way. Managers should not put up with incompetence, whether from their boss or subordinates. Of course, the theme of this book is that although you cannot completely eliminate incompetence, you can manage it so that it is less disrupting to your work.

Will Setting Goals Make a Difference?

If you do not set goals for your unit, they will be set implicitly by your subordinates. Goals will emerge from the group when no formal goals are stated, and your subordinates' goals will often be contrary to your own.

In setting goals, you should not do it autocratically. Rather, use a participative approach that allows subordinates to have significant input. (You can ignore the input of incompetent employees but do not avoid participation merely because you have some incompetent people working for you.) Subordinates will have greater commitment to goals that they have helped set.

But the point is that goals must be set under your direction. If not, those that emerge—and they *will* emerge—are likely to be contrary to those the group should be striving toward. Only in cases where there is much role consensus and mutual understanding among work group members would group goals emerge that are consistent with formally set goals

Why are goals important? Consider this example.

ANTS IN THE BASEMENT

"It's all a question of priorities, ladies and gentlemen. You don't want to stomp on ants in the basement while elephants run wild on the first floor. Instead, put your effort on important matters. Don't waste your time on the trivial. Go after the important. Get the biggest bang for your buck.

"You are all good supervisors. We've got one of the best billing operations of any insurance company around. You people know your job, but sometimes you get sidetracked. You know what needs to be done, so let's do it. Let's get that error rate reduced."

With that, Janet Kowalski concluded her weekly staff meeting. During the past three or four meetings, Janet had tried to impress upon her subordinates the need for setting priorities and working toward important goals. She felt many subordinates were spending too much time on wheel spinning and not enough on important activities. For example, the error rate in some units had increased from the company standard of three per 1,000 to eight per 1,000 premiums processed. Janet believed that even the standard of three was too high. Yet some supervisors did not seem concerned about the error rate of eight per 1,000. They complained that if they concentrated on reducing the error rate, they missed the deadlines for mailing the premium notices. Janet had indicated that it was better to be a little late on notices than to send some out in error.

Late that afternoon during a meeting Janet had with her boss, Mike Rutledge, the following discussion took place.

Mike: Well, how are things going, Janet? Have you gotten that error rate under control yet?

Janet: Well, almost, but not quite, Mike. We're working on it. It seems that when we get the error rate down we begin to miss our mailing deadlines.

Mike: Oh, don't miss those. We can't get behind in our mailings. They're even more important than our accuracy rate.

Janet: Really? I thought accuracy was more important.

Mike: Well, we want both; but we've got to get the notices out on time so we get our payments early. Anyway, most customers can't tell if their premium notices are accurate.

Janet: But the State Insurance Commission can.

Mike: Yes, that's true, but remember, we can't afford to miss those deadlines.

Janet: OK, Mike, I'll see what I can do. See you.

As Janet left Mike's office, she was confused. The error rate was just one example of where priorities had changed. She wondered how she could be expected to enforce priorities when her boss changed them. She also wondered whether her boss's boss might have put pressure on him to change priorities and whether a different priority might come forth in a few weeks. How then could she ask her subordinates to deal with important priorities when they kept changing? Talk about ants and elephants, she mused, soon we won't even be able to tell the difference between the two.

Analysis

Many organizations have the problem of both communicating and maintaining priorities and yet changing them as conditions change. What should have been done in this case to solve the problem? What should Janet do now? If you suggest that she meet with her subordinates again, what should she tell them? What action, if any, should Janet now take with Mike?

Competent people can distinguish important from unimportant matters. Incompetent people cannot, and so lose a sense of priority. Here Janet is being asked to enforce a set of priorities that seem to be changing. So the case involves two key issues. First, how can Mike's ability to communicate priorities to Janet be improved? Second, how can the company maintain and enforce priorities and yet change them when necessary?

If incompetence is to be kept to a minimum, a clear sense of priorities must be maintained. People must be able to distinguish ants from elephants. This entails a good list of specific company objectives from the top down, objectives that are internally consistent from one level to the next. It also involves the necessity of setting, maintaining, and communicating priorities of objectives throughout the organization. Perhaps a formal system of objective setting such as Management by Objectives (MBO) is needed. If this is adopted, it must involve participation and agreement between management levels if it is to operate properly and achieve effective communication and integration of activities. That such a system seems to be missing calls into question the competence of Mike and his boss more than of Janet.

Incompetent people don't care about goals or priorities. Competent people do. Goals and priorities serve as motivating devices and guides to behavior, giving us someting to strive for and to organize our efforts around. They are the reason for work. They also serve as a way to measure performance and as benchmarks for comparison that tell us how much is achieved relative to what we set out to achieve.

Incompetent people are not interested in goals, because they do not want to be evaluated against a desired target. Such an evaluation enables everybody else to see their failure to achieve. Incompetent people want fuzzy goals like loyalty, getting along with others, working hard, and so on, since these are very subjective and open to differing interpretations; fuzzy goals are almost no goals at all. How can we argue with an incompetent person's failure if we don't interpret the goal in the same way? It's hard to document incompetence when the goals are fuzzy.

How Can I Work *with* People, Not *for* Them?

When subordinates work under an incompetent superior, the superior usually has a "me against them" attitude, viewing subordinates as people to be ordered around at will, as people working *for* him or her, not *with* him or her.

If you as a subordinate find yourself working with an incompetent superior with this type of attitude, it is necessary to shift the frame of reference from "me against them" to "us," so the superior will view the work unit as a group cooperating to achieve common goals. This change in perception is not easily accomplished, but it can be done. For example, when communicating, use the pronouns "we" and "us" more than "I" and "you." Try to convince the superior to get goals *with* the group, not for it. Share in work rewards. When a good job is done, make sure all get their share of credit, including the superior. These are but a few ways to try to change the superior's perception.

A second way to get caught in the with-versus-for syndrome is to have an incompetent subordinate or two try to make you as a superior work *for* them. This is how they view their relationship with you. Strange as this may seem, they acually expect you to bail them out, solve their problems, correct their errors, and do their work for them. In reality, therefore, you *are* working for them.

How can you get subordinates to work for you instead of you for them? Don't do their work for them. Don't bail them out. Don't solve their problems. Provide guidance and counseling when needed, but let them sink or swim on their own performance. It's difficult to stop doing these things when you've been doing them all along, but stop you must.

You can stop gradually. For example, when a subordinate comes to you with a minor problem, provide minimum guidance and ask him or her to try solving it first. Successful experience in solving a minor problem will build confidence for solving larger problems. If a subordinate errs, have him or her redo the work; don't redo it yourself. Do this even if it means missing a deadline. But don't personally take the blame for missing the deadline; let the person who messed up take the blame. Incompetent people have got to be held accountable. If they suffer no penalties for poor performance, they will very likely repeat it. You know that ultimately you are responsible for the performance of your subordinates. But this does not mean that you do not hold them accountable for the performance of the duties assigned to them. You *do* hold them accountable, just as you're held accountable. This chain of accountability is required in every organization. If performance of subordinates is low, then it's up to the superior to correct it by either reorienting, retraining, or transferring the subordinate. We'll discuss these and other steps to manage incompetence in later chapters.

Summary

The key for coping with incompetence is to recognize it head-on and deal with it from a managerial perspective. Incompetence will always be with us, at every level in every type of organization regardless of industry. It's found in business as well as government. It cannot be ignored.

If managers do not manage incompetent performers, they will be managed *by* them. Demands made by incompetent members of the organization will consume vast amounts of time and effort of those who are competent. Preventing incompetence and minimizing its effects are real challenges for every manager.

2

The Poor Shall Always Be with You

Why are there always incompetent people around us? Why does an organization always seem unable to completely eliminate incompetent employees? We began examining these questions in the last chapter and saw that the issues of entitlement, equality, narcissism, and legalism all play a role in incompetence. These are basically social reasons that encourage the growth of incompetence in our organizations, but there are also organization and personal reasons.

What makes a person incompetent? We have used the term incompetence as if it were absolute. It is not. It is not like pregnancy; you cannot be a little bit pregnant, but you can be somewhat incompetent. Some people are competent in some fields and incompetent in others. For example, I consider myself competent to teach a class in management, conduct a research project, or complete a management consulting assignment, but I certainly would be an incompetent brain surgeon. Probably no matter how much training I had, I would never be a competent one. I don't have the aptitude, ability, and interest to learn these skills.

People also differ as to how well they can perform a job. Not everyone is a superior performer. Some are average performers, but we do not regard the average performer as incompetent. Generally, we regard someone as incompetent who is unable to complete the job satisfactorily; that is, incompetent people fail to meet even *minimum* standards required on the job.

Furthermore, a person need not fail to meet *all* minimum job standards to be incompetent; missing just one or two key standards may be enough. For example, a quality control inspector may be able to make 24 of the 25 measurement checks on a product but not the twenty-fifth. Assuming that all checks are important, the inability to make the last one is significant. It is an indication of incompetence.

Why Are Some People Unable to Meet Minimum Standards?

There are many reasons, some of which are:

◆ Insufficient training to perform the job.
◆ Poor job placement. The person is in the wrong job.
◆ A lack of direction from above.
◆ A lack of aptitude and/or ability to do the job regardless of the amount or type of training provided.
◆ A lack of interest in the job.
◆ A lack of feedback on performance. The person does not know whether the job is being performed properly or not and repeats the same mistake.
◆ Inadequate physical resources—tools, space, equipment, energy, and so on.
◆ Incompetent subordinates.
◆ A lack of adequate support staff for planning, financial management, and other staff work.
◆ An incompetent superior.
◆ A poorly defined job and associated job standards.
◆ A lack of clear agreement between superior and subordinate on job expectations.
◆ An economic recession which causes sales and markets to dry up.

Each or all of these reasons can explain incompetent job behavior. Some are within the control of the job-holder, such as interest or aptitude, but many are beyond his or her control. What

A Humorous Approach to
Performance Appraisal

EMPLOYEE: _____   RATER: _____

DATE: _____   DEPARTMENT: _____

1) This form will help you determine which of your employees are incompetent. Rate the employee by placing an X in the space beside the description that most nearly expresses your judgment.
2) Consider only one performance factor at a time.
3) Consider the individual's entire work performance on each factor. Don't base your judgment on only one or two occurrences.
4) Use the back for comments and explanations.

Quality: 5 ( ) Leaps tall buildings with a single bound.
                  4 ( ) Must take running start to leap over tall buildings.
                  3 ( ) Can leap over only short or medium-sized buildings with no spires.
                  2 ( ) Crashes into buildings when attempting to jump over them.
                  1 ( ) Cannot recognize buildings at all, much less jump over them.

Timeliness: 5 ( ) Is faster than a speeding bullet.
                  4 ( ) Is not quite as fast as a speeding bullet.
                  3 ( ) Would you believe a slow bullet?
                  2 ( ) Has difficulty shooting gun.
                  1 ( ) Plays Russian roulette and loses.

Initiative: 5 ( ) Is more powerful than a locomotive.
                  4 ( ) Is not quite as powerful as a locomotive.
                  3 ( ) Whistles as loudly as a locomotive.
                  2 ( ) Consistently misses trains.
                  1 ( ) Plays with toy trains on the job.

Adaptability: 5 ( ) Walks on water consistently.
                  4 ( ) Walks on water in emergencies.
                  3 ( ) Washes with water.
                  2 ( ) Drinks water.
                  1 ( ) Cannot drink water without spilling it.

Communication: 5 ( ) Talks with God.
                  4 ( ) Talks with the angels.
                  3 ( ) Talks to himself.
                  2 ( ) Argues with himself.
                  1 ( ) Loses those arguments.

TOTAL SCORE: _____

can a subordinate do about an incompetent superior? How can a job-holder get feedback on performance if it is not forthcoming? How can more support staff be obtained? How can a recession be prevented? Of course, even though these problems are actually beyond individual control, they are not beyond influence. In other words, many of the reasons for substandard job behavior listed above can be influenced, although not controlled, by a job-holder.

How Can Employees Influence Negative Job Factors That Are Beyond Their Control?

The influence process is informal within the organization. Employees cannot fire incompetent superiors, but they can do other things to improve a superior's performance. A subordinate can set an example, counsel informally, provide suggestions, try to get agreement on goals, and so on, all in the hope of making a superior a better performer. (We'll look at other steps later in this chapter.)

Also, a job-holder has some responsibility to ask for feedback, to help set job standards if none exist, to initiate role clarification sessions, to improve competence of subordinates, and to request a transfer if placed in the wrong job. If incompetence is caused by any of these, the incompetent employee should take some responsibility to correct the situation even if he or she has no direct control over it. The problem, however, is that most incompetent employees are incompetent not only at doing their jobs but also at using the influence process. So they cannot take action to correct a situation causing their incompetence even though they have a responsibility to do so.

Who Should Deal with Employee Incompetence?

As we saw in Chapter 1, managers in the organization have the primary responsibility to manage incompetence even when the subordinate is somewhat responsible. If a manager is incompetent, then the manager's superior has the responsibility to correct the situation. If the superior is incompetent, then the superior's superior has the responsibility, and so on up the chain of command.

Sometimes incompetence is so widespread in an organization that a complete housecleaning is needed. A board of directors, or a board of commissioners or trustees in a nonprofit organization, may need to appoint a new chief executive officer from the outside with the mandate to clean house. In some cases this is the only way to rid the organization of pervasive incompetence.

Sometimes managers can improve training and development to reduce incompetence, but it doesn't always work. Consider this situation:

OLD DOGS AND NEW TRICKS

Mark could see the eyes of half of those in the group actually glaze over as he went into his presentation on human resource management. He knew that even though he was making his presentation as simple as possible, it was still over the heads of at least five of the ten people in the room.

Mark was an organization development specialist hired by Dentrex Corporation to conduct management workshops for middle-level managers of various divisions of the company. Ten managers attended this first worshop session. These were a mixture of old and new managers who Dentrex believed needed management training to improve their effectiveness and efficiency. The workshop consisted of three mornings of lecture/discussion on key human resource concepts—leadership, communication, performance appraisal, and coaching and counseling. During each afternoon session the participants applied the concepts in case analysis and role playing.

As was true in so many groups Mark had worked with, he noticed that the younger employees were picking up on the ideas, but the older employees seemed to be having difficulty. This perception was confirmed during the first afternoon workshop, in which the class was divided into two groups of five each. Each group was asked to analyze the same two cases describing two organizations with problems in human resource management. Each group had to identify the problems and develop feasible solutions, which were then presented to the entire class for critique.

Mark observed that the older employees, whom he guessed to be between 50 and 60 years of age, participated very little in the small group discussions. When each group made its presentation, the older managers asked very few questions and made few comments. At day's end, Mark believed that while the younger managers had gotten quite a lot from the program, the older employees were no better off. He even believed they could be worse off, since their frustration may have been increased as they realized their inadequacies to deal with these new concepts.

This experience only confirmed Mark's previous opinion: You just can't teach an old dog new tricks.

Analysis

Do you agree that older managers have difficulty learning and applying new management concepts? What does this have to do with management competence? Is it fair for Mark to judge management competence based on a manager's performance in a workshop case analysis?

Perhaps such a judgment based on one day in a management seminar is not fair. The older managers may well be competent but unable to demonstrate this competence in a seminar. They may feel intimidated by the group and instructor or they may only be unfamiliar with case analysis procedures used in management seminars. Also, if Mark is young they may consider him to have low credibility and may feel there is little if anything a "kid wet behind the ears" can teach them.

On the other hand, most competent managers are used to problem solving and decision making in small groups, where they are also skilled at asking probing questions and in presenting their ideas. Therefore, these managers may very well have some deficiencies that the seminar brought to light.

What can be done about these deficiencies? Can you teach an old dog new tricks? Of course you can. It might not be possible in a three-day seminar—or in a three-week seminar, for that matter—but this is true of any manager who needs significant improvement of skills, regardless of age.

It is important for a manager to be motivated to learn. Motivation is a prerequisite for effective learning. Some older managers may just be putting in time until retirement, without much incentive to learn. Of course, this can be true of any manager regardless of age. We are all familiar with unhappy managers who are only awaiting a job opportunity in another organization.

Thus, whether you can teach an old dog new tricks is not the central issue. The issue is whether any manager of any age, with low incentive to learn, can acquire and practice new management concepts and skills.

> Knowledge that is acquired under compulsion has no hold on the mind.
>
> *Plato*

The Myth of Termination: Why Won't Managers Fire Incompetent Employees?

Most managers are reluctant to fire incompetent employees. Sometimes their reluctance is due to certain protections the employee has, such as civil service for government employees or a union contract that constrains action to terminate. Some employees may allege racial, sexual, or age discrimination if fired, and managers don't want to get caught up in lengthy commission hearings or receive adverse publicity. Still other employees may threaten to sue a manager and/or the organization for violation of various employment rights.

While these are genuine reasons why managers resist terminating an employee, there are other, more basic reasons. First is a misplaced sense of compassion. Managers will do almost anything rather than fire an employee, because they feel sorry for the job-holder. A sense of compassion is important, but it is not healthy when it results in retaining employees who hurt the organization. Not only does the organization suffer, but so does the employee, who must contend with continual frustration and disappointment at work. Instead of giving an employee a third, fourth, or fifth chance, the manager may be giving the employee a third, fourth, or fifth opportunity to fail. This is surely not true compassion.

Second, managers too often let an employee's personal circumstances cloud job decisions. We hate to put a person with a family out on the street, especially the sole breadwinner. But if this person's performance is harming the organization, why make others pay for his or her incompetence? Is this fair to other employees?

Third, and related to the above, many managers feel that their organization can absorb some incompetence without any real damage. The "assistant to" position is created for the 55-year-old, once-productive employee to tide him or her over until early retirement. Placed in a relatively innocuous position, the employee can do little harm awaiting the retirement date. Although this is a waste of resources for an organization, managers engage in it because they want to protect the company's reputation in the community as a good place to work. A government organization can more easily absorb this practice, but a profit-making business cannot. In a sense, such action deprives stockholders of a greater return on their investments and deprives customers of products or services at a lower price. It may also deny other employees wage increases, as salary funds are siphoned off for nonproductive work.

Fourth, many managers want to avoid a personal confrontation. They just do not have the guts to sit down with an employee and say that he or she has been canned. This is difficult for any of us to do, but it is a manager's essential responsibility. Many managers resist this confrontation because they just don't know how to carry out a termination in an effective yet tactful manner. Very little training and development is provided managers on how to handle any confrontation, let alone a termination. And most managers do not learn this from experience because most have never had to fire an employee. For example, let's look at Rona Zambelli's situation.

RED CIRCLE

Indelible, Inc., a large graphics and printing firm, has a policy that requires graphic artists, drafters, copy editors, and other professionals in the organization to work an 8:00 A.M. to 4:30 P.M. work shift each day. The employee signs in and out on a time card, stating the exact time of arrival and departure. In the past the company was fairly lenient enforcing the sign-in-and-out procedure, since it was realized that many of its professionals work in spurts of creativity and often put in two or three hours at night at the office or at home. Because there was no union the company wished to maintain maximum flexibility.

During the past few weeks, however, Rona Zambelli, the Layout Department manager, began to enforce the policy more strictly with Vera, one of her employees. It seemed that the quality and quantity of Vera's work had begun to fall off considerably. Rona counseled with Vera several times on this issue but it did not seem to help. Therefore, Rona decided to enforce the 8:00 A.M. to 4:30 P.M. workday and the sign-in-and-out policy more strictly with Vera.

On four occasions during the last three weeks, Rona observed that Vera had come in to work anywhere from one to seven minutes late but had indicated on her card that she had arrived at 8:00. On each occasion, Rona pulled Vera's card and wrote above "8:00" the actual time she observed Vera coming in. She circled this in red ink and replaced the card in the holder at the front of the office. Later each morning she discussed this action with Vera.

Vera became quite upset with Rona's actions, which was fine with Rona. In fact, Rona hoped Vera would resign over the issue so that she would not be forced to terminate her. Even though Rona's red circling caused a lot of office talk and some dissatisfaction among the employees, Rona planned to continue it for the foreseeable future.

Analysis

Do you agree with Rona's strategy on this issue? If not, what would you have done differently? Would this situation be different if a union were present? If so, how? What should Rona do if Vera refuses to resign in the foreseeable future? What should Rona do about the dissatisfaction she is causing other employees in the office?

Rona does not have the courage to fire a weak employee. She is hoping to harass the employee into quitting, a step that may backfire on her because Vera may continue on the job and other employees in the office may become so disgruntled that their work will suffer.

Many managers follow Rona's strategy with poor performers. If a union were present or if Vera were in a government organization and protected by civil service, Rona's behavior would get her in serious difficulty because she would likely be viewed as arbitrary and capricious in selectively enforcing company policy, and an arbitrator or civil service board would likely rule against her.

The consequences of Rona's present course of action on the other employees could be very serious. Graphic artists and other creative professionals tend to have a somewhat "free spirit" method of operating, and Rona's actions must certainly aggravate a number of them. Rona must be careful that she doesn't create a situation that causes a walkout, slowdown, or other form of mass rebellion.

At this point, Rona should either terminate Vera or begin an intensive counseling and development program with her. If she is a valuable employee and salvageable, the second course of action is recommended.

A fifth reason why managers are reluctant to terminate is because they often do very little outplacement, although this is changing. A survey completed by Drake-Beam, Inc., a New York consulting firm, and reported on page one of the November 6, 1979 issue of *The Wall Street Journal* indicated that more and more firms are engaging in outplacement, but most firms still spent inadequate time and effort on it. If managers spend some time in helping a soon-to-be-terminated employee locate another job, they may be more willing to terminate, since some of their guilt will be assuaged.

Sixth, some managers don't fire because they don't feel they can find a replacement. In tight labor markets a half-ass engineer may be better than no engineer at all, or so they reason. The problem with this is that they do not realize the real harm done to the organization by retaining an incompetent employee. This person screws up not only his or her own work but usually the work of others as well. This can cost the organization significant amounts of money. Besides that, mediocrity soon becomes the standard by which we judge performance. We become concerned just with getting the job done at some bare minimum level rather than with getting the job done right.

Finally, some managers won't terminate because they hope someone else will do it for them. They shirk their responsibility in this area and expect either their boss or the personnel department to step in and bail them out. This behavior is especially prevalent when a manager is soon likely to be promoted, to be transferred, or to otherwise leave the present position. Such a manager doesn't worry about confronting a termination because soon "it'll be someone else's problem."

All these reasons make managers reluctant to terminate incompetent employees. The overall condition is very different than it was 50 years ago when most employers were too quick to terminate and employees could be fired at the drop of a hat. Various legal protections and social morès that have developed since then probably have caused the pendulum to swing too far the other way. Many managers won't terminate because they are not sure they have documented the case sufficiently or they have not followed their organization's termination procedures to the letter. In other words, they're afraid their decision to terminate will be overturned because of a technicality.

These protections of employee rights are necessary and certainly have corrected arbitrary and capricious abuses in the past, but they should not serve as an excuse not to terminate. Termination should still be a viable management option and must be exercised periodically when dealing with incompetent employees. Of course, a manager must adequately document the termination case and must ensure that company termination procedures are known and followed.

How Can I Learn to Live with Incompetence?

Even though managers should terminate, they often do not, so that people in organizations must learn to live with incompetent fellow employees who may be superiors, subordinates, or peer managers and professionals. Sometimes the termination decision may be beyond an individual manager's authority. After all, a manager can't terminate a superior or a subordinate of another manager in another unit.

The primary objective in learning to live with incompetence is to minimize the damage an incompetent person can do to your career and to the unit for which you work. If the organization is going to tolerate incompetence, there is no reason why you have to tolerate it. Let's look at what you can do if you work with an incompetent superior, subordinates, or peers.

An Incompetent Superior

First, prior to taking a new job, promotion, or transfer, be sure of the qualifications of the person you will be working for. Knowing this is just as important as learning about the organization and the unit in which you'll be working. Working for an incompetent superior will make your job many times harder. Refuse any job that requires you to work for a dud.

Neither do the ignorant seek after wisdom. For herein is the evil of ignorance, that he who is neither good nor wise is nevertheless satisfied with himself; he has no desire for that of which he feels no want.

Plato

However, if you find yourself working for an incompetent superior, here's what you can do:

1. *Modeling.* A subordinate can serve as a model of effectiveness for a superior. By actions and example, effective performance can be demonstrated. This should be done tactfully and in subtle ways so as to be nonthreatening to the superior. For example, if you believe your superior has difficulty writing clear reports, you can demonstrate effective report writing when there is an opportunity to submit a report to your superior.

2. *Information transfer.* The subordinate often has greater access to certain types of information than the boss. Such information may be in a particular area of a subordinate's expertise or may deal with a personnel or morale matter regarding other subordinates. This information can be shared with the superior to im-

prove the superior's decision making. For example, a computer programmer working for a billing supervisor can share information about computer capabilities with the supervisor.

Furthermore, subordinates can share informative articles and the results of professional or trade conferences with superiors.

3. *Incremental change.* Sometimes all that a subordinate can hope for is to make a few small changes in one or two key areas of a superior's performance rather than to completely revamp a superior's total style of management. For example, just getting a superior to set clear, measurable goals with you can lead to significant improvements in job output.

4. *Appeal to an outside authority.* Work through others who have some influence and can pressure the superior to change. This outside authority may be a consultant, the superior's superior, or a competitor who is doing something well. The point is that perhaps someone other than yourself can get a superior to improve performance.

5. *Refusal to act.* You can always say "no" to something that a superior asks you to do. While there are risks to this approach, it is an option when working for an incompetent superior. This is such an important and risky step that we devote Chapter 7 of this book to examining it.

6. *Shared decision making.* Encouraging the superior to involve you and other subordinates in decision making via task forces, committees, or staff meetings can improve the superior's decisions. While this is often resisted, it can have results if done tactfully and on a gradual basis.

7. *Training and development.* You can encourage your superior to take advantage of training and development opportunities by bringing them to his or her attention. And encouragement to attend trade conferences and conventions may help bring your superior up to the "state of the art" in the industry.

8. *Objective performance appraisal.* Subordinates can work to have superiors use measureable goals for evaluating unit performance rather than subjective standards of performance. A more objective basis of evaluation can lead to insights for the whole unit as to how performance can be improved.

Incompetent Subordinates

As a superior you really don't have to tolerate incompetent subordinates since you have authority over them. You can:

1. See that they get proper training and development to overcome their incompetence.
2. Transfer them to another unit more suited to their talents, interests, and aspirations.
3. Switch them to a more suitable job in your unit.
4. Create a new position for them that minimizes the damage they will do.
5. Overwork them and be very critical of their performance, hoping that they see the handwriting on the wall and quit.
6. Recommend them for a promotion to another unit and make them "someone else's" problem.
7. Counsel with them to overcome the areas of problem performance.
8. Ostracize them—give them the "cold shoulder" and ask other subordinates to do likewise.
9. Terminate them.

Of course, dangers exist with each of the above actions, but the key is to determine whether these costs outweigh the costs of doing nothing and letting the situation continue.

Incompetent Peer Managers and Professionals

Sometimes we must work with other managers and professionals (such as engineers, accountants, and others) who are incompetent. What can we do?

1. Refuse to work with them as soon as the incompetence is recognized. Refuse to return phone calls, don't attend meetings, resign from committees and task forces, and just generally avoid the incompetent person.
2. Ask to have the incompetent person removed from the task force or committee.

3. Work to get the incompetent person transferred to another unit in the organization.
4. Work to get the incompetent person terminated.
5. Refuse to do the incompetent person's work. Make the person do his or her own share and be held accountable for it.
6. Don't place the incompetent person on any important sub-committee. Place the person on subcommittees where little damage can be done.
7. Try to get your job redefined so that you don't have to work with an incompetent person.
8. Have one of your subordinates serve on a committee or task force, or otherwise interact with the incompetent person in your place.

Again, there are risks in taking the above steps, but the costs of working with an incompetent peer manager or professional may well outweigh the risks of acting to resolve the situation. If this is so, then action must be taken.

Even though all these moves are viable, sometimes conditions are so bad that a complete housecleaning is needed. For example:

DOCTOR, HEAL THYSELF

Dr. Brian Rambo was in the final series of interviews for selection as director of the Mental Health Unit of a large (1,000 bed) municipal hospital. The unit was made up primarily of psychologists (with Ph.D.s), psychiatrists, and nurses who work with mentally ill patients.

The hospital had an excellent reputation, not only in the immediate community but throughout a four-state region. However, the reputation of the Mental Health Unit was not equal to that of other hospital units. Dr. Rambo was being considered as a replacement for the former head of the unit who recently had resigned his administrative position but who was still employed as a staff psychologist by the hospital. At present the unit was headed by an acting director.

Dr. Peter Malik was chief of the medical staff at the hospital and would make the final selection of the new Mental Health Director. Dr. Rambo was one of three names recommended to him after an extensive six-month national search by an advisory selection committee made up of members of the community and the mental health staff. At the time,

Dr. Rambo held a position, similar to the one he was being interviewed for, at a smaller private hospital in a neighboring state.

After an extensive series of interviews with various members of the mental health and hospital staff over the previous two days, Dr. Rambo was in Dr. Malik's office for a final interview before departing that evening. Following is an excerpt.

Dr. Malik: Well, Brian, I hope everything has gone well for you during the past two days. I know you've made quite an impression on the staff.

Dr. Rambo: Yes. It's been a good two days. I've enjoyed my visit and I appreciate your time and hospitality.

Dr. Malik: As you know, you are the third and last candidate we will be interviewing. Although I haven't yet talked it over in depth with everyone, we will probably be making you the offer. Should such an offer be forthcoming at an appropriate salary, of course, what would be your reaction?

Dr. Rambo: Well, of course, I am interested in the job or I wouldn't be here. But there are some things that concern me. You've got a lot of dead wood in mental health. There are some staff that never should have been hired and some who should have taken early retirement several years ago. I get the impression that there is a "good old boy" network at work in the unit.

Dr. Malik: Be more specific if you could.

Dr. Rambo: Well, for example, you have not hired very many new psychologists during the past five years, and I believe during the past two years you have not hired anyone at all. I'm concerned about the fresh flow of new ideas into the unit under these conditions. Also, I get the impression that promotion and pay increases are very heavily influenced by time in grade more than by meritorious performance.

Dr. Malik: Well, there is some of that, but I'm not sure it is as bad as you may think.

> *Dr. Rambo:* If I can be candid with you, Peter, if this job were to be offered to me and I were to take it, I'd have to have a pretty free hand to make some major changes.

> *Dr. Malik:* Sure, I understand. We'd want you to make some improvements.

> *Dr. Rambo:* Well, I'm referring to some drastic measures. A number of staff would have to be terminated. Some could be transferred out of the unit, I suppose. Others are salvageable and would need intensive professional retraining and development to bring them up to current practices. I'd want to replace some supervisors with other people. Also, I'd like at least five new—net additional—positions at a competitive salary to attract some top-flight psychologists at the entry level. All of this is likely to cause quite a bit of conflict and turmoil among the staff, but in my view it needs to be done. I'd need your full support in carrying out these actions.

> *Dr. Malik:* Well, I don't know what you have in mind specifically, but I think I could support such actions. I know change is needed. The previous director served for twelve years and during the last five he performed basically a caretaker role.

> *Dr. Rambo:* Well, the staff is likely to go over my head and put a lot of pressure on you to block some of the things I want to do. Some of the people who may be asked to go could be personal friends of yours.

> *Dr. Malik:* Hmmmm. Well, that could get sticky, but I think I could support your efforts. We need some changes.

> *Dr. Rambo:* OK. Let me think about it.

> *Dr. Malik:* Sure. We'll be in touch.

Later that evening on the flight home, Dr. Rambo pondered the situation. He felt that he would likely receive the job offer, but he wasn't certain whether he would accept it. He knew Dr. Malik had served as chief of staff for the past ten years, and he wondered why Malik had allowed the mental health unit to deteriorate as much as it had. He knew the previous mental health director had voluntarily stepped down, but he was uncertain how much pressure Malik had placed on him to resign. He was just not sure Malik would be strongly supportive of his efforts and questioned whether Malik's perception of the needed changes were as drastic as his own. How could Malik have let the situation deteriorate so much without taking strong action, Rambo wondered. Maybe he's the real cause of the problems in mental health.

Analysis

If the job is offered, should Rambo accept? What factors should he weigh in his decision? Is Malik's basic management competence at issue here? Is an outside person like Rambo in a better position to bargain and make changes compared with an internal candidate who could be promoted to the job?

Depending on how bad conditions are in mental health, Dr. Malik's competence as a manager is certainly an issue here. If the situation has deteriorated as much as Rambo believes, one must ask why Malik did not take any decisive action to improve conditions. One must also ask how likely he will be to support actions taken by Rambo.

On the other hand, an outside person is in a better bargaining position and, compared with an inside person, often is able to bring about more change. If Malik wants Rambo bad enough, perhaps he can use him as his hatchet man to bring about the needed changes that the previous mental health director would not make. While Malik need not support Rambo on each and every change, he must work with him and be very supportive, especially on the first few changes Rambo initiates, so as to bolster Rambo's credibility. Of course, Rambo must work with Malik in planning these changes so as to get a reading on how far he can go.

Organizations that let a unit deteriorate as much as this one often find it very difficult turning things around. It usually takes an outside person with a fresh approach who does not have friends, loyalties, and debts in the organization. Yet if conditions are too bad, it's difficult to attract such a person. Who wants to walk into a hornet's nest?

Of course, the situation would be different if Malik were a new appointment. Rambo could then rationalize that the problem in mental health was caused by the former chief of staff and mental health director. A new chief of staff would convey to Rambo real desire and support for change on the part of the hospital. It is for this reason that many organizations in similar situations often start at the top when replacing people.

Summary

The theme of this chapter is that sometime in your career, either as a superior, subordinate, or peer/professional, you will likely have to work with incompetent people. Even though it may not be possible to avoid this situation, you don't have to accept it. It is true that in today's organizations managers are reluctant to fire incompetent people, but this does not mean that there are no other steps that can be taken.

We have explored some reasons why people are incompetent. Some of these can be corrected by others in the organization; better job training and placement, better job standards and expectations, and more feedback and job counseling can help correct incompetence. However, if a person has low motivation, interest, and aptitude, these usually cannot be corrected by someone else. The incompetent person must work to correct these.

We also saw that there are some specific steps you can take when dealing with an incompetent superior, subordinate, or peer manager/professional. Each of these entails risk. Yet the costs to your career and to your organization of not taking action may very well outweigh the risks of the action itself.

In the next chapter we'll see how important it is to associate yourself with competent people in the organization.

3

Hitch Your Career to a Star

On one of my first jobs I had to work for an incompetent manager. Here I was, a young, naive management trainee fresh out of business school, working for a person whose behavior flouted nearly every management concept and principle I had learned. He would give me a project due the next afternoon only to interrupt me an hour later with a project due at noon. He would not plan or schedule his activities, which made it difficult for me to plan and schedule mine.

He did not return phone calls and frequently either missed or was late for meetings. He'd call meetings of his own staff on a moment's notice to discuss a so-called "emergency." (Would you believe one concerned the enforcement of payment in the office coffee fund?) He provided little guidance and constructive feedback and appraisal of subordinates. Once when I asked him what the criteria were for annual merit salary increases and promotions, he replied by saying, "Just keep your nose clean and stay out of trouble." I hardly found those words reassuring for an objective performance-appraisal system.

After a couple of months, I quit and went with another organization. Why? Because one of the most important things for a new person trying to establish visibility and credibility in an organization is to be associated with competent people who have credibility in the organization. Let's face it—we are judged by the company we keep. Of course, it is possible to succeed *in spite of* an incompetent boss; but the probabilities of success are enhanced when working for a competent person.

Why Is It Important to Associate with Competent People?

What can competent people do for you? First, they make you look better. There surely are many football players of All-American caliber on poor or fair college teams, but how often are they chosen as All-American? Not very often, indeed.

Second, competent people make your job easier. There is a synergistic effect when working with competent people. The whole is greater than the sum of its parts. One plus one equals three. The effect of a group of competent people working together is greater than the sum of the efforts of each individual involved. We see this synergistic effect in team sports.

Third, competent people can serve as excellent role models, particularly for new employees. Think back over your career. I'm sure you can think of one or two key people who provided you with exceptional learning experiences on your job. This is very important, especially for newly hired employees.

Fourth, working for a competent superior means you are likely to be promoted more rapidly. As he or she is promoted because of exceptional competence, chances are you will move up too when this superior builds a new staff at each level in the organization. If you've demonstrated your competence to this fast riser, you'll be in a position to move up with him or her. Your career will be enhanced.

Fifth, you'll be better able to meet both your unit and personal job goals working for and with competent people. Incompetent people usually are not goal oriented. Visible achievement of solid goals will enhance your position in the organization.

Sixth, your job mobility will be enhanced by working with and for competent people. Competent people are known in the profession, trade, or industry. When it comes time to take advantage of a job opportunity with another organization, your position will be enhanced because you have worked with respected, known people in the field.

Some managers place a great deal of emphasis on having competent subordinates. Consider this statement made by a manager of a large manufacturing concern.

SWEET ISOLATION

You're only as good as your subordinates. Show me a manager with good subordinates and I'll show you a good manager. No matter how incompetent you might think a manager to be, if the guy has a good group of subordinates to get out the work and cover for him he'll look good.

After all, what is management? It is getting things done through others—that's what it is. And who does a manager get things done through? Why, his subordinates of course. Thus, the better your subordinates, the more you'll get done and the better you'll look.

So I agree that managers must associate themselves with competent people in the organization, especially with competent subordinates. They must select, hire, train, and place good subordinates. If they do this, the shop will run itself. Heaven help those managers who cannot hire their own subordinates. If a guy can't put together his own team, don't blame him for the unit's failures. The manager isn't incompetent; the organization is for allowing such a stupid situation to exist. You can't hold someone responsible for performance if he doesn't have the authority to pull together a team that can perform.

Analysis

Do you agree with this person's last statement? Why, or why not? In your experience, can managers usually put together their own teams? If they cannot, because of organization policy, what are the implications for performance? What are the implications of this person's argument at each level in the organization?

The fact is, one mark of managerial competence is the ability to pull together a team of competent subordinates. Good managers tend to attract good subordinates. Incompetent managers tend to have trouble getting good people to work for them. Management is getting things done through others, but making things happen requires managerial skill.

Seldom do managers have the authority to completely reconstitute their team of subordinates. They may be able to make a few personnel changes, but usually they must do the best they can with what they have. In fact, one mark of managerial incompetence is the inability of a new manager to get higher productivity out of a low-performing group. So the excuse of "I can't pick my own team" becomes a hollow rationalization for low performance.

Finally, if every manager at every level in the organization had the authority to reconstitute his group of subordinates, there would be an extremely high number of transfers, terminations, and social upheavals every time a new manager near the top of the organization was appointed. A domino effect would be felt down through the entire organization. While some change in personnel is expected when a new manager is appointed, a change this drastic on a regular basis would be very dysfunctional.

Why Should I Ride on Another Person's Coattails? I Want to Make It on My Own

I'm not suggesting that you try to ride the crest of someone else's performance. No matter who your associates are, if you don't perform it will have little if any effect. In fact, your sub-par performance will seem even more apparent if you're working with competent people. The point is, in today's large organizations a person's visibility is important for merit salary increases and advancement. This is particularly true for new employees. Besides this, competent people enhance other people's performance.

Yet a person should avoid the appearance of being a social climber or name dropper. Most people can see through this behavior immediately. Such transparent action raises doubts in other people's minds as to competence, since it then appears that you cannot make it on the basis of your own performance but must rely on the reputation of others. So creating conditions where you can associate with competent people must be done tactfully. Here are some guidelines on how to go about it.

First, at the time of initial job interviews find out with and for whom you'll be working. Learn their backgrounds. What experience have they had? How long have they been with the organization? What is their education? How fast are they likely to be promoted in the future?

Second, find out all you can about the organization unit or division in which you'll be working. Is it a glamour division of the company? Is it a fast-growth unit? Is it a new unit? What is its contribution to the company's profit? What kind of people are sent to the unit? (Is it a graveyard or a way station to retirement?) I once knew a person who went to work for a major growth company and was placed in the purchasing unit of a division that had product lines in the mature to declining stage of the product life cycle. He stagnated for 18 months before he finally realized there was little future in the division. Unfortunately, he was unable to obtain another position in another division of the company since people from his division were generally typecast as losers in the company.

You want to be in an organization unit that has strong growth products and makes a substantial contribution to the company's profits. This will enable you to associate with aggressive fellow employees who are valued greatly by the company. It will also give you the opportunity and visibility to demonstrate your competence.

Third, when you work on a special task force or committee with competent people from other units, use this as an opportunity to get to know them and demonstrate your competence. This might enable you to request a transfer to their unit when the opportunity arises, or perhaps you can even be promoted by one of them to a better position in their unit. I know a person who served on a task force to implement an EDP system in an insurance company several years ago. The task force did an exceptional job and he was able to receive a substantial promotion to another unit in the company as a result of his performance. The task force chairman, who was well regarded in the company, decided he wanted that individual to work for him on a permanent basis and requested that the person be promoted once the committee completed its work.

Fourth, it's possible sometimes to make contact through social and civic organizations. We are all familiar with contacts established on a golf course, tennis court, or fishing trip. But excellent contacts can also be established through activities of neighborhood home associations, political committees, or civic clubs like Kiwanis, Lions, or Civitan International. Often these contacts are not with people in your own company, but with competent people in other organizations. A word of warning is appropriate here, however: you don't want to develop a reputation as a social climber or user of people. In other words, you don't want to develop a reputation of meeting and knowing people just for your own personal enhancement. You must be interested in the person first and enjoy meeting new people and making new friends. Using people as contacts solely to enhance your own position is so transparent that most people easily see through it and will avoid you because of it.

Fifth, never burn your bridges behind you. You may want to rely on associates from a previous job for future recommendations. If you leave an organization—through either voluntary exit or termination—try to make the experience as pleasant and smooth as possible. You never know when you will need to rely on a previous employer for a key recommendation. You also can never be sure when a future employer might call a previous employer without your knowledge for a *sub-rosa* reference check.

Maintaining your "bridges" is not always easy, especially if you were fired or asked to resign. Yet by placing the situation in perspective you may decide that the costs of fighting your dismissal outweigh any potential benefits. There's no need to fight such an action and perhaps destroy past associations just for your own satisfaction or because you are angry. How will this help you obtain a job in the future? By the way, this also goes for people who retire early. Who knows, it is possible to decide to work again a year or two after retirement for either the same organization or another one. People do change their minds.

Each of these ways can be used to build a network of associations with competent people in order to enhance your job performance.

How Can I Avoid Being a Janitor and Cleaning Up After Others?

Most people will let you do their jobs if you try hard enough. Don't get sucked into this trap. Managers spend far too much time being "janitors"—cleaning up or redoing the work of subordinates, bailing out their own boss, or taking over job responsibilities of peer associates. When two or more people work on the same task to the detriment of achieving a goal, this is called *organization overlap*. It occurs when people try to do other people's jobs.

I know a high-level administrator in a telephone company who was not content to delegate authority properly and hold people accountable. Instead he not only often tried to do his subordinates' jobs, but often meddled in the jobs of *their* subordinates! Needless to say, this man put in a 60 to 70 hour workweek and was quite proud of it. No one else in the company worked as hard as he did. He often called people at home at 11:30 P.M. while he was at the office still working because of some "emergency." He was not content to let subordinates do their job under proper guidance and to terminate or transfer them if they failed.

When an outside consultant confronted him with the undesirable consequences of this behavior, the man claimed that he faced so much pressure by the state's public service commission that this was the only way he could stay on top of things to get his job done. The man was soon transferred to another division of the company. After a few weeks of adjustment, his replacement was able to complete the same job in 40 to 45 hours per week at no fall-off in division performance or service! He was able to do this because he refused to be a janitor and clean up after other people. He let them rise or fall on their own performance. If they were incompetent, he replaced them.

Here's another situation:

SOUR GRAPES

> *Bob:* Ted, I'm afraid we're going to have to terminate you. Your performance during the past six months has not really been

that good. I've talked with Carol about your performance at length and we've reached this decision. I'm sorry it hasn't worked out.

Ted: I guess I'm not surprised. Carol has spoken with me about my performance on several occasions. I know she's somewhat disappointed, but I don't think I'm entirely at fault. She's a difficult manager to work for.

Bob: What do you mean?

Ted: Well, she gives little guidance and she frequently contradicts herself. She'll ask me to do one thing and then turn around and ask me to do something else. Then she'll completely ignore me for long periods of time. I didn't know how to interpret that. I didn't know whether she was happy with what I was doing and saw no need to talk with me, or if she was so disappointed that she thought I was beyond help. Sometimes I'd just feel lost. You know, this is a very big company and it's easy for new people to get lost, especially if they work for a poor manager.

Bob: Yes, we are big, but our department heads know they have a responsibility to orientate and help new people. Some do a better job than others.

Ted: A couple of people who were in the MBA program with me at Indiana are with companies that use a mentor system. This protects them from being stuck with a poor supervisor right off the bat. Their mentor, who is fairly high up in the organization, takes a personal interest in them and helps them out. That system can work well, especially since the mentor is not in a superior–subordinate relationship.

Bob: Yes, I've heard about the mentor system, but you shouldn't need that if you've got capable supervisors. You know, Ted, I'm pleased that you are taking this in such a mature fashion. You're not acting like a 25-year-old kid. We should have had this talk earlier.

Ted: Yes, we should have. I did try to see you on several occasions, but I guess you were always busy. You really need to do something about Carol, though. She is not a good supervisor. I was planning on quitting soon anyway if I had to continue under her much longer.

Bob: Well, I'm sorry, Ted, that things just didn't work out. Let me know if I can be of assistance with any recommendations or whatever.

Bob was ambivalent. On the one hand, he thought Ted had the potential for being a good employee. On the other, he thought Ted was unhappy having to work for a female supervisor. Ted believed Carol was reasonably competent. She seemed to get along well with her other subordinates and peer managers. Certainly Bob felt that he had a good relationship with her. Yet Bob didn't believe Carol had done the best job she could have with Ted. He thought maybe he should have been more involved than he was earlier, but he hated to meddle in his subordinates' problems unless asked. He wondered whether Ted's feelings about Carol were just sour grapes, or perhaps he really was losing a valuable employee.

Analysis

Why did Bob tell Ted of his termination without having Carol present, especially since Bob did not want to meddle in his subordinates' problems? How much and in what way did Ted's working for a woman influence this situation? If you were Bob, what if anything further would you do now? Would you reverse your decision and ask Ted to stay on? Why, or why not?

Chalk this one up as Bob's mistake. While there could be some sour grapes on Ted's part because he worked for a female, Bob should have been involved with this situation long before, especially if he is the one with the authority to actually terminate his subordinates' subordinates, which is apparently the case here. He does have the responsibility to support his subordinates, but he should work with them in trying to solve problems such as this one before they reach the termination stage. For example, he could have tried to counsel with Carol and

Ted to improve Ted's performance. If this failed, a transfer of Ted to another unit might have been appropriate.

There is some evidence that Ted is a capable employee. First, he handled himself well in the discussion with Bob. Second, he has an MBA from a good school and may not have had a chance in just six months to show what he can do. Also, there may be age bias against Ted. Bob says that Ted is "not acting like a 25-year-old kid," which indicates that Bob may be prejudiced against new people fresh out of school. This could easily prevent Bob from making an objective appraisal of a person's performance, especially when he is unlikely to get the full story because he does not want to meddle in his subordinates' affairs.

If Bob and other managers at his level are expected to exercise termination authority, the organization must ensure that they are more involved with their subordinates' subordinates. Otherwise they'll be making decisions with incomplete knowledge. If Bob had been thus involved, he'd have been better able to determine whether Ted really did have a point, or if he was just voicing sour grapes.

Can't a Manager Lose Control If Delegation Is Widely Practiced?

Of course. A manager must delegate judiciously. Proper delegation to competent subordinates keeps a manager from having constantly to play janitor. On some occasions, one will have to redo a subordinate's work, but these should be few and far between. It should not happen regularly.

A manager should *manage by exception*. That is, a superior manager should become involved in an issue only when it becomes so far out of line or complex that the subordinate manager cannot handle it. But the manager should *manage*; this is a management process—it is *not* an excuse for not managing.

I know a president of a large research/consulting organization who believes that managing by exception means giving subordinates enough rope to hang themselves. He believes that letting subordinates decide what needs to be done and letting them do it with virtually no guidance from above is the best approach. The idea of management by exception does not occur to him until the situation becomes a critical emergency and he *must* get involved.

There are many disadvantages to this laid-back style of management, not the least of which is that important decisions which only the president can make remain unmade. The man is unwilling to act on certain key decisions for fear of alienating certain groups. He pushes the decision down in the organization and asks someone to make it who really should not have the authority to make it because of its widespread effect throughout the entire organization. When these decisions are bucked back up to him for his action, he sits on them hoping they'll go away. On decisions that subordinates have already made but which are appealed to him for review, he echoes their decisions.

This is not proper delegation regardless of why it's done. It is a perverse shifting of responsibility to others. Fear of alienating certain groups should not become an excuse for inaction at the top.

How Can I Avoid Doing My Subordinates' Work for Them If They Expect It?

This is the law of the self-fulfilling prophecy. You believe subordinates will screw up so you do their work for them. You stop doing their work and sure enough, they screw up. So you go back to doing their work for them.

This law works in many areas. If every major stockholder in GM believed the price of stock was going to fall and rushed to sell, it would indeed fall since the supply of stock would be greater than the demand at the existing price. When Johnny Carson said there would be a toilet paper shortage, sure enough there was, because all his listeners ran out to buy toilet paper the next day and depleted grocer shelves.

If your subordinates expect you to clean up after them when they make a mistake, they are more likely to make a mistake, knowing you'll be there to bail them out. As soon as you delegate, they make a mistake. The law takes hold. You see the mistake and clean up. The cycle repeats itself.

This behavior is only natural on the part of subordinates. My daughter won't make her school lunch in the morning when Mamma's home because she knows Mamma will make it. Yet when Mamma's out of town, she makes it and does not rely on me to do it for her. Mamma returns and she does not do it. Mamma does it because she knows if she doesn't the child will have no lunch.

To break the cycle of the self-fulfilling prophecy, let those who want to eat make their own lunch. A few lunchless days and they'll soon remember to make it. It's a question of habit, expectations, and responsibility. You need to put subordinates on notice that from hereafter this is what you expect of them. You need to do

---

Excuses for a Closed Mind

Incompetent people often have closed minds and usually give a variety of reasons. Be prepared for excuses such as these:

We can't get the money for it.

We tried that before.

Our situation is different.

It costs too much.

That's beyond our responsibility.

We're all too busy to do that.

That's not my job.

It's too radical a change.

We don't have the time.

Not enough help.

That will make what we are doing obsolete.

Let's make a study of it first.

Our operation is too small for it.

Not practical for operating people.

The others will never buy it.

We've never done it before.

It's against policy.

Runs up our overhead.

We don't have the authority.

That's too ivory-tower.

Let's get back to reality.

That's not our problem.

this through consensus and expectations derived from meetings between you and subordinates, which need to be held *before* you stop doing their work for them. Don't just stop doing their work, or they *will* screw up, expecting you to cover for them. Put them on notice, then gradually pull out of their work and let them stand on their own. Be available for guidance and counsel and provide it liberally at first, but gradually encourage the subordinates to exercise their own judgment. Those who cannot handle this should be trained, transferred, or terminated. This will soon get you out of the business of doing your subordinates' jobs.

Can I Use the Same Techniques with My Superior?

Yes and no. Consensus and expectations meetings can be requested by you to set out what you will and will not do, but enforcing these meetings with a superior who knows you've always bailed him or her out in the past will be difficult. Many superiors actually expect subordinates to cover for them on a regular basis. In fact, they expect the primary role of a subordinate to be that of cover and support. Of course this is wrong. Just as a subordinate must stand on his or her own two feet, so must a superior.

This does not mean that superiors and subordinates should not work together as a team and occasionally cover for one another. This should happen, and teamwork is essential. But it does mean that subordinates should not do the superior's job. That is not their responsibility, and in most cases they are not paid enough to do it.

If consensus meetings don't resolve this problem, it might be necessary for the subordinate to break the chain of command and go to the superior's boss. There is some risk to this as we've seen already, but it is sometimes necessary.

Refusal to act on the part of the subordinate may be appropriate but could be devastating for the superior and the subordinate alike. Failure to cover may expose the superior's failings for all to see, and as he fails he may drag you down with him. However, if you can divorce yourself from your superior's behavior, refusing to cover his mistakes may be an appropriate course of action.

Of course, if these moves fail, transfer and quitting are other ways to remove yourself from having to continuously cover for your superior.

Don't I Put My Job in Jeopardy If I Don't Cover for My Boss When It's Expected?

Yes, to some extent, but the key word is *expected.* You've got to change these expectations—which may be tough if the entire organization is managed this way and your boss is not just an isolated case. In other words, if he is covering for his boss, and so on up the line, you'll not likely get this pervasive management style or your boss's expectations changed. This is another reason why it's so important to carefully assess the management style of those you'll be working for prior to accepting the job. Here's a situation where a manager and his subordinates had very different expectations.

LATE, BUT GREAT

John Hanson is State Bureau Chief of Workers' Compensation in a large industrial state. John's bureau is in a Division of Employment which is a major division within the State Department of Labor. John supervises six section heads, each of whom has four to seven subsection heads reporting to them. Each subsection head supervises 12 to 15 employees who process workers' compensation claims filed by firms in the state.

The state has standards for claim processing that are either the same as or slightly different from the national standards of the federal government. (States are expected to try to meet these federal standards but are not required to do so.)

Working for John as a section head is Sally Iacampo. Over the past six months, Sally's unit has been the bureau's best, consistently exceeding the work-output standards while remaining far below the error standards. John has been quite proud of this performance, but lately some difficulty has begun to develop with other section heads. The state has several work rules that some section heads claim are being violated by Sally's section. For example, even though the official work-day is 8:00 A.M. to 5:00 PM. with one hour off for lunch, other section heads know that Sally does not enforce this schedule too strictly with her subsection heads. People are allowed to come in 30 to 45 minutes late occasionally and to leave 10 to 20 minutes early without indicating this on their time cards. Since all employees are on a biweekly salary, they are paid for 40 hours of work each week even though they may have worked an hour or two less.

Sally also lets her subordinates leave work two or three hours early occasionally to run personal errands without taking the personal leave time required by the state. She also does not object if employees take a little longer for lunch. Of course, since she doesn't enforce these rules with her subordinates she really does not expect them to enforce them with their subordinates. She has told her subsection heads that as long as productivity remains as high as it is, she will look the other way.

John has talked with Sally about this issue only once. Sally simply indicated that her section was doing a far better job than anyone else's, and as long as this continued, she was not going to stop the loose-hours practice. She said that she hoped John would allow her to con-tinue with this, so John was hesitant to bring the issue up again.

Lately, however, two other section heads have complained to John about Sally's deviation from state policy on work hours. It appears that considerable pressure has been brought on them by their subsection heads to also allow them and their subordinates to deviate from state work-hour rules. John responded to these two section heads by telling them that Sally's section was producing so much more than the others that it was OK with him if she were a little lenient. Their response was that the reason Sally's section was producing so much more was be-cause her unit was overstaffed relative to theirs, had newer equipment, and processed claims that were easier to handle. While John thought they might have a point on the equipment, he did know that Sally's staffing was within the applied staffing formula. He was not sure about the easier claims, but promised them he would do a work sample to test their assertion.

When John informed Sally of his plans to do the work sample, she became somewhat defensive, telling John her unit was doing the same work as everyone and doing a better job. Sally said the reason why they were so much more efficient was because she had good subsection heads who had created an excellent work environment that had not only substantially reduced turnover, but had also increased motivational levels of individual employees. She indicated that other sections had poor supervisory relationships that caused low morale and high turnover.

John agreed that turnover was higher in the other sections—the figures spoke for themselves—but he believed a work sample was still needed. Yet he hesitated to go ahead with it without Sally's support, especially if it so disrupted her section that turnover increased and work output fell. He did feel, however, that he was treading on thin ice by allowing Sally to let her section deviate so much from established policy.

Analysis

If you were John, what would you do now? Why? Is enforcing work-hours policy more important than high output? Why, or why not? Would this situation be different if it were a private insurance company processing claims? Why, or why not?

State agencies are usually very bureaucratic in nature. Often, they are more concerned that rules, policy, and procedure be followed than that performance be high. Bureaucracies do not inspire managerial and employee competence. If the Division of Employment Security and the Department of Labor in this state are very bureaucratic, then John better be careful. If any of the disaffected section heads decides to break the chain of command and go directly to the division or department director, John could be placed in a very difficult situation. He will be pressured not only from section heads below him, but from his superiors as well.

John must carefully document the productivity of Sally's unit. He will need accurate figures on output levels, error rates, turnover, and staffing levels for Sally's section compared with other sections. He will also need to conduct the work sample of all sections so that he can document for his superiors and other section heads the difficulty of the claims Sally's section processes compared with other sections.

Prior to conducting the work sample, John needs to have a meeting with Sally and her subsection heads to fully explain the reason for the procedure. He should explain that all sections will be sampled, not just those under Sally's authority. This should reduce any feelings of being singled out. He should also use this opportunity to praise and otherwise reinforce the high productivity of Sally's section. If the work sample shows that the claims being processed by Sally's section are less difficult and time consuming than those of other sections, John should inform Sally and her subsection heads of this and then make a more equitable workload distribution among the sections.

Regardless of the work sample results, John must take action with other section heads to reduce turnover and increase output in each section. He should examine and improve bureau hiring, placement, and training policies and procedures. He may wish to introduce contests among sections. He may need to replace some heads with more capable managers.

The issue for John may not be why Sally's section output is so high; instead it may be why the output of other sections is so low. This is the key area for analysis. Work-hour schedules are orderly means to achieve ends of high productivity and low errors. Unfortunately, in government, ends sometimes become the means. Form is valued over content; process is valued over product. This may be true in John's case and he may simply have to comply and find some other means to reward Sally's section.

Summary

Associating with competent superiors, subordinates, and peer managers is critical for successful job performance. It will not guarantee success, but through synergism, it will sure make job performance easier.

We should not play the role of janitor, cleaning up after superiors, subordinates, or peer managers in the organization. This takes time and effort away from our critical job tasks and prevents us from performing as well as we could. Also, most of us are not paid enough to do the jobs of others as well as our own. Breaking this habit is difficult, however, because of the law of the self-fulfilling prophecy and the expectations it creates. This is why meetings to generate consensus and expectations between superiors, subordinates, and peers are so important.

In the next chapter, we'll look at rewards on the job: specifically, the role that money plays as a reward and measure of individual and organization performance. Money and rewards are critical for encouraging and maintaining competence on the job.

4

Money Isn't Everything; It's the Only Thing

Rewards must follow performance. Competent performance must be rewarded; incompetent behavior must not be rewarded. This simple fact is obvious, yet it is violated daily in most organizations. People are paid for the time they put in on the job rather than the goods or services they produce. Promotions are based on time in the organization not capacity to perform. People are hired because they will "fit in" rather than because they will be top producers. Incompetent people often receive standard, across-the-board pay raises equal to those received by competent performers.

All of these actions condone incompetence by failing to distinguish between competent and incompetent behavior through the organization's reward system. Employees are told, in effect, that no matter what they do they'll get rewarded. By not differentiating rewards based on performance, the reward system loses all of its intended meaning.

Why Do Reward Systems Often Fail to Reward?

There are many reasons why managers do not use the reward system properly to reward competent performance. Not all of these are within a manager's control. But if incompetence is to be managed, managers must make a concerted effort to influence the reward system as much as possible so that competent, and not incompetent, behavior is rewarded. Following are some common reasons why reward systems don't reward.

Sometimes it's difficult to tell when someone has done a good job. Some performance is hard to measure. This is particularly true in service industries like government or education. How do we know, for example, when a social worker has provided good service to a client? What hard measures are there of exceptional performance for an elementary school teacher? Most job performance measures in these areas are fuzzy. Usually these types of organization have not put the required time and effort into developing better performance measures. Fuzzy criteria are open to widely differing interpretations as to what constitutes superior performance.

Closely related to the problem described above is the argument that any merit system of rewards is fraught with managerial favoritism and bias. In other words, if we have trouble distinguishing good performance from bad, then all we are doing when we reward is to take care of our favorites. This leads to charges of paternalism, nepotism, and capriciousness. It is for this reason that unions so often argue for seniority as the primary basis for annual wage increases and promotions. They want to reduce the amount of discretion—and hence favoritism—management can exercise.

Inflation presents another problem to reward systems. During times of high inflation, such as that experienced in the United States during the late 1970s and early 1980s, the argument is often made that everyone should receive a large across-the-board annual wage increase just to keep even with inflation. So if inflation runs about 13 percent per year as in 1979, the argument is made that everyone should receive a 13 percent annual wage increase. Since this usually exhausts money available for wage increases, any merit increases are forfeited that year.

Consider Mary's situation.

MARY, MARY, QUITE CONTRARY

Mary Stevens is a family services counselor in a State Health and Rehabilitative Services (HRS) office. She has been with HRS for almost four years. During her first two years she was an outstanding employee. However, although her performance began to deteriorate during her third year, still she received an overall outstanding evaluation on her annual performance appraisal.

During the past year, Fred Albrecht was appointed as Mary's supervisor. Fred quickly noticed that Mary's work habits were rather poor. During the past six months, she has had problems getting along with other employees in the office, and she has been shaving time: she has been 15 minutes late for work four times each of the past two months, she has often taken long lunch hours, and she has frequently left work early. In addition, on several occasions Fred has overheard her on the telephone and in the office talking with clients in a condescending, curt manner.

Last month Fred spoke with Mary about these problems, hoping to find a way to resolve them. After about an hour's discussion, in which Mary seemed evasive and had many excuses, she concluded the meeting by saying, "Look, they don't pay me enough to do this work. My pay hasn't even kept pace with inflation over the past two years. Inflation has averaged 10 percent each year, and my pay increase has averaged 6 percent. What do you expect?"

It is Fred's responsibility to complete Mary's annual performance evaluation for 1979, which will be used to compute a small annual merit increase (one to 4 percent) that can be received by a deserving employee. All employees also receive a 4 percent across-the-board annual raise. Inflation during 1979, the period of the review, was 13 percent. Mary is protected by state career-service regulations that make it very difficult to terminate her.

Analysis

What should Fred do? What effect does inflation have on the reward system? Can Mary be compensated now for superior performance that occurred during her first two years?

Obviously, since Mary's annual wage increases have not kept up with inflation, she feels she has suffered a real wage cut, which she has. For 1979, even if she received the highest merit increase plus the 4 percent across-the-board increase, she will still be five percentage points below the inflation rate. Such is the price public employees often have to pay in return for job security.

Fred must make it clear to Mary that her job is much safer than if she were in private business, and that even though her wages have not kept pace with inflation as certain industrial workers' may have, she is not subject to frequent layoffs as are auto or rubber workers. This job security is part of the total reward package for government employees. But Fred must also make it clear that unless her performance improves, she could be subject to termination, difficult as this procedure might be to carry out in civil service.

Finally, Fred should avoid granting Mary any merit salary increase at all. To grant her a large increase so she can keep up with inflation merely rewards her poor performance during the past year. She needs to understand that good performance creates the possibility of her raise climbing from 4 percent to 8 percent. While 8 percent is still below the inflation rate of 13 percent, it is twice a 4 percent raise.

Even though the total raise package is below the annual inflation rate, the variation in the merit raise received by each individual connotes a rating of that person's performance relative to others. Whether salary information is shared formally or informally (and it is likely to be public information—and thus shared formally—in a state agency), each employee will know how he or she fares relative to others. The annual merit increase can be used to differentiate and reward performance even if it is below the annual rate of increase in consumer prices.

Sometimes an organization simply cannot afford to pay. Suppose a firm has a bad year or a government agency faces a major budget cut in a particular year; it may not be possible to provide any wage increases or promotions the following year. In fact, wage reductions might be necessary. We saw this in 1980 with the Chrysler Corporation. Managers and executives had their salaries cut, and rank-and-file factory workers forfeited portions of future wage increases for a three-year period. Obviously, if no money is available for wage increases for anyone, then monetary rewards cannot be used to reward competent performance.

Unions attempt to reduce the amount of discretion management can exercise in all areas. In particular, two areas where a union applies pressure are annual wage and promotion decisions. Unions want tenure or seniority to be used as a basis for promotions as well as for across-the-board wage increases. Thus, if an organization faces a powerful union with this philosophy, it will be more difficult to reward competent performance.

When unions or employee associations make length of service the primary consideration for wage increases, promotions, vacations, layoffs, and dismissals, then employees have *de facto* tenure. In the university environment, faculty members are awarded tenure after a specified length of time of proven performance, usually five to seven years. This is done in the name of academic freedom: established faculty should not be fired for unpopular views expressed in class or in print.

In an industrial setting, union employees begin earning a type of tenure after a probationary period of usually 30 to 90 days. This length-of-service tenure soon affects all decisions regarding job assignment, promotion (assuming the employee has the minimum skills), wage increase, layoff, and termination. Of course, tenure, be it academic or *de facto* based on seniority, greatly reduces a manager's discretion to reward competent behavior. Consider this example.

TENURE?

Jack Haroldson is a 52-year-old research chemist in a large petroleum company. After earning his Ph.D. at the age of 26, Jack taught at a university for ten years, and then joined his present employer.

Jack was promoted to the highest rank of research chemist four years ago and is now at the highest salary level for that rank. Over the years, he has made a substantial contribution to new product development, presented papers to professional organizations, and published articles in learned journals. During the last two years, however, Jack's research output has fallen off considerably. Even though publication is not required by the company, he has not published an article or presented a paper for three years and has none under development. Furthermore, while research chemists have flexible work hours, his absenteeism has increased to an average of three days a month over the past six months.

Jim Racine, Jack's department head, has discussed these issues with Jack on several occasions over the past several weeks. Jack indicated that he was about to hit on something major for the company and was in a very creative stage. He needed time to think. Yet as time passed, Jim saw little evidence that Jack's creative efforts were bearing fruit.

Finally, after Jack had been out three days in a row, Jim stopped by his office near the lab and saw Jack sitting with his feet propped up on his desk, as if asleep. "Hey, Jack!" exclaimed Jim, "Wake up!"

"I am awake," replied Jack. "I'm thinking."

"You're thinking, hell. You were asleep."

"No I wasn't, Jim. I was thinking. I'm really on to something big."

"What? I'd like to start seeing some results," said Jim.

"You're too young to remember, but I was the one who developed that new polymer that is the lifeblood of this division today. Take that away and this company would be zilch."

"I know you were involved in that, Jack, but so were others. And, yes, it was a godsend for the company. But that was five years ago."

"Larry [the division president] really appreciated that one. It got him promoted. Did you know that, Jim?"

"Well, I don't know about that, Jack. He . . ."

"Well, I guess that little ole' invention earned me tenure around here, didn't it, Jim?"

Analysis

Does Jack have *de facto* tenure? Can and should Jim do anything about this situation? If so, what?

It's clear Jack feels he has earned tenure in the company whether he has been officially awarded it or not. He made a substantial contribution in previous years, and apparently the product he helped develop was a key one for the division. He appears to have the complete confidence of the division president and is at the top of his rank and pay scale. As a professional with an academic background, he feels he has earned his tenure and may be entitled to cut back some. After all, he has worked hard.

Ridiculous! At age 52 he is too young to retire physically or mentally. No doubt with proper incentives and guidance he can once again become a top performer. While tenure—*de facto* or academic—is helpful to an organization, it can lead people to literally fall asleep on the job if some care is not exercised. Professionals with tenure have some protection against arbitrary discharge, but they usually can be dismissed for gross incompetence or moral terpitude—which could happen to Jack if his performance does not improve.

Dismissal, however, should be an action of last resort. Prior to that, Jim should work with Jack and help him close his present project. But if the project is just a smoke screen, Jim should encourage interest in a new project. Perhaps more laboratory assistance is needed, or perhaps he could pair Jack with a new, eager chemist to start on a new project. Maybe Jim can again interest Jack in becoming active in a professional organization so as to receive recognition from peers, which often motivates professionals and seems to have worked in the past with Jack.

The point is, tenure should not become an excuse for inactivity and incompetence. Unless an organization monitors its tenured people and is willing to take some corrective action when needed, tenure can sometimes serve as a cocoon that protects the incompetent.

Giving a competent subordinate a wage increase for superior performance means denying a poor performer a similar increase. Thus, a manager has to say "no" to some subordinates. Many managers feel uncomfortable doing this and don't wish to hurt some subordinates and cause tension and conflict in the workplace. So it's easier just to give everyone the same annual wage increase than to tell some they will be receiving less money than others.

Sometimes an employee works on a job where it is difficult to control output. Other people at or outside the job affect performance. For example, salespersons on a commission or bonus often complain that those who make the highest commissions have the easiest territories. Even though sales managers try to adjust the commission rate to the sales territory, some inequities no doubt remain.

I once worked on an assembly line where we were payed a group bonus based on how much we produced each day. Yet our output depended directly on the output of another assembly line. If its output was low, ours was too, no matter what we did, because we did not have product components to work on. We were penalized for the poor performance of others, and even though we wished to work hard, we often could not because not enough components were available. Of course, in a situation like this a more equitable bonus system should have been set up, one that did not penalize us for the failure of another group. But after several experiments management decided such a system was impossible to design and they did away with the bonus, putting everyone on a straight hourly basis to reduce dissension.

Often managers use an incentive system, such as the group bonus described above, that directly relates money earned to performance. Piece rate, sales commissions, profit sharing, and cost reduction plans, like the Scanlon Plan, are examples of incentive systems.

Sometimes these systems are so complicated it's difficult for employees to understand how their individual payments are computed. In the group bonus system described above, one factor that continually frustrated us was that we could never figure out exactly how the complex set of formulas worked for each of us in determining weekly bonus. This is even more amazing since I was a senior management student studying personnel at a major university, employed only during the summer, and I could not understand the system. For the average employee it was completely beyond comprehension. Such a complicated system makes it difficult for the employees to see how their output is related to increased wages. They are not sure how much is required for a reward or if management will "retime the job" if they produce too much. That the incentive system was so complex also led to its demise.

Each of the above conditions for not having a reward system tied to performance can be substantially altered or even eliminated. In fact, this must be done for the reward system to work properly. People must believe that their performance will be rewarded.

How Can the Pitfalls of an Inadequate Reward System Be Overcome?

First, *expectancy theory* tells us that employees must expect that a certain desirable reward will follow a given level of performance.

In other words, employees must first want the reward and then expect that it will be forthcoming at a given level of effort and output. Complicated systems that are always being retimed to set new rates are frustrating. They make employees feel like they are being exploited. It is necessary to have clear systems with specific and fair guidelines for retiming.

Second, *equity theory* tells us that employees compare their performance and rewards with those of others. In other words:

$$\frac{\text{my rewards}}{\text{my effort and output}} \quad \text{are compared with} \quad \frac{\text{others' rewards}}{\text{their effort and output}}$$

If there are substantial differences, I will make an adjustment. If I perceive my rewards relative to my effort and output as low compared with others', I will seek to do one of the following:

1. Raise my rewards.
2. Reduce my effort and output.
3. Reduce the rewards of others.
4. Increase the effort and output of others.

If, on the other hand, I perceive my rewards to be higher than those of others relative to my and their outputs, I will try to:

1. Increase my effort and output.
2. Increase the rewards of others.
3. Reduce the effort and output of others.

(Notice that in this case I will not seek to reduce my rewards.)

Thus, the second requirement for an effective reward system that distinguishes competent from incompetent behavior is that it must be perceived by employees as fair and equitable. Appropriate rewards must be related to appropriate levels of effort and output.

The Peter Principle: In a hierarchy, every employee tends to rise to his level of incompetence.

Laurence J. Peter and Raymond Hull

Third, *motivation theory* tells us that rewards should act to satisfy unfulfilled needs of employees. So far, this chapter has stressed money as the primary reward, because for most people money is a need satisfier. It is not the *only* need satisfier, but research shows that it is one of the most important, because money represents so many other things: status, prestige, and recognition, as well as inherent purchasing power. Frederick Herzberg's Dual Factor Theory states that money does not motivate (its absence causes dissatisfaction; its presence does not cause satisfaction), but much research shows that money will motivate if tied directly to performance and output.

Yet a reward system should also provide other compensation besides money. For example, a good reward system will also include the following:

1. Promotion to jobs of higher authority and responsibility.
2. Certain perquisites such as club membership, executive dining room privileges, reserved parking spaces, and others.
3. Praise—both oral and written.
4. A comprehensive health and benefits package, including a sound pension plan.
5. Interesting jobs that have challenging and satisfying tasks built into them.
6. Status symbols like job titles, service award pins, certain office locations, types of desks, and so on.
7. Opportunities for time off with pay, such as vacation, holidays, sabbaticals, or personal leave time.
8. Company-paid vacation trips for employee and family.

For these rewards to work properly, however, they must be earned. Often they are provided to everyone regardless of performance level (for example, a health and benefits package) or are based on years of service regardless of performance (such as vacation time). While there has to be some minimum level of health insurance and vacation time provided for everyone, additional insurance and time off could be tied to superior levels of performance. When this is done, these factors take on added meaning and serve as incentives for superior performance. They motivate people toward competent levels of performance.

Finally, *goal-path theory* tells us that employees must desire a particular goal and believe a certain path will lead to that goal. If I desire a promotion I must believe that doing a good job will get it for me. Also, goal-path theory holds that I must want and be able to follow the required path. If I see that promotions are based upon apple-polishing for the boss and I'm opposed to this, I will not do it and will therefore not be motivated by promotion. So goal-path theory tells us the following:

1. I must desire the goal.
2. I must see the path that leads to the goal.
3. I must have the ability to follow the path.
4. I must want to follow the path.

Obviously, many reward systems fail because not all of these four items are present.

What Can an Individual Manager Do?

So many managers believe they can't do anything to improve their organization's reward system in order to reward competent behavior. They feel that their hands are tied and they have little authority to effect change, feeling blocked by personnel departments, higher management, or some other group.

These feelings of helplessness are especially prevalent in large bureaucracies like government agencies. But they can also exist in medium-sized firms where the personnel department has too much authority over the reward system or where a particularly powerful union exists.

As long as a substantial group of managers in an organization believes this, the reward system is unlikely to be changed. Consider this person's statement:

BURNED UP

Sure I believe reward systems should reward competent behavior and not reward incompetent behavior. Any manager worth his salt should believe this. But around here, rewards are based primarily on political factors. It's "promotion by surprise." A person is promoted and no one knows why, except that he must have an in with the boss.

Raises are handed out almost willy-nilly. Salaries are kept confidential by the company and no one really knows for sure what kind of increases other people are getting. All we hear is lunchroom and office gossip. As a department head I have a pretty good idea of what the supervisors below me are making, but I really do not know what people in other units make. It's as if the company is so unsure of its salary system for managers that they want to keep it a big secret.

We know what all our people at the worker level make because we have a union and the rates are printed in the contract. But the union exists primarily to reward seniority. Everybody gets the same percentage raise each year no matter how he or she did. Our gutless wonders in Industrial Relations won't stand up to the union so as to institute some incentive system or to try to make merit the basis of wage increases. Giving everyone these big raises each year just makes inflation worse since people get an increase even if their productivity has not gone up at all. How can we survive as a nation when we give people an annual raise no matter how poor their performance during the past year?

So what am I to do? What power do I have to change things? None. All of us department heads feel the same. Top management won't listen to us. I guess I'm stuck with the present system and I don't like it. Sometimes I get so burned up about this I feel like quitting, but what good would that do? I'll just have to lump it, I guess.

Analysis

This person feels the frustration common to many managers in large organizations who have basically lost their authority to reward. The constraints imposed by personnel, top management, and the union have so narrowed their authority that they feel helpless. What can managers do who find themselves in this position?

First, in this case, the department heads could act together to lay out the problem and a recommended solution to top management. Instead of acting individually, they should approach top management as a group, demonstrating that the concern is not isolated but is a major one of a group of middle managers. Also, by presenting a suggested solution the department heads are not just "bitching" about the present state of affairs, but have a viable solution.

Second, the role of the middle managers with regard to collective bargaining negotiations needs to be redefined. Apparently they are not being consulted enough by the firm's I.R. negotiating team for information to use at the bargaining table. While unions do tend to emphasize seniority and across-the-board raises, it *doesn't* have to be this way. A company doesn't always have to give in to this demand. There is no reason why a system of incentives or merit wage increases cannot be used in addition to some across-the-board increase. The department heads need to make their position known on this and to press regularly for this demand with the company negotiators.

Third, the department heads are able to control other aspects of the reward system. They can recommend supervisors for promotion, offer oral and written praise, use job assignment (for non-union employees) as part of the reward system, complete accurate performance appraisal records that reflect true performance, and use status symbols and certain perks as rewards. These actions show that even when managers feel their hands are tied by the wage and salary and promotion systems, they still have other ways to reward competent performance.

Individuals like the one quoted above are often looking for a scapegoat to blame for their own failures to make the reward system work. While a manager can indeed be hamstrung by top management, personnel, or a union, the manager should not throw his hands up in disgust and refuse to improve the system. It is the responsibility of every manager to work for system improvement so that competent behavior is rewarded.

Don't Managers Try to Make or Save Money for the Organization?

In the early days of industrial activity, managers of the organization were its owners, founders, and entrepreneurs. We had Ford, Carnegie, Mellon, Kroger, Chrysler, Firestone, and so on, as corporate leaders. As time went on, the organization's owner-founders were replaced as managers by a professional staff with little or no ownership. John Kenneth Galbraith has long recognized this problem of the separation of ownership and management. The professional manager does not have the same dedication and loyalty to profit maximization as the owner. Although companies have tried to overcome this limitation through stock purchase plans, profit sharing, and large executive bonuses, the manager today still works *for* the corporation. The corporation does not work for him as in the past. It is no longer an extension of the founder's or owner's personality.

Whether this is good or bad or, indeed, can even be changed today is not part of this discussion. What matters is the lack of incentive for top management to maximize profit, or reduce costs in the case of a not-for-profit organization. Organization owners today are, by and large, not really interested in anything other than a dividend check. They give up their vote through proxy, holding so few shares that they believe their vote doesn't really matter. Or they own stock indirectly through institutions like pension or mutual funds and have no voting rights. What owners want today is not profit maximization, but long-term growth and stability in dividends. What salaried managers want is a steady job, a good income which rises annually, and a periodic bonus as icing on the cake. Their identification with the organization as a way to build personal wealth is not as strong as the owner-manager's. In fact, many managers today may have very little of their own wealth invested in the company they manage. They may own certificates of deposit, stocks and bonds of other companies, or shares of insurance and pension funds—virtually unheard of in the owner-manager days.

Therefore, what real incentive does top management have today to maximize the assets and wealth of the corporation? Very little incentive exists. Not only are they without this incentive, but they are pushed and pulled by competing interest groups—government agencies, consumers, labor, charitable organizations, and others—for a piece of the corporate pie. Maximizing profits is no longer the objective; rather, as Herbert A. Simon says in his book *Administrative Behavior* (1957), it is to *satisfice* profits. Satisficing means that management needs to maintain some reasonable, satisfactory level of profits in order to ensure continued stable growth and the company's survival. This has replaced the objective of maximizing profit.

This causes all sorts of behavior that may not be in the best interests of maximizing owner return on assets. Evaluation of competing capital expenditures is not based on profit maximization, but according to the best chance for a reasonable level of return over the long term. Instead of high risks that could result in high profits, more conservative risks are taken that are more likely to result in a lower but surer return. Instead of standing up to labor on an outrageous wage demand, to the point of a strike or lockout, management makes settlements to ensure the uninterrupted operations of the company. Gone is the desire to maximize profits. In its place is the desire to achieve stable, long-term, reasonable profits. Where is the incentive to go the extra mile? It's missing.

Yet company managers *do* have the responsibility to maximize return on investment and to reduce costs.

How Can an Organization Create a Sense of Ownership Among Its Managers?

This is, indeed, difficult to accomplish, yet it is important and should be done so as to improve managerial effectiveness. As we've seen, many companies use stock option plans, profit sharing, and executive bonuses to build a sense of ownership. The problem with these, however, is that they are often of relatively small value, except for a very few key, top-level executives. The issue then is how to spread these benefits among other top managers as well as middle- and lower-level managers.

One method used successfully by a number of firms is the profit center concept, sometimes called entrepreneurial bonus plans since they treat managers as proprietors of an independent business. Compensation depends on the success of that business. By decentralizing and using cost accounting principles and structured goal setting—MBO, for example—it is possible to create semi-autonomous units, and then to hold the managers of these units accountable for profits. Earnings can then be shared among these managers in a significant fashion through stock ownership or profit sharing. Decentralization of authority and responsiblity should be followed by decentralization of partial ownership and thus rewards.

Another way to create wealth for the manager is an investment program tied to corporate performance. While such a wealth-creating program is usually linked to common stock ownership, it can go beyond this. In addition to common stock ownership, preferred stock, bond, and other corporate obligations can be purchased in the manager's name, so the corporation becomes the primary vehicle for the manager's investment income. Theoretically, the better the company does, the greater the return on personal investment and the greater the increase in the wealth of the manager, who has a personal stake in the health and growth of the organization beyond salary or an occasional bonus.

A third method is called cost reduction. It relies, not on generating a profit, but on reducing costs. Although it was developed in the steel industry, its greatest potential is in not-for-profit organizations like government agencies.

The Scanlon and Kaiser plans are the best known of this type. Managers, their superiors, and employees decide on a realistic, acceptable cost of production or operation at the beginning of a specified time period, say a year, in order to produce a given level of output or a certain service level. If the production or service level is reached, at acceptable quality levels and at a cost lower than that agreed to, the cost difference is shared among the organization, managers, and the employees as a year-end bonus. Of course, effective cost reduction depends upon forecasting production costs with integrity and realism. This is not always easy to do, especially if there is little trust among managers and employees. Yet with proper cost forecasts and certain cost checks, the program can work and has worked successfully. Even in not-for-profit organizations people can be given a real incentive to do well, feel a sense of ownership, and work for the organization's success.

Finally, some top executives use another approach that is somewhat different from the three mentioned. It does not rely on creating a sense of ownership for managers. Rather, it creates a sense of urgency among managers to maximize their income. Consider this manager's ideas:

IN DEBT

In today's large complex organization it's very difficult to create a sense of ownership among key managers. Stock option plans, bonuses, and profit-sharing plans usually don't provide enough incentive for the average manager. So I take another approach. I want my people to be so far in debt that they have to work their tails off just to meet their monthly bills. In other words, instead of *pulling* them to work harder through incentives, I like to *push* them to work harder through fear—fear that they won't meet their monthly bills. Fear can be a strong motivator.

Therefore, I like to see my managers buy new expensive houses, cars, campers, boats, clothes, country club membership, and so on. The monthly pressure of meeting high bills drives them to work harder and harder. They *want* to maximize their income because they *need* to.

Now when I tie bonuses, profit sharing, and other financial incentives to superior performance, it has real meaning for them. It's not a nice extra, but a necessity. Thus I can make incentive payments really work. If my executives tried to maintain a moderate or average standard of living, why would they strive for a high bonus? They've got to be kept hungry for more money.

Analysis

What do you think of this strategy? Is it proper for an organization to encourage high spending levels among its executives and managers? This person has tried to make discretionary spending permanent. He wants his people to be so locked into debt that the constant need for more money spurs them to higher efforts. But while this strategy may work with some people, it can have a devastating effect on others. High levels of debt can cause stress, heavy drinking, domestic problems, and even divorce. Should organizations encourage such behavior?

Summary

Rewards must follow performance. It is through the reward system that organizations recognize and encourage competent performance and discourage incompetent performance. Across-the-board wage increases, standard hourly wages, or weekly and monthly salaries pay people for *time* put in on the job, not for *performance* on the job. Managers must use pay and the entire reward system to differentiate good performance from average. A person must know that if a good job is done, a meaningful reward follows. If not, where is the incentive for superior performance? Of course, this system requires that managers are able to tell the difference between superior and average performance. It means organizations need hard measures of performance that are accurate and understood by all. Playing favorites or rewarding buddies through the "old boy network" is not appropriate. Performance, well measured and well rewarded, is the key to encouraging competence.

5

Fat Cats and Rats

Why do so many top executives isolate themselves from the rest of the organization, creating buffers and layers between them and others? How does this isolation contribute to the problem of managing incompetence?

Top-level executives often live in a surreal world. They are picked up at their mansion by their chauffeurs, driven to the corporate jet for a meeting in the Bahamas, returned to their downtown club for dinner, and whisked back home in the evening. They associate primarily with others of their status and background at private clubs, on the golf course, in their neighborhoods, and at the best resorts. They dine at the finest restaurants and clubs, work amid the plushest office surroundings, and vacation at the most exclusive spots in the world. Their children attend exclusive private schools. Gardeners, maids, and servants attend their homes. They worry little about inflation, school integration, weekly trips to the market, picking up the dry cleaning, or running their children all over town to 101 activities.

While this description certainly does not characterize all corporate executives, the lifestyle of a typical top-level executive is vastly different from that of a mid-level or supervisory manager and that of a rank-and-file worker. This lifestyle is usually justified on the basis of entitlement: they've earned it and it befits their position in life.

They also justify their isolation from the rest of the company with the argument that their demanding job requires time for long-range planning, policy making, and strategic decision making. They do not have time to get involved in routine problem solving or decision making. Others can do this. If they got involved in small decisions, who would make the big ones?

While there is some truth to this way of thinking, there is also danger. Small decisions can become catastrophic problems, as we saw in the Watergate trauma. Yet executives cannot have their noses everywhere in the organization.

The key to solving this dilemma is accessibility. How accessible should top-level executives be to people, information, and ideas in and outside of the organization? What are the consequences of inaccessibility? How can top-level executives carry out their major responsibilities, including meeting with various outside groups, and avoid becoming isolated from internal affairs?

This is not easy to solve, and yet the problem must be properly addressed if managing incompetence is to be effective. The final responsibility for managing incompetence rests with the organization's top executive staff. If they ignore this problem, it will remain unaddressed. People in organizations do what top executives watch. We know that unless top management is committed and attentive to something and visibly indicates this, people down through the organization won't be committed to it. Commitment for a project or idea from top management is not sufficient for its successful conclusion or implementation, but it is *necessary*.

How Do Top Brass Spin Cocoons?

Top executives are quite successful at developing a complex web of rules, procedures, and offices that can effectively isolate them from most of the organization. They have assistants, executive secretaries, receptionists, rows of offices between them and outer offices, tight appointment schedules, and other barriers to entry. The chief executive doesn't return calls, someone else does. Letters and memos are written (and often signed) by others in the executive's name. Problems directed at the executive's office are usually examined, and sometimes solved, by others. This is all to limit the top executive's involvement in day-to-day issues. There is only so much time in a day and the top executive must spend it on the important issues of concern to the organization as a whole. The sheer volume of information, requests, and contacts directed toward a top executive is physically impossible for one person to handle.

Yet this cadre of executive screeners and buffers can soon become "yea-sayers" to the detriment of the organization, more concerned with remaining in the executive's good graces than with accurately communicating information that could be construed as having a negative impact on the organization. Not many relish the role of one who carries bad news to the mountain top. Just as the Greek messengers were killed if they brought bad news to the generals, carriers of disconcerting organization news are sometimes rejected by executives. No one likes to be banished from the inner circle.

This problem of telling top executives only what they want to hear is a serious one and prevents correction of incompetent action. How can corrective steps be taken if the top executives don't know problems exist? I recently had an experience that exemplifies this situation.

BAD NEWS BEARERS

A couple of years ago we were involved in a major development project for a large state agency. An initial step in this project was to conduct an organization assessment or audit to pinpoint the strengths and weaknesses of the agency. To do so we decided to use the interview-survey-feedback technique. We planned to interview lower- and mid-level managers, gather and analyze their responses, and feed the information back to them in workshop sessions. During these sessions, solution strategies would be designed for each problem identified.

Soon after we signed the contract for the program, we met with the agency head to tell him what we would be doing and to alert him to the fact that we would be exposing agency problems as part of the assessment. We did not want him to be embarrassed because we were making a conscious effort to pinpoint problems in the agency so they could be dealt with forthrightly. Without hesitating, he agreed to this plan.

We then asked him for the name of a person in his office with whom we could meet periodically to discuss our progress and any issues or blocks we might encounter. He immediately named the chief of his executive staff. At the conclusion of the meeting he took us to her office and introduced us, and we talked with her for about 45 minutes. We agreed to meet again in one month.

We were very pleased after our two initial meetings, which occurred in January. We felt the agency head supported our efforts, and we believed we had a direct line to him through his chief of staff.

In February, as agreed, we met again with the chief of staff, explained to her our plans for the assessment, and reviewed the instrument we would use to interview each manager. She was enthusiastic and looked forward to reviewing some preliminary data at our next meeting in March.

At that meeting, we reviewed with her data collected from the first group of 25 middle managers. These data, compiled and tabulated so that it was not possible to associate responses with particular individuals, would serve as the basis for our workshop with the middle managers. While reviewing the data, the chief of staff was somewhat surprised at the breadth and depth of the problems identified. After about 30 minutes of discussion we left, but she was clearly troubled.

At the end of March we had difficulty reaching her to arrange our April meeting. After several calls to her secretary, we finally got through and arranged a time for early April. But the day prior to the meeting, her secretary called to cancel it, indicating the chief of staff could not set up a new meeting time until the following week. She would call and let us know. Next week passed and then the next. Our phone calls to the chief and her secretary were not returned. Finally, three weeks after the initial date for the April meeting, we were able to set a new date for early May.

At the May meeting, the chief of staff pleasantly apologized for being unable to find a time for us in April. She said we would begin meeting monthly again in the future. After a fruitful discussion of another set of data from the second group of 25 middle managers, we left her office, agreeing to set up a new meeting for the first week in June.

Once again we experienced difficulty in arranging a time. By June 5, it had still not been set, and our phone calls to the chief of staff were again not returned. At this point I called the head of the agency. Two calls were not returned. I wrote a letter to him detailing the problem and asking that we meet with him personally. No reply was received.

Finally, at the end of June, I received a call from the chief of staff's secretary, who said that from now on we were to deal with a new man named Raleigh on our project. He had been with the agency for several years and was a rather unusual person. In asking a few knowledgeable persons in the agency (as well as the managers with whom we were working in the development program) about him, we were told that Raleigh had little credibility in the field of development and was generally thought of as a real "character." We also found that our direct link to the agency head's office was now far removed, since Raleigh was five levels below him. In other words, instead of working with a person who was close to the agency head on a daily basis, we were now to deal with a person who had nothing to do with the agency head and, indeed, was five offices removed from him.

After one meeting with Raleigh at the end of June it was soon apparent what had happened. The chief of staff was not removed from our project because she was too busy. Raleigh had not been appointed because he had more time for us and would give us better service. Rather, the agency head did not want to hear about the problems and issues we were uncovering. He made Raleigh our liaison so that the information we gave to Raleigh would never get to him and so that we would be discredited by association with a person of low credibility.

Analysis

This rather long example shows the lengths to which some managers will go to avoid hearing things they don't want to hear. "Yes, I'm open, I want to know" often really means "I want to hear good things about my big happy family."

Granted, we were outsiders, but we had been invited to the agency because it had very real problems that needed attention. The agency executives also believed that a comprehensive organization and management development program was needed to correct these problems, not traditional management training of the two- or three-day variety.

But as we continued with the program, it indeed became more traditional. The organization assessment ceased. The survey-feedback method stopped. The management development sessions became two- or three-day "dog and pony shows." It was obvious that the higher-level agency executives did not want middle and lower managers to deal with real problems in an open forum.

An interesting phenomenon of this whole process was "denial of the data." It started with the agency head, but it eventually continued down through the organization. People denied that the data applied to them. Comments like "This cannot be accurate" and "These are not our managers" were frequent. Related to this was the "denial of ownership" syndrome. In some cases middle managers would accept the data but claim it was not their problem. They believed nothing they could do would correct it. The problem had to be solved by someone else—preferably top management.

These two reactions—denial of the data and denial of ownership of the problem—were defensive reactions on the part of managers who felt helpless in dealing with problems and issues of great magnitude and who felt that only top management could solve them. Top management believed that while there were some problems, they were relatively minor and most things were going along fine. They really didn't want to hear about any serious problems. Thus a stalemate was created and the development program slipped from an organizationally focused and diagnostic one to typical dog and pony show training. Incompetent performance by many managers in several units continued, because in essence top management did not want to believe it existed in the first place.

How Does Isolation of Top Management Lead to Excessive Loyalty?

The top manager's group of buffers and screeners becomes an inner circle—a ruling clique. If conditions become rough and bad news filters in, the inner circle belittles it. Comments like "It's just a few spoiled apples in the barrel," "There are always some complainers," "They don't represent the feelings of all employees," "It's just a passing fad," and "Don't worry, they don't know what they're talking about" become very common. Like the pioneer settlers, staff members pull the wagons into a circle to keep out bad influences. Any advisor who suggests there might be some validity to the complaints is viewed as a traitor—one who has sided with the enemy.

A "we versus them" mentality develops and soon colors all actions of the group. Anyone who deviates from this approach is viewed as disloyal. Advisors no longer give objective advice, but rather reinforce the position and attitudes of the executive. Perceived disloyal members of this inner circle are discredited and even transferred or fired for not being a "team player."

How can this situation be prevented? To some extent, any top executive must have an inner circle. There is no way he or she can be accessible to all. So the issue is not how to do away with this group, but how to make it more effective.

First, inner group members should be rotated periodically. Secretarial staff should be changed and new advisors and key assistants should be appointed every two or three years. In fact, service within this inner circle would be excellent training for up-and-rising junior executives. Also, top-level outside consultants should be invited to meet with this group quarterly or even monthly to discuss issues of concern.

Many managers bring a trusted staff assistant or two with them as they move up the ladder. This is OK but should be limited to one or two key aides.

Second, the top executive should clearly define each person's role along three dimensions: (1) It should be made clear that the executive expects objective advice and that there is no room for yea-sayers; (2) It should be indicated that the executive does want to be accessible and that the inner circle is not to screen *everything* out; (3) The executive should stress that those in the inner circle are serving only for a specified period of time, for example, 18 to 24 months. It should be made clear that no one has a perpetual lock on their position.

Third, the top executive should occasionally leave the office and visit the troops. Some executives of certain motel/hotel chains stay in the firm's hotels under an assumed name as customers. Executives of large restaurant chains similarly dine at their establishments. Still other top executives do likewise in the airline, railroad, and bus industries. Some corporate chiefs of small- to medium-sized manufacturing firms will spend a day at one of the factory jobs. Since they are often founders of the compamy, they

---

More Excuses for a Closed Mind

Why change it? It's still working OK.

I don't like the idea.

You're right, but . . .

You're two years ahead of your time.

We're not ready for that.

We don't have the money, equipment, room, or personnel.

It isn't in the budget.

Can't teach an old dog new tricks.

Good thought, but impractical.

How are you going to prove it?

Top leaders would never go for it.

Let's put it in writing.

We'll be the laughing stock.

Not that again.

We'd lose in the long run.

Where'd you dig that one up?

We did all right without it.

That's what we can expect from staff.

It's never been tried before.

The problems that creates are . . .

Let's form a committee.

Let's give it more thought.

---

probably have worked at a number of the jobs in the not too distant past and can pick up on them fairly easily. Of course, this may be more difficult to do in a union shop where work rules prevent people from doing other workers' jobs.

Florida Governor Bob Graham has made it a policy to spend one day a month doing a different job someplace in his state. He started these workdays as a campaign tactic but is continuing them in office and asking his cabinet members also to work one day a month on different jobs. The governor has worked as a road paver, high school teacher, fruit picker, police officer, and farmer, among other jobs.

Graham is a wealthy individual and the whole idea behind this workday activity was to show the public that he hasn't lost touch with them. It was a successful campaign strategy—it got him elected—and it has probably given him a more realistic perspective on people's problems since he's been in office. It is also good publicity.

Another top-level Florida executive became exposed to field operations of the state's health and rehabilitative services agency. A newly appointed district director, who happened to be black, visited one of the agency's offices disguised as a client applying for food stamps. He was surprised at the long wait, poor level of service, and the general runaround he received, and later instituted a series of programs, procedures, and quality-control measures to improve operations. Had he not posed as a client, he likely would not have known about the serious deficiencies and incompetent performance in the food stamp offices.

A fourth way for top executives to keep from being isolated by a group of yea-sayers is to actively recruit advisors who are likely to disagree. Instead of pulling together a management team of people who all think alike, a conscious effort is made to appoint advisors of differing opinions so that various viewpoints are represented. Of course, there are some dangers to this approach if the executive does not emphasize that dissent is tolerated only during the decision-formulation stage. Once a decision is made, the executive's advisors should support it even if they disagree. Nonsupport, especially if made public through the press, undermines the executive's position. Dissent following a decision is not acceptable.

This situation existed in the early months of the Carter Administration. In his efforts to avoid the mistakes of the Nixon Administration, Carter purposely brought together advisors and aides with diverse views. This was OK, except that after decisions were made some advisors voiced their disagreement with the decision openly, often to the press. This was unacceptable because it gave the impression that the Carter Administration lacked direction and that Carter could not lead. Dissent and disagreement prior to a decision are fine; afterward they are not.

How Can Managers Avoid Pouring Resources Down Rat Holes?

Top executives—in fact, all managers—must be able to recognize and admit a mistake. It's senseless to throw good money after bad. In the last section we saw that once a decision is made, the top executive can expect support for the decision from advisors. But blind support is dangerous. There is little sense in forcing through a poor decision. The executive must be able to recognize it and take corrective action as soon as possible. Why waste resources trying to make bad decisions work? It's like pouring money down a rat hole.

To recognize a bad decision, managers must receive feedback and have access to information indicating how well a decision is working. Obviously it is difficult to get this if the executive is heavily isolated from the organization's operations and thus cannot see a decision's effects. What advisor wants to tell the executive that the decision he or she has made is a failure? This is a criticism that the executive erred and implies a personal weakness. Many executives cannot separate criticism of a bad decision from criticism of their person. Consider the following case:

ROSE-COLORED GLASSES

"I'm not going to tell him! Would you? He'll blow his stack. You know how he takes bad news. All hell will break loose!"

"Well, if you don't tell him, I don't know who will. At least you've got his full confidence. He listens to you more than he does to the rest of us."

"What about Burt? Maybe he would tell him. Or Joan or Bob; he listens to them."

"Maybe, but I think you'd do the best job."

"Why don't we just let the figures speak for themselves? Let's just give him the report and let him read it."

"Hell, he doesn't read reports. Anyway, as soon as he saw those figures, he'd be calling one of us in for an explanation. Do you want to explain them to him?"

"Not me, but someone should. I just don't know what to do. I advised against purchasing that company last year. It was a weak firm.

The first six months of sales and expense figures were horrible. Things did get better for a few months, but look at these last two months! Now it's time to give him the quarterly report. Maybe he ought to monitor the thing monthly. What's worse is that he appointed Richards to run the damn thing and he trusts him."

"Yeah, his old fraternity buddy who isn't worth a damn. He's going to have to take some action and get Richards out of there if we're ever to see any improvement in that company. It's a drag on our profits now, but with proper management, a complete overhaul of personnel, and a complete reinvestment in new capital equipment, the company would generate some profit for us."

"Might as well start our own firm if all that needs to be done. I say we should sell the damn company. Write it off. Admit we made a mistake. Why pour all that money into a losing venture?"

"How are you going to convince the old man that's what we should do? He's wanted to get into the chemical business so bad for so long, he bought that company blindly. The chemical business does fit well with our tree fiber and wood pulp business and it is a good alternative to even higher-priced petrochemicals, but I think we just bought the wrong chemical company."

"Yeah, he sees that little company through rose-colored glasses. It's going to be tough to convince him he made a mistake. Who's going to tell him?"

Analysis

Who's at fault for a situation like this where advisors are afraid to be candid with their boss? Is the chief executive officer too far removed from daily operations? That is, should he see monthly figures on this company instead of quarterly reports?

The chief executive should monitor this new company on a *weekly* basis. Even monthly is not frequent enough, let alone quarterly. Apparently, the chief wants to manage by exception and not be bothered with details. But in order to manage this way, he needs staffers who can advise him freely. Apparently, however, his advisors do not now feel this way. Which is dangerous. Any CEO who manages by exception needs to be made aware of situations that are exceptions—situations where the CEO's attention is definitely required. The newly purchased chemical company is precisely that type of situation.

Not only must the advisors inform the CEO of the very serious profit drag the new company is having on the firm, they must also convince him that immediate action is needed. Personal friendships have no place in a situation like this. Bias caused by personal loyalties can easily divert a manager from the logical and proper decision. The company must cut its losses, and if it means Richards must go, then he must go. Using the sales and profit figures, the two advisors must convince the CEO that such action is needed.

When advisors can no longer freely provide advice, the *raison d'etre* for their job vanishes. They must either provide advice or resign. It's now up to these two individuals to make that decision.

How Far Should You Go to Salvage a Project or Person?

You project the costs and benefits of salvaging and decide if it's worth it. None of us believes it's right to simply give up when we initially encounter problems with either a project or a person. We take action to correct the situation and turn things around. But at some point, spending more and more time, effort, and money to salvage a project or person in the organization becomes *dysfunctional*—costs exceed any potential benefits.

The costs involved in trying to save a project or person include:

◆ Effort and attention to sift through the facts and come up with a recommended course of corrective action.
◆ Time that could have been spent on other projects. This is a real opportunity cost. Perhaps we could spend our time in another area giving us a greater return.
◆ Psychological costs of tension, stress, and frustration as we attempt to deal with the problem but meet recurring roadblocks.
◆ Financial costs as more and more money is used to try to save the project or person.
◆ Political costs of alienating someone powerful in the organization by cutting his or her pet project or terminating his or her friend.

These costs must be weighed against projected benefits, which include:

◆ Profit that the project or individual may contribute to the company. (The contribution may not be immediate but may occur in the long run.)
◆ Cost savings that may be generated by the project or individual even though no direct profit contribution is made.
◆ The salvaged ego or esteem of an individual who is not terminated.
◆ An enhanced community reputation. We may continue a money-losing project because it is good P.R. for us within the community.

Obviously these costs and benefits are difficult to project, and their accuracy is directly related to the quality of planning and forecasting within the organization. The greatest difficulty occurs in trying to salvage an individual since individual behavior is especially hard to predict. How many second, third, and fourth chances do you give a person? How much training and retraining should you provide to enhance skills? How much job coaching and counseling are appropriate before you give up on the person as a lost cause? Naturally, managers' responses differ greatly on these questions, but the point is that a person cannot be retained whose performance has a serious adverse effect on organization health and long-term growth. But just how far can you go? Let's look at this example.

RAINY DAZE

Harry Edwards: 56 years old; Bachelor of Business Administration degree 1948; joined company 1968; previous employment with Duke Power Company and Jefferson Controls Corporation; Korean War vet. Disabilities: alcoholic.

"Umm," thought Brad Dillford, "at least it's formally noted in his record."

Brad Dillford had recently been appointed vice-president for human resources for Wakeenah Power Corporation and was reviewing some notes located in the file of Harry Edwards, Wakeenah's training manager. Harry reported to Brad, as did the employee relations manager, industrial relations director, and EEO director. Brad had recently been hired from another large utility company. His position was created by Wakeenah to consolidate all personnel-related functions.

Harry has had some difficult times with the company. He has held four different jobs during the past three years—none of them considered promotions. After a rather quick rise within the company, he developed a severe drinking problem. His performance suffered considerably but he was kept on. Finally, the firm started an Employee Assistance Program to help people like Harry who had alcohol, drug, or severe emotional problems. The program seemed to help Harry and other employees.

Wakeenah prided itself on being a responsible corporate citizen of the community. For years it paid a higher than average wage in the utility industry and was quick to provide new benefits for its employees, such as comprehensive health care insurance (including dental coverage) and a liberal pension plan. It also took a strong leadership role in the community's annual United Way drive, gave liberally to two universities within the community, and started and continues to coordinate Second Chance, a summer camp for local disadvantaged children.

Even though the firm is unionized, it has maintained harmonious labor relations and believes its employees are the company's most important asset. This is evidenced by the fact that the firm has not only an industrial relations director, who handles union matters, but also an employee relations director, who handles all other employment functions, such as hiring, placement, health and benefits administration, and employee problems, and administers the Employment Assistance Program.

The company has always had a philosophy of maintaining a strong image of corporate responsibility to the community and its employees, but it was heightened during the mid- and late seventies. The continuing price hikes by OPEC nations caused the average customer's electric bill to triple during the same decade. So the company believed it had to counteract the unfavorable publicity created by these soaring rates, and desired even more the image of a responsible citizen of the community and of a good place to work. Consequently, the Employee Assistance Program was developed to do everything possible for employees who run into temporary emotional problems. The company believes a good employee should be salvaged and not cut loose.

This brings us back to Harry Edwards. During his first ten years with Wakeenah, Harry had been a solid performer. While not a real star, he performed at a level that got him promoted quite regularly. But during the last three years, he has had periodic bouts with drinking and drying out and his performance has fallen off considerably. His three months in the Employee Assistance Program seemed to help; at least Harry seemed no longer to be drinking. According to his program counselor, Harry indicated that he attends Alcoholics Anonymous meetings regularly. However, his actual job performance is mediocre. For example, he has been training manager for three months and has yet to develop a training plan for the company. Also, Brad has received reports from outside training consultants that Harry is rather difficult to work with. At meetings with outsiders he tends to dominate and "grandstand."

Brad has been in his new position for two months and has talked with Harry on two occasions about his role and his responsibility for developing a training plan. Harry said he was working on the plan and would have it soon, but Brad doubted such a plan would ever be written.

Harry was a likable fellow. He seemed to get along fairly well with everyone he had contact with in the company and usually had a good joke at meetings or at lunch. Yet he had the image of being something of a buffoon, and also had some peculiar mannerisms that a number of people found amusing. One was to "French-inhale" when smoking cigarettes. He was very fastidious and compulsively neat. His office and desk were spick-and-span, with everything in its place—no papers on his desk, shelves, or filing cabinets. Harry hated anything out of order and would go so far as to rearrange pictures, ashtrays, and pencil holders on other people's desks while he talked with them. And he would often walk up and down the halls mumbling to himself, oblivious of his surroundings. Occasionally he would sit at his desk, arms outstretched, palms up, chanting a mantra. If someone entered his office, he kept right at it as if in a daze.

Brad believed that having Harry as company training manager gave the training function low credibility. Brad wanted a strong and prestigious role for training. Too often in the past he had seen marginal employees appointed training manager in other firms because they couldn't hack it in operations. Training was where the organization dregs ended up. Brad certainly did not want that to happen at Wakeenah.

Yet apparently Harry had recovered from his bouts with the bottle. He was an example of success for the Employee Assistance Program, and Brad as well as other managers in the firm were quite proud of this. It showed the program could work. Furthermore, Brad believed that terminating Harry would be bad for the company's image as a responsible corporate citizen and a good place to work, but he saw no place to transfer Harry since he doubted any operating division would take him. In fact, Harry had been bumped around to four different jobs during the past three years.

So Brad was stymied. If he fired Harry it would damage the company's image. If he kept Harry as training director it would give training a poor image and low credibility. If he tried to transfer Harry, no unit would take him.

"What a problem to face right off the bat," thought Brad. "What do you do with a guy who walks around as if he were in a daze half the time?"

Analysis

What do you do? Is Harry salvageable? Should he be salvaged?

At 56 Harry may be eligible for early retirement. If so, Brad should encourage him to take it. Transferring Harry to another unit is out of the question; he's been transferred before and he has the image of a buffoon. What division would take him? Leaving him as training director will seriously hurt the firm's training function and make Brad's job more difficult. Sending Harry to training or counseling sessions will probably be futile. He's already had extensive counseling and likely would not benefit from training, given his experience and present stage in the career cycle. Creating an assistant-to spot for Harry where he can live out his company life while doing little damage is just adding fat to overhead.

If Harry is not willing to take early retirement, Brad should terminate him. The costs of keeping him are greater than the benefits of maintaining the company image as a responsible employer. Perhaps Brad could help Harry get a job with another local organization. Harry might even be a prime employee for a nonprofit firm in the rehabilitation field. After all, he's been there and back.

Companies like Wakeenah Power often face similar situations. The desire to maintain a good image begins to outweigh the desire for operating efficiency. Even though Wakeenah is a regulated utility in a monopoly situation, and does not feel the competitive pressures of a manufacturing firm, it still must meet profit and expense objectives. It also must meet operating regulations established by the state public utilities agency. The firm has done enough for Harry. It's time to cut the strings.

Summary

Top-level executives commit a serious error when they isolate themselves from their company's operations. This then makes it very difficult to spot incompetent performance. In fact, such isolation, when reinforced by excessively loyal advisors, can actually present to the executive a false picture that all is going well. If top management doesn't commit itself to rooting out incompetence, neither will middle- and lower-level managers. It takes a conscious effort at the top to deal with incompetent behavior.

Top managers not only have to know about projects, programs, or people that aren't working out, they must be willing and able to do something about it. The key question is: How far do you go to salvage a project, program, or person? Most of us do not immediately cut a project or program without at least some minimum effort to save it. But at what point do the costs of trying to save a poor project or marginal employee outweigh any benefits? This is not easy to answer; the solution depends upon the manager's ability to accurately forecast costs and benefits. At some point, trying to turn around incompetence in either a project or person becomes a futile effort of throwing good money after bad, and the organization has to cut the program, project, or person.

6

Courtroom, Cops and Robbers, and Other Games

Organization life is full of game playing. Some games serve a useful purpose; most do not. Our concern is with the use of corporate game playing as a way to mask incompetent performance. Managers and employees who have difficulty performing their jobs will often adapt various subterfuges to cover their incompetence. Even though playing games is a fact of organization life and will likely never be eliminated, it's up to managers to ensure that the games are not used to mask incompetence.

How can this be done? Managers can take two very important steps: (1) play organization games to win; (2) make the rules and call the shots. Games cannot be prevented, but they can and should be reduced. As long as others will play games, you need to ensure that you do not get the short end of the stick in any game involving you, and that games are not dysfunctional to company operations.

What Are Some of the Games Commonly Played?

Various authors have written about organization games. Our purpose is not to describe every game—which has been done—but to highlight a few of the more common games.

Courtroom. In this game, staff and other organization meetings are transformed into courtroom drama. Either by design or spontaneously, members begin examining and cross-examining a meeting participant about a certain program or project involving him or her. The participant tries to defend the project or program before the group and the meeting moderator, who plays the role of judge. Examination and cross-examination go on in a somewhat threatening rather than supportive atmosphere, and later the participants will often gloat over the victim. Comments like "Boy, old John sure was sweating for a while" or "We turned Elaine every which way but loose. She didn't know whether she was coming or going" are common.

Cops and Robbers. Participants try to answer the question, "Who are the good guys and who are the bad guys?" People are typed as good or bad based on whom they know and whether they are on the "right" side of important issues. Once people are typed, it's up to the "cops," or the good guys, to "catch" the "robbers," the bad guys, who are caught in any number of ways. Organization rules that are usually bent are enforced more strictly for the bad guys. Important information is shared only among the good guys and kept from the bad guys as if it were a secret. When the bad guys make mistakes because they did not possess the important information, they are pounced upon. Or bad guys are given a Herculean task to do with extremely limited resources. When it is not completed on time they are called on the carpet.

Dress for Success. It's the clothes that make the person, and nothing else. The organization has a uniform down to the color and type of shoe. However, the details of the uniform are never verbalized, orally or in writing. Those that are "in" know the standards. Those that don't and hence don't follow them are, by definition, out. Performance, competence, and results become secondary. Appearance is primary. People in organizations where this game is played believe in the axiom, "He looks successful, therefore he must be successful."

Don't Confound Me with the Facts. Managers who play this game have settled ideas and opinions, and no amount of objective data will change them. In fact, presenting properly gathered and analyzed data to these managers is actually dysfunctional. It challenges their core attitudes and beliefs. For example, I knew a manager of a car dealership in the late 1970s who believed that big cars would always sell because Americans were hooked on luxury. No amount of talk and presentation of data on OPEC oil-price increases, small-car sales of competitors (foreign and domestic), or surveys of consumer buying preferences would change his mind. Americans liked big cars and that was that. Today the man is bankrupt and out of business.

Plunder. We try to steal resources from other units for our own. This may be done quite subtly during budget presentations or quite openly by removing furniture and office equipment from other units at night. Managers who play this game have, as their number-one preoccupation, the desire to build an empire: The more budget allocations, equipment, staff, and programs they have under their direction, the greater their status and importance. No person or program in the organization is safe from the power-hungry grabs of managers playing this game. Though they have trumped-up rationalizations for more staff or budget, all they really want is to build their empire by taking resources away from you. This game is very popular in government agencies.

Party. Keeping up your organization contacts through off-hours entertaining and partying is the theme of this game. Participants invite the "right" people over for cocktails and dinner or eat lunch with those in the know. They join the "right" country clubs and live in the "right" neighborhoods to further develop the "right" social contacts. Younger, fast-moving managers often play this game as they vie for power and influence. They fight to be associated socially with key executives and often try to outdo each other with elaborate dinners and parties to impress these officers.

Let's You and Him Fight. We all played this game as children. The idea is to get two or more managers or units fighting with one another, and then either sit back and be amused by it or maneuver around the units while they are thus preoccupied. One executive I know used this game quite successfully to direct attention away from problems in his unit. The attention of top management was focused on two other units in conflict—conflict which the manager of the third unit started.

Scapegoat. We're all familiar with this game. We look for others to blame for failure or problems in our unit. Sales didn't do its job; parts did not arrive on time; there was a strike caused by union militants; the economy entered a recession; and so on. The reasons are limitless and we can always find someone else to blame. In organizations where this game is widely played, the buck never stops anywhere. Points of accountability are diffused. Decisions are made by committee. Something is everyone's responsibility, therefore, it's no one's responsibility.

It's Showtime. There are those who like to grandstand. Certain organization hot dogs like to impress others during staff meetings and presentations with their talk and ideas. They tend to dominate discussion, and if asked to make a presentation, they do an elaborate job with flip charts, overhead transparencies, slides, handouts, and the like. It becomes a case of media overkill. Furthermore, if these individuals are in charge of setting up and conducting a meeting, they go to extensive lengths to orchestrate a happening. Nothing is too elaborate. The meeting is conducted not to inform but to impress. Where this game is not discouraged, people soon try to outdo one another. The organization becomes an entertainment production company.

Consultant. Consultants can be used as pawns in a game of company chess. They are hired for their ability not to study and inform, but to confirm a desired course of action or to act as a scapegoat. In the first case, consultants are given only so much information—all of the "right" type—so the only conclusion the consultant can reach is the one a manager wanted in the first place. The consultant thus lends credibility and legitimacy to a course of action a manager had already decided to take.

In the second case, consultants can be blamed for failure. One is hired and then fed biased information that results in a poor recommended course of action. The project fails, and the manager sits back and says, "See, I told you this would never work." The manager did not want the project to succeed in the first place.

Hi-Lo. Also known as good news-bad news, this game involves organization members who like to be deliverers of the latest news. They get a thrill presenting good news-bad news to others. For example, a staff analyst in budgeting might gloat in announcing to others that sales increased 10 percent but that sales expenses increased 15 percent. Sometimes the bad news is announced first and then tempered by the good news. Such announcements are usually followed by a little chuckle. People who play this game like to surprise and shock. It makes them feel important as they scurry around from one office to the next with their news and gossipy tidbits. As more and more people play the game, they try to outdo one another in the shock value of their news.

Ain't It Awful. A variation of *Hi-Lo,* this involves discussing only bad news. People try to outdo each other in gossiping and complaining about all the bad aspects of the organization without suggesting positive means of improving things. They also focus on negative aspects of individual personalities. "Did you hear about the chewing out Fred got from Roger?" and "Did you see Sally's sales figures? She's really goofing off" are examples of comments frequently heard where this game is played.

Setup. The objective is to set someone up for failure by feeding the person biased or incomplete information, hoping he or she will act on it. Since the information is so poor, the action is programmed for failure. The purpose is to embarrass someone or to have someone commit a fatal mistake that results in termination.

There are other organization games, but these are the more common. They can damage an organization. Not only can they mask incompetence, but they can drain much productive energy from more worthwhile endeavors. As was stated before, however, all a person can hope to do is reduce the incidence of game playing, work to change the rules, or play them to win. Games cannot be eliminated.

How Can Games Be Played to Win?

A conscientious member of an organization can take several steps to cope with a game-laden environment.

First, you must know the game rules. Each is played differently in each organization. For example, in *Ain't It Awful,* some organizations do not permit individual fellow co-workers to be discussed; instead it's always a nebulous "they." "They are really screwing up" and "They don't know how hard we work down

here" are frequent. Usually "they" refers vaguely to top management or some other powerful group.

Second, avoid games you cannot win. If you are not
Machiavellian, do not try to play Machiavellian games. Why enter
a race without a good chance of winning? A person is better off
avoiding a losing situation than participating in it hoping that
somehow things will turn out all right.

Third, discourage games that are clearly dysfunctional to the
organization. Don't become involved in them, and actively discourage others from participating. Winning a dysfunctional game,
which serves only to further nonproductive energy and effort,
should not be viewed as an accomplishment. Comments like
"This is really hurting our company" and "Let's move on to more
productive endeavors" can help put a stop to these games.

Fourth, know when a game is being played and when it is not.
Often an organization allows games to be played as a test of managerial ability. For example, if *Consultant* is being played, don't
put much credibility in the consultant's report. It's been wired—a
facade. Acting on it in the belief that it's legitimate will get a
person in a lot of difficulty. When it's a game, treat it as a game.
On the other hand, if the company is not playing *Consultant*, treat
consultants' reports with credibility and respect. You can tell
whether *Consultant* is being played or not by watching what happens to the reports. Ask these questions: How are they used? Who
uses them? What kind of follow-up and evaluation is made on
consultant recommendations?

However, it's not always easy to recognize games, nor are
they easily played. Consider this manager's approach:

NECESSITY IS THE MOTHER OF INVENTION
You should try to make new managers uncomfortable. They ought to
experience some difficulty in the first few weeks on the job. They will
eventually experience difficulties so you might as well make it happen
early rather than later—before you have a lot of time, effort, and money
invested in the manager. If the man or woman cannot cut it, let's find
out early.

If there are no difficulties at the time of appointment, they should
be created. You might as well build pressures early to see how the

person reacts. Some of the things I do to create these pressures include transferring a key subordinate from the manager, giving the new person a complex project to do with a tight deadline, and arranging for the manager a two-week visit to plants or other offices in the company. If the person is hired near budget time, I cut his or her budget request 10–15 percent just to see the reaction. I may not actually implement it; I'm more interested in how the potential cut is dealt with.

I know this is a game, but the new manager doesn't. I think we'd all be better off if we did these kinds of things when a new manager is appointed. It gives us a better reading of the person's abilities. Is the manager really creative? Can the individual solve problems? Is he or she willing to be innovative? How can a boss know these things unless the new manager is tested? After all, necessity is the mother of invention.

Analysis

The game suggested by this manager can be useful or it can backfire. It can so pressure a capable new manager that failure occurs. Any new manager, no matter how competent, needs a few weeks to learn the job. Is it fair to pull the rug out from under the person immediately? Also, a sharp manager may see through this facade. No doubt this boss's approach and reputation are well known in the company, so the new manager could learn from others what to expect.

Another problem created by this approach is credibility. How believable will this boss be in the future if the new manager sees what is going on? This game is not necessarily the best way to establish trust, respect, and confidence between the new manager and the superior.

But the approach does have merit. In fact, simulation-testing and assessment centers rely on a similar tool, but in an artificial (laboratory) setting. A subordinate's real skills and abilities are often unknown unless tested by real problems. But this test can be controlled, and many organizations now do so. Controlled simulation has the advantage of giving a superior a better reading because it is closely monitored. It also keeps an on-the-job error by the new manager from devastating the organization or the manager.

While this game may work for the manager quoted above, it is not a prudent way of operating. A manager may fail this test and still be competent.

How Can I Make the Rules and Call the Shots?

Managers with power and authority have the responsibility to ensure that games do not damage the organization. Not only should games be functional and played to win, but the game rules and the operating methods should be set by the competent and not the incompetent managers.

Game rules can be changed through influence, persuasion, negotiation, bargaining, and consensus. In short, by using key political skills in a *tactful* manner. Failure to be tactful is unlikely to result in any rule changes. Groups have norms—understood and accepted patterns of behavior—that are resistant to change. Games are often a big part of these norms, so any overt, frontal attack on the games is likely to be strongly resisted by the group. Here's an example of how *not* to try to change game rules:

Some Humorous Ways to Describe an Incompetent Person

He's two bubbles left of center.

She needs to be fine-tuned.

She's empty between the ears.

He's out to lunch.

He doesn't know which way is up.

She's dead in the water.

She's working with frayed wires.

His bells ring a little early.

She can't get all four burners to work.

She's not playing with a full deck.

He doesn't have his keel in the water.

He's always on hold.

Her cork doesn't float on top of the water.

She goes out the "in" door and in the "out" door.

His sail is always at fluff.

He's about a brick short of a full load.

If she took a trip, any road would get her there.

His coil is too tightly wound.

FIRE IN THE MORNING

Lori Bashinsky had recently become corporate customer services manager for a large discount chain department store. The firm had 23 locations throughout the southeastern United States, and Lori's office was at the company's chief store in Florida. She reported to the vice-president of marketing, Burt Higgins. Lori had reporting to her each of the chain's customer services managers and had been such a manager herself prior to promotion.

Her charge at the time of her appointment was to "straighten out the customer services mess" existing at most stores. It was Mr. Higgins's belief that Lori's predecessor had not paid close enough attention to the actual customer services operation at each store and had "let things get out of hand" in most stores. Higgins felt that the company policy on customer service was a good one but had not been properly enforced. While it was the store manager's responsibility to enforce the policy, it was also the corporate customer services manager's responsibility to help each store manager on this issue and to monitor the store manager's performance.

Customer service has to perform the following functions:

1. Resolve customer complaints and requests for refunds and exchanges.
2. Resolve customer complaints on billing by working with the credit department in each store.
3. Provide a storewide service for gift wrapping.

Lori had been told that the primary problem was in customer refunds and exchanges. Some stores were very liberal with these while others were stringent. The company policy on refunds and exchanges read as follows:

> A satisfied customer is our primary goal. Therefore, our stores will refund or exchange a defective product if the original purchase and sales receipt is returned to the store within thirty days of purchase, unless manufacturer's warranty stipulates otherwise.

The problem was that some stores followed this policy to the letter, and some did not. Those that did created animosity, especially with long-term good customers. If refused refund or exchange, these customers would close their charge accounts and vow never to shop at the store again. Their business would be lost. Those stores that were more liberal had extremely high rates of return and refund, which severely cut into profits.

Lori had noticed these problems through informal discussions with other store customer services managers prior to her promotion. Since becoming corporate customer services manager, she had had an opportunity to review each store's history on the matter and agreed that the policy was being unevenly and inconsistently applied among the 23 stores. After giving the issue considerable thought, she called a one-day meeting of all 23 store customer services managers at the home store in Florida.

Preparing for the meeting, Lori felt she had to do two things: First, she had to establish her credibility as the managers' boss. Lori had recently been one of them, and although most of the customer services managers were women, Lori's predecessor was a male. Second, she had to ensure that they understood the policy and would enforce it. Lori felt she really had to make a good impression, not only for the above reasons, but also because this was the first time the chain's customer service managers had ever met as a group.

Lori's strategy was to strongly threaten them in the morning and then slack off in the afternoon. She wanted to hit them really hard with a straightforward presentation that detailed the policy and showed them how important it was to follow it in order to enhance profits. She hoped this would fire them up and make them willing to take action. In the afternoon she planned to have role-playing sessions to give them an opportunity to learn how to handle various types of complaints under the policy. Using this strategy, Lori hoped to make them fearful and insecure in the morning so as to convince them the firm meant business in enforcing the policy. In the afternoon she would teach them how to comply with the policy.

Lori believed this approach not only would bring about the awakening she wanted of the store's customer services managers, but would also establish her credibility with them and her boss. In particular, she believed her one-day presentation would include hard content that, in her opinion, would be a change from most of the presentations she'd witnessed at corporate headquarters since being promoted. She felt those she had seen were well orchestrated and conducted with all sorts of graphics, but they were all fluff—done to impress, but not communicate. Lori vowed to make her presentation different. She would tie the refund and exchange policy to the bottom line—profit. Instead of relying on a fancy orchestrated presentation to get their attention, she would use a sense of fear and insecurity. That, she thought, should grab them.

The meeting went as planned except that Mr. Higgins attended most of the morning session. When she arrived the morning after the meeting, Lori was pleased to see a note on her desk that Higgins wanted to see her immediately. Expecting to be congratulated, Lori walked into Higgins' office and heard him say:

"Come on in, Lori. Glad you could make it so early. Look, let me get straight to the point. We've got a problem. You scared the hell out of those people yesterday. My phone's been ringing off the hook since they left yesterday afternoon. They even called me at home late last night. Two called this morning. I sat through yesterday morning, as you know, and I think you were too hard on them. Plus, you had few charts, transparencies, or other graphics to back up your points. Quite frankly, I thought it was a horrible presentation. All you kept talking about was how the policy affected the bottom line. Those people don't care about the bottom line. What do they know about profits? They can't understand our accounting system. All they want is to do their job from 9 to 6 and then go home. They can't identify with the big picture. Maybe you could when you were one of them, but you're unusual.

"I'm afraid you really messed things up now. I just don't know if you're cut out for this kind of work."

Lori was speechless.

Analysis

Lori tried to change the rules of the game, *It's Showtime.* She wanted to give a straightforward presentation devoid of all fluff. She failed because she attacked head-on an honored corporate tradition of fancy presentations apparently made to impress rather than communicate. Her straightforward attack on this approach and on the customer services managers upset them and her boss. She probably would have been better off using some aspects of the orchestrated presentation and tying these directly to solid content. She also should have reviewed her presentation with Higgins prior to the meeting. And she should have avoided the game she used—fear—in dealing with the customer services managers. While she may have been right in a theoretical sense, her approach so deviated from company norms that her job is now jeopardized. You should not try to change a sacred corporate game unless you have first established good credibility in your position. You should also not try to substitute one bad game or poor set of rules for another.

How Can the Rules Be Rewritten to Enhance Performance?

Simply rewriting corporate game rules is not enough. The "right" rules must be substituted for the "wrong" rules. The right rules are those that enable the game to help the organization achieve its goals; the wrong rules are those that make games dysfunctional. Substituting one set of poor rules for another does nothing to make the game function for performance. For example, in *Ain't It Awful,* the rules could be changed so that anyone heard complaining about the organization would be required to draft a two- to three-page memorandum to his or her boss suggesting a means of resolving the complaint. This changes the rules of a dysfunctional game to make it functional. In *Courtroom* we might change the rules so that everyone must take a turn in the barrel—no exceptions. In *Cops and Robbers* we can encourage public debate on a whole host of corporate issues so that it becomes difficult to stereotype a person on the basis of a stand on one or two issues. This encourages open and candid communication—a real plus for any organization.

In changing corporate game rules we first must decide what the organization's goals are, and then determine how our present games help us reach these goals. Where these games don't help, we must either eliminate them or change the rules so they do help.

The best way to change game laws is by being a competent performer. Actions speak louder than words, and a person who is clearly competent can change a game and will be listened to with respect. Here's a conversation between two bank executives who are playing *Dress for Success:*

GORK

Bud: He's what we used to call a "Gork" in college. You know the type—real screwy dresser, funny mannerisms, peculiar behavior—they just don't fit in.

Lou: Yeah, we called them Dinks. I guess I'm of a different generation. But you know, you can't argue with success. Harvey *has* been successful. He's the first branch manager that has been able to turn a profit at that place. That's tough in that location. Look at his clientele. Poor blacks and Mexicans.

Bud: But he just doesn't portray the image we want to portray to the board and the community. Those bow ties are ridiculous. His pink shirts are too loud. And those white shoes and polyester pants. Let's face it, he doesn't portray the image of a bank manager. Have you ever seen the way he walks with that limp wrist? His long skinny neck reminds me of Ichabod Crane.

Lou: But how can you argue with success? I think you'd be making a mistake to replace Harvey. His loans are up and his default rate is the lowest I've ever seen it at that branch. In fact, it's below our company average. He's not had one robbery in 18 months. That place used to be hit about once a quarter. He really has a good relationship with that community. He takes a personal interest in his clients—knows most of them by name. And he's white! It's really incredible.

Bud: Yeah, I know, but it's really embarrassing to me when he comes to the executive committee and board meetings dressed like a clown. I've talked to him about this but it just doesn't do any good. His response is, "What difference does it make what I wear as long as I do the job?" He's got a point, but as president of this banking operation, I have the responsibility to uphold a proper professional business image for the bank. Harvey's an eccentric. He just doesn't fit in. There's no room for eccentrics in the banking business. Why can't we have someone who is both competent and a good dresser?

Analysis

Dress for Success is a very difficult game to change. During the late sixties and early seventies there was some relaxation of the rigid dress codes in many corporate offices, but this seems to have abated. Today it's back to dark three-piece suits at many firms. The only moderating influence on *Dress for Success* is high energy costs resulting in cold offices in the winter and hot offices in the summer. If the energy crisis worsens significantly, we may see a corresponding change in the dress game.

Respectable dress for business is important, but overemphasis on clothes relative to a person's ability is not functional for performance. Dress is overemphasized for two reasons. First, if it's difficult to measure performance and output, the focus may shift to non-output, or to such factors as dress. Second, appropriate dress *is* important for jobs where performance is directly linked to the image of the person. This is often true in sales positions, for example. It is reasoned that you cannot be a good salesperson unless you *look* like a good salesperson. For some jobs, we do read a book by its cover, forming an immediate impression of an individual based on the clothes worn. A new salesperson may have to look the part to get in the front door.

According to the conversation between Bud and Lou, Harvey has proved himself. There is no need to make his dress and peculiar mannerisms an issue. Even if he is promoted to the bank's main offices, there is no need to ask him to change his dress. What does this bank want—a modeling agency or top-flight managers?

Summary

Corporate games are a fact of organization life, but they should not be used as a cover for incompetent behavior. Smart managers try to take three courses of action with regard to games. First, they eliminate all games masking incompetence and hurting unit and company performance. Second, they change the rules of games that cannot be eliminated so that the games help the organization achieve its goals. Third, they play games to win. Where functional games are played, smart managers try to maximize game results to enhance their own and the organization's performance.

Some would argue that there is absolutely no place for any games in an organization, that all games should be eliminated. But this denies human nature. People are game oriented and somewhat political. Corporate games recognize this fact and can be used as functional factors for organization performance.

7

Avoiding Intimidation: The Fine Art of Saying No

It's 3:00 P.M. Friday afternoon. You're hoping to leave a little early for a weekend camping trip with your family that has been planned for several weeks. Suddenly your boss enters your office with a stack of papers. Your heart sinks. He's done it before. He needs a report for a 9:00 Monday morning staff meeting with his boss and he wants you to put it together over the weekend. Do you do it?

Or suppose you find yourself in this situation. It's 9:00 Monday morning. You look at your daily appointment sheet and see exactly 45 minutes of time today when you won't be in a meeting. As you flip through your calendar, you notice that almost all your time for the week is scheduled in meetings. You wonder why other people are scheduling your time for you and whether you will have time to get your work done. How can you gain control over your work schedule?

Consider one more situation. It's 4:00 P.M. Monday. You're to leave on a four-day trip at 6:30 A.M. the next day. As you look through some material needed for the trip, you note that one important report is incomplete. The person responsible for completing it is out of town. You decide that you will need to stay at the office to do it. You call your spouse to explain the situation and say that you probably will not be home until 10:00 or 11:00. You're told you are foolish for letting yourself be used by an incompetent staff member. What should you do?

Most of us have found ourselves in similar situations in the past. We allow ourselves to become intimidated and pushed into uncomfortable and inconvenient positions. It doesn't have to be this way. But it happens because certain people in the organization have not done their job competently. We pay for their mistakes and poor performance; but we don't have to. We must learn to say no—no to a subordinate, a colleague, a staff member, and occasionally even to our boss. Unless we are willing to say no, we will continue to be intimidated by others.

Isn't Assertiveness More of a Problem for Women?

For years women have been pushed around and discriminated against at work. Even though there are now legal remedies to correct this, many women still fall into a docile and subservient role. This is especially true of newly appointed women managers. In order to correct this situation and make women managers more aggressive, assertiveness training has been developed to teach them how to stand up for their work rights, negotiate and bargain for job opportunities, give an order and make it stick, and tactfully refuse to carry out a request or demand.

The training rests on the theory that people can be aggressive and assertive without being obnoxious. It also rests on the belief that people can create and shape their own work environment. These are key ideas and they apply to men as well as to women. While we cannot control everything in our work environment, we can shape it. We can create certain conditions and reduce or eliminate others. We can amplify certain forces and reduce or deflect others.

Being assertive without being obnoxious requires forcefulness and tactfulness. It also requires the person to have a pretty clear-cut idea of what needs to be accomplished and how to get there. This means that an integration of personal and company goals is necessary. Also, the means to achieve the goals must be clearly understood by the individual.

Much of what is being taught in assertiveness training is nothing more than watered-down leadership principles and concepts. One theory that is particularly useful for developing assertiveness is *goal-path theory,* the basic premise of which is that people must have a clear conception of the goals to be achieved in a job and must see a path that is instrumental in achieving them. They can then organize their work around these paths. Anything that causes a deviation from the path can be resisted, and what facilitates movement along the path can be enhanced. The person can then be in a position to say, "No, I cannot do that for you since it will cause me not to achieve this goal." If the goal has been participatively set by consensus among those concerned with it, it soon becomes clear to the person making the request that if the request is pursued, the goal will either be delayed or not achieved.

Acceding to all requests, never saying no, creates the impression that you don't have enough to do. Soon you are receiving requests right and left for all sorts of special projects and tasks, especially if you do a good job on them. But at some point, the quality of your work will suffer as your load becomes too heavy. You cannot be all things to all people. Project deadlines are missed, performance suffers, and your job goals are not achieved. This downward spiral feeds on itself. You work longer and longer hours and become frustrated because you cannot achieve everything you promise. Soon your career with the organization is damaged. This is a terrible situation to be in, and it requires assertive behavior to pull out of it, as we see in this situation:

BREAKING AWAY

"Tom, it looks like you're going to have to go to Washington next week and testify for us on that depreciation write-off bill in the Senate. You'd do a good job for us."

"But I thought Ralph was going up. He's our P.R./Government Relations man."

"Hell, Ralph is OK for some things, but he wouldn't do a good job on this. He couldn't hold up in front of Senators and staff. You would though. You present a good image. Besides, they'd much rather hear from a high-level line manager—especially one with a strong accounting background such as yours—than the P.R. type. You'd do more good for our company and our industry than Ralph would."

"But, Larry, I just got back from New York. Two weeks ago I was in L.A., and Chicago before that. When am I to get my job done? And what about my family?"

"You'll only be gone two days. Do you have that much pressing work to do?"

"I sure do, Larry. Things have piled up. You know what's involved in a division V.P. job with this company. You were one not too long ago. But you're the boss, and if you think I should go, I guess I will."

"Good, Tom. I appreciate that. Better see Nancy before you go and she'll fill you in on what you need to know."

Next week on the plane, Tom thought about his conversation with Larry. Since that conversation two additional minor crises had arisen which needed his immediate attention. He knew they would be waiting for him when he returned. While he was flattered that Larry and the company had so much faith in his abilities, he felt he was being used and that his job pressures were closing in. He vowed to schedule a meeting with Larry as soon as he returned to settle the issue once and for all.

Analysis

There are at least four issues at work in this situation that need to be resolved by Tom. First, Tom is being asked to play an *organization boundary spanning role,* but as a line division V.P. he is not in a boundary spanning *position.* This situation occurs frequently today since organizations have become more concerned with maintaining linkages with their external environment. All sorts of complications arise from this situation, not the least of which is determining who is to manage the unit while the line manager is away.

Second, Tom's position and function are becoming implicitly redefined. Every job rests on tenuous building blocks of expectations about job duties, formed through tradition and agreement between superior and subordinate. These blocks usually shift over time on an implicit rather than explicit basis. Even where a written job description explicitly sets out duties and responsibilities, there will be implicit shifts in tasks, functions, and emphasis over time. For Tom's position there is probably no job description since it is at such a high level in the organization. This implicit redefinition of job duties and functions can cause several problems, because it usually means a person is taking on new duties without giving up old ones.

Third, Tom is apparently unable or unwilling to delegate some of his duties to subordinates. He cannot continue to carry out these boundary-interface linkages *and* do his regular job too.

The fourth issue is Tom's responsibility for assertiveness. He is the one who must initiate any corrective action. It's *his* job that is being implicitly redefined. It's *his* work that isn't getting done. Tom is not being as assertive as he should be.

Given these issues, the suggested move is for Tom to renegotiate his job description with Larry. He may very well continue with his external interface work if he is that valuable to the company in that role. But if he does, he'll have to delegate many of his internal duties to subordinates. If he has no one to delegate to, he should demand someone from Larry. If he has people now but does not believe them capable of handling increased delegation, he'll need to get them trained and developed or transfer or terminate them and hire replacements. But he'll need to take the initiative on this since it is obvious that Larry won't. Tom should not have to pay the price of incompetent subordinates when a superior is having so dramatic an impact on his job.

If Tom is unable to create conditions where delegation is possible, then he must tell Larry that he'll be unable to continue these outside duties for the firm in the future. Tom must be willing to take the consequences of Larry's reaction, which might include his transfer. On the other hand, such assertiveness could earn Tom additional respect from Larry, since he stood up for an issue central to his job. At any rate, the present condition cannot continue much longer without severely affecting Tom's performance and his emotional health.

How Can I Be Assertive Without Being Obnoxious?

You can disagree without being disagreeable. Consider this example:

> *Mark:* No, Ray, I can't get it for you by Friday. I'm too busy. I think you're being unreasonable in asking me to do it.
>
> *Ray:* Look, Mark, I'm not being unreasonable. I need the damn report by Friday. No excuses.
>
> *Mark:* Well, I can't get it for you by then. You're always picking on me. Why do you expect me to perform superhuman efforts and not others in this organization?
>
> *Ray:* I'm not telling you to do something superhuman. Any twit could get the job done by Friday.

Not a very productive conversation, is it? Mark comes across rather strong, putting Ray on the defensive. Even if Mark gets the report done by Friday, Ray will probably still be unhappy because of their conversation.

Suppose it had gone like this instead:

> *Mark:* Ray, I'm going to have difficulty getting that report to you by Friday. You may not know it but I've got to be out of town on Wednesday and I've got a project for Fred also due on Friday.
>
> *Ray:* Oh, I see. Well, I sure would like to have it Friday.
>
> *Mark:* How about if I get it to you by 5:00 P.M. the following Monday? I'll have some free time this weekend to work on it.
>
> *Ray:* Well, I guess. Is that the best you can do?
>
> *Mark:* Yes it is, Ray. I wish I could get it to you by Friday but it's virtually impossible. But next time around your report will receive my first priority. Is that OK?
>
> *Ray:* Yeah, I guess so. It's a deal.
>
> *Mark:* Great. I appreciate it.

Notice that Mark explained why he couldn't meet Ray's deadline (out of town and another report due). He also promised two things in exchange for being released from the deadline: He would get the report done by 5:00 the next Monday, and Ray's next report would recieve his first priority. Notice also that by promising Ray's report Monday, Mark shows that he's willing to sacrifice free weekend time to get the report done.

Also note the number of questions asked by the two men in the second incident (three) compared with the first (one). Questions enhance two-way communication by requiring a verbal response from the other party; orders do not.

In the second case, Mark got what he was after: a delay in the due date of the report. In the first case he did not. We can be assertive without being obnoxious by using tact, by encouraging two-way communication, and most of all by indicating what other work will suffer if the demand or request is met. Finally, instead of telling people what you *cannot* do for them (first incident), tell them what you *can* do for them (second). But again, don't promise more than you can deliver. Mark had damn well better get that report done by 5:00 Monday and give Ray's next project first priority.

Business demands assertive behavior. It's the nature of the competitive system. People are expected to be aggressive. Even in government we need to be somewhat aggressive to avoid drowning in the sea of bureaucracy. If you do not stand up for your own job rights, no one else will. It's expected in our system. Of course, you will not get all you ask for, but you will certainly get more than if you said nothing. Most company recruiters will tell you that aggressiveness (assertiveness) is something they look for in a promising job candidate.

Does Collective Action Help Assertiveness?

In numbers there is strength. Unionized employees learned long ago that they are likely to get more by acting as a group than by acting as individuals. Group effort enhances bargaining power. In politics it is well recognized today that group effort enhances the impact of special interests on the legislative process. Witness the tremendous increase in lobbying by farmers, teachers, business people, veterans, disabled and older Americans, and homosexuals to influence legislation at the national, state, and local levels. All these groups and many more exert political pressure on the legislative process so that their demands are met. Very often they work through professional and trade associations to influence various legislators and the public and educate them to the righteousness of their demands.

Resorting to collective action in some ways goes against the emphasis on individuality that traditionally has been a value of U.S. culture. Yet collective action so enhances a group's bargaining power that likely we would never have had major pieces of social legislation passed without it. Women's suffrage, civil rights, consumer and environmental protection, occupational safety and health, and countless other laws in other fields were all passed because interested and concerned people acted as a group to place pressure on the legislative process.

The collective process can also be used without having to harm a union. Managers and professionals act in a collective manner all the time in their organizations; it's called *consensus building* or *forming coalitions*. People seek out respected key figures in the organization and attempt to convince them to join them in presenting an idea or making a demand to another group. How many times have you been asked "What does Joe think on this?" or "Have you discussed this with Nancy?" when you've presented an idea to someone? Or have you ever been told "You haven't got your ducks in a row" when presenting an idea? All these questions and statements indicate that many managers *expect* others to touch base with certain people before presenting new ideas. This touching base is a mild form of collective action.

Building coalitions to sell an idea or new policy is a political process. It usually involves some horse trading. You agree to support someone else's cause if he or she agrees to support yours. Politics in organizations is a fact of life, and while it can be disruptive and distracting at times, it does serve a useful purpose if practiced in moderation. However, there are times when it is not helpful.

FLASH IN THE PAN

John was known as an idea man. He seemed to have a new idea every day, and most had some merit. The trouble was, he had difficulty selling them to key people in the organization.

Akbar Company, a medium-sized manufacturer of steel rods and fittings, had three plants in the midwestern United States but sold internationally through its own sales force and independent middle-men. John was recently appointed Akbar's director of planning. (The firm desired to increase its product markets and to develop new products, so John's position had been created three months before.) Prior to assuming his new position, John had been personnel manager at one of the plants.

It was generally recognized by top management that John was a man of vision with good ideas. It was also believed that he had trouble focusing his efforts and always seemed to have 25 or 30 projects going at once. Seldom were these completed on time, if at all. John seemed to initiate a lot of action but had trouble bringing closure. He was frequently referred to as "Flash" (short for Flash in the Pan) since many managers felt his ideas were nothing more than that.

The company relied on a rather elaborate set of informal rules and policies to get things done. Yearly corporate goals were formed mainly as public relations tools rather than as working targets for management. Few policies were reduced to writing. Managers were very conscious of status symbols like office furnishings and location. Most had known each other for years, having grown up in the company together. In fact, one might say the firm was ruled by a "good old boy" network.

As part of its informal management style, the firm relied on an elaborate political system. "If you scratch my back, I'll scratch yours" seemed to be the firm's motto. This informality appeared to work well in getting things done, and the firm was quite profitable in the industry.

John did not fit well into this network. He was generally a loner. He drove a late model Corvette; other managers drove sedans. He wore the latest fashions; other managers wore conservative polyester suits. He lived in a rustic wood house in the country; others lived in conventional suburbs. He grew up in California; the others were reared in the Midwest.

John detested Akbar's political games. He thought his ideas had enough merit to sell themselves. He was disappointed that so few were accepted. He was also disappointed at his inability to complete so many of his projects, which he attributed to a lack of cooperation from others.

John had higher hopes for his new position. To him the appointment meant that the company might have finally realized the valuable contribution he would make to the company's future growth and direction. However, he was unsure as to what management style he should adopt to sell his ideas. He sure didn't want to play the political game if he could help it.

Analysis

This is a situation where a company is letting its political environment interfere with its long-term growth and survival. In today's internationally competitive market, it's important for a firm to pay much more attention to the strategic planning function. (A front-page article in *The Wall Street Journal* on August 26, 1980, indicated that more and more firms are creating and filling the position of vice-president, corporate planning.) The purpose of strategic planning is to forecast economic, social, technological, and market trends and to suggest new ways companies can develop products and services to meet them.

Apparently Akbar Company feels a need for more planning and sees John as a person suited for this position. The question is, will it accept his ideas? Unless John is willing to play the political game to some extent, chances are that not too many of his plans will be accepted. If he is not willing to play the game, perhaps he can argue for more staff to help him implement his ideas. Perhaps he could work through them. This course of action, however, may be unlikely in a company the size of Akbar.

John's situation is not unusual. As corporate planners are added to management staff, there has been the problem of getting line management to accept the planning staff's work. John's situation is also compounded by his very different management style. Perhaps having John report directly to the CEO will give him direct access for selling his ideas. Whether this is allowed depends on how serious the CEO is about enhancing the strategic planning function and John's credibility in the firm.

At any rate, in this situation excessive reliance on the informal political network is having a dysfunctional effect on the need to take advantage of new ideas useful to corporate strategic planning.

Are Those with the Most Numbers Always Right?

Besides politics, there is another danger to following a collective-action approach: the majority may be wrong. It takes a strong leader to sometimes oppose prevailing opinion. The ability to gain the support of others does not mean that the advocated cause is the right one, or the best one for the organization. It only means there is broad support that enhances the power behind the suggested course.

Building this power base, however, is precisely what a person must do to be assertive and avoid intimidation, which is the focus of this chapter. But the base itself may be built around a wrong idea or poor course of action, thus increasing the chance that this idea or action is accepted. This is why individual managerial responsibility is so important. Standing up for the wrong ideas is worse than not standing up at all.

Our concern is with avoiding intimidation as a way of managing incompetence. A manager should not let an incompetent superior, subordinate, or peer intimidate. These people must be stood up to. Using coalitions to stand up to incompetent action is the method suggested. This does not mean that the person with the strongest coalition is always right. Far from it. In fact, you may find yourself at the other end—having to face many incompetents acting as a group or coalition.

> Great spirits have always found violent opposition from mediocrities. The latter cannot understand it when a man does not thoughtlessly submit to hereditary prejudices but honestly and courageously uses his intelligence and fulfills the duty to express the results of his thought in clear form.
> *Albert Einstein*

We sometimes see this in the academic world. In some university departments all major decisions are made by only the senior tenured faculty, who may be the least competent faculty. Often it is the new assistant professor who is current in the literature and latest research methods, who is trying to publish to get promoted, while the senior full professor is out consulting, writing his life's work, or just plain asleep. Yet, since tenure protects these professors, they cannot be dismissed. When they make all department decisions on promotion, tenure, curriculum, and policy, they are in effect acting as a group against the perhaps more competent assistant professors.

This conflict between the old and the new guard is often dramatic in the academic environment, but it also occurs in the business world. The new hirees are looked at as young turks— wet-behind-the-ears college kids who haven't learned from the school of hard knocks. Many senior managers resist the ideas and suggestions that a fresh face can bring to the job. Read what this engineering manager had to say to a group of newly hired engineers who presented him with some changes in the application of engineering concepts on the job.

BULL IN A CHINA CLOSET

The trouble with you young guys is that you just want to barge ahead without fully thinking of the consequences. You don't appreciate all of the background or history on some of these issues. Most of the problems you see have been around a long time. It isn't that we haven't tried to do something about them; we have, but we haven't been completely successful.

These problems have built up over a long time. There are a lot of personalities involved. You're dealing with people who've been around a long time and don't see much need to change. Sometimes you've got to accept people for what they are. You can't always change them. You can't always change the situation. Learning to live and work in the situation you find yourself in requires patience, tolerance, and understanding. Coming in and trying to shake things up right off the bat doesn't enhance your credibility and image around here.

We have ways of doing things. There are proper channels that must be followed. Forms must be completed. Approvals must be obtained.

Reviews must be held. These processes often take weeks if not months. We don't want to make change just for change's sake. We want to make sure the change is absolutely needed before we go ahead with it. Now go to your office and get back to work. Concentrate on getting your jobs done right instead of wanting to charge ahead like a bull in a china closet.

Analysis

People must have credibility to bring about change in an organization. Unfortunately, new people often do not, even though they sometimes have the best ideas for change because they are not wedded to the status quo. While they might not understand the complex history of an issue, they usually don't have a vested interest to protect.

The manager in the example above makes many statements to thwart change. "We have ways of proceeding," "You don't understand the history," and "You've got to accept things as they are" are all standard responses from the old guard who see no need for change. Yet these engineers are probably better educated than the senior staff. It's estimated that the half-life of knowledge for an engineer is five years, so unless senior engineers make a conscientious effort to keep up to date, they will be woefully incompetent on the latest concepts.

The young engineers in this case must first establish their competence through good work, and then present their ideas as a group. If the senior engineers are unwilling to entertain suggested changes, the firm will likely find itself in serious financial difficulties.

Summary

Incompetent people like to intimidate others. They do so both explicitly and implicitly. Therefore, to properly manage incompetence we must be willing and able to avoid intimidation. This means saying no to subordinates, to peers, and occasionally to our boss. It also means forming coalitions to enhance our power base to make the "no" stick.

Being assertive and forming coalitions need not be done in an obnoxious or highly political manner. Aggressiveness is something prized and expected. Politics is present in all organizations and need not be dysfunctional if kept in proper perspective.

8

Using Power
Without Abusing It

In the preceding chapter we saw that increasing one's power by being assertive or by forming coalitions is an important way to deal with incompetence. In this chapter we are concerned with the abuse of power as it relates to incompetence. Incompetent people who are also very powerful are extremely difficult to deal with and present to a manager a special challenge requiring rather unusual tactics.

Must Power Always Corrupt?

In the United States we have always been very suspicious of large concentrations of power. Our system of government checks and balances served as a key building block when our country was founded. Large concentrations of power, whether in industry, labor unions, or one branch of government, have been countered by other government units, such as the courts, or by other social institutions. Inherent in these checks is the assumption that there is indeed a strong tendency for power to corrupt. A person or institution with great power faces great temptation. The assumption is that it is almost humanly impossible to resist the urge to abuse the power available. In other words, there can be no benevolent dictators.

    The basis for this assumption was the experience of our country's founders with the monarchy of England. But their beliefs are with us today. For example, recent anti-trust actions of the U.S. Department of Justice were taken against large corporations solely because of their size and market domination, not for any actual illegalities. That is, these corporations are being sued not because they have abused power, but because of their *potential* to abuse power. Also, there is an increasingly common feeling that the federal government has become too large and has intruded too deeply into our personal and business lives. We still resist power concentrations and expect some institution or persons in society to do something about it when it occurs.

Power does not always corrupt. Some people can maintain their humility and a sense of perspective even when holding great power. Former President Harry S. Truman is a good example. On the other hand, former President Richard M. Nixon attempted to use the power of the presidency to its utmost, even to the point of abuse during the Watergate cover-up events.

Most organizations have elaborate controls to prevent the abuse of power, such as independent and internal audits, management reviews, and quarterly performance reviews. Because of these and other control systems, as well as the new, post-Watergate demands for accountability and ethical behavior, managers today may be less likely to be corrupted by power than in the past. Therefore, power does not necessarily always lead to abuse and corruption.

What Exactly Is Power, Anyway?

Traditionally, power has been defined as the ability to get people to do something they would not ordinarily do. This implies that power is an influence process much like leadership. Effective leaders are able to wield power, but their effectiveness depends on other qualities besides the mere ability to use power, such as trust, compassion, expertise, honesty, perseverance, and others.

For our purposes, we broaden the traditional definition of power to cover resources other than people. Recognizing that managers also use information, money, and physical resources, we can define power as the *ability to command resource usage.* Power can be exercised over a budget, materials, equipment, and information as well as over people. Therefore, although influencing other people to act as they ordinarily would not is an important part of power, our definition includes any influence over any resource base. The person running a million-dollar machine has a certain power over that machine.

How Can a Manager Build a Base of Power?

Management literature has long recognized at least six bases of power. Managers must build their power on as broad a set of bases as possible. Also, a manager must recognize the bases for an incompetent person's power in order to deal with that person effectively.

Rational/Legal Power

This derives from a person's position in, and is officially sanctioned by, the organization and society. It is the power exercised when we attempt to "pull rank" to get something done. In this respect it is very similar to the concept of authority. We listen to the judge in the courtroom because society has given him the power (authority) to run the court. We obey a police officer because she was duly appointed to carry out certain functions. We defer to our boss because he has been designated our superior manager.

Every manager has some rational/legal power by virtue of his or her position. Yet even among managers at the same level in an organization the amount of this power can vary. It depends on the degree to which others in the organization view the *legitimacy* of the person's official appointment. For example, we all know someone who is in a position not because of performance or competence but because of close friendship to a higher-level manager. When managers are appointed through nepotism or cronyism, their level of rational/legal power is reduced. The person's legitimacy is questioned. The level of credibility is low. It could conceivably be so low that while the person has *authority of position*, he or she has virtually no power.

Reward Power

A second power base rests on the ability of a person to dispense rewards to others. A manager who has the ability to recommend merit salary increases or promotions has more power over subordinates than those without this prerogative. Parents frequently use this power over their children. They promise ice cream or a special television privilege provided that "Susie makes her bed every morning" or "Johnny feeds the dog daily."

This is a good power base since we know from the literature of behavior modification and positive reinforcement that people tend to repeat rewarded, but not unrewarded, behavior. However, for this power base to work well, people must see the relationship between the action and the reward. They must also want the reward. And they must believe the person can actually give it. If I am told that if I perform well as an engineer my boss will recommend me for promotion to engineering supervisor, I must want to become a supervisor, believe my boss can recommend me, and see the tie between present job performance and future promotion. If, as time goes by, I see people being promoted because of political reasons or on someone else's recommendation, my boss's reward power over me will be low.

Coercive Power

The flip side of the reward coin is coercion or penalty: when a person can inflict a penalty—an undesirable consequence—on someone. Again, parents use this frequently with children. They are spanked, are sent to their room, lose television privileges, or are grounded because they did or did not do something. Coercion rests on punishment and is also well grounded in the behavior-modification literature. The theory is that a person will avoid actions that bring an unpleasant consequence. I have to touch a hot stove but once to learn not to do it again.

Despite recent admonitions to use more rewards and less coercion, managers still rely on coercion. People are sent home without pay as a form of punishment. They are sometimes demoted or even terminated for a serious offense. These are meant to serve as deterrents for certain behavior, which people are expected to avoid because they do not want the consequences. As with reward power, however, people must see the connection between the behavior and its consequence, must *not* want the consequence, and must believe their boss can inflict the consequence. To the extent that any of these three elements is missing, coercive power is reduced.

Referent Power

Identification with a person who has power is called referent power. There are two types. First is where the association or identification is known to the person. For example, the secretary of a high-level manager has a certain amount of power over other secretaries at the same rank simply because of the association with a high-level manager. Or perhaps I have a certain amount of power over my peer managers just because I'm a good friend of the company president. I have power because of whom I know and associate with. Name droppers use referent power.

The second type of referent power is exercised in a more impersonal way. It is akin to hero worship. A famous movie star or athlete can influence dress, hair style, and other behavior of many people virtually without knowing it. Emulation of rich and famous people is a form of referent power. Evel Knievel now warns his spectators, especially children, not to try his jumps since some people so closely identify with him that they put themselves in danger.

People who possess this type of referent power are often unaware of how much they have. A casual remark or change in clothing style can start a whole new fad, while the person is initially unaware of this effect. Witness the drastic change in hair styles brought about by the Beatles and later by Farrah Fawcett.

Charisma

This is the power of a dynamic, gregarious, almost mystical personality. Some of the most powerful political leaders—for good or evil—have had strong charisma. Hitler had charisma for the German people, and among American political leaders, former presidents Franklin D. Roosevelt and John F. Kennedy had it. Many religious leaders owe their popularity to charisma.

Charisma tends to be group-specific. Charles Manson and Jim Jones both had charismatic personalities limited to a cult following. Even a popular president like FDR was resisted and detested by many people. What may seem charismatic to some is not to others. Managers who rely on charisma may find they have strong power over one group of subordinates but not over another.

Expertise

The final power base generally recognized in the management literature derives from a person's expertise in an area. An individual is respected because he or she knows or can do something valued by the organization.

I can recall an incident of several years ago when the power of expertise was used in a major oil company. The firm had recently installed an electronic data processing system for customer billing and record keeping. The firm's CEO would continually call the new computer programmer to ask if a particular set of calculations could be computed. Whatever the programmer said was accepted. Since the CEO knew nothing about computer operations, he deferred to the judgment of the head programmer. There was consequently a period of time when the chief programmer virtually ran the company.

Even today, programmers have much power because of their

expertise. In most organizations, few people really understand the mystical workings of the magical machine, and these tend to have great power because most organizations are so dependent on computers.

Expertise as a power base has grown over the last few decades as organization life has become more complex and sophisticated. For example, personnel managers and lawyers have the predominant say-so in hiring, promotion, and termination decisions because of the existing complex Equal Employment Opportunity legal framework. It seems that line managers can no longer take even a simple personnel action without first clearing it with personnel and the legal staff.

People have also become much more specialized than in the past. The days of the managerial generalist appear to be numbered. Now people move up the corporate ladder because of a particular expertise in finance, accounting, marketing, law, or personnel. Their inability to take a broad-based integrative view of operations once they become top managers can present some real problems for the organization.

Yet there is real advantage to the trend of expertise becoming an increasingly common power base. Perhaps people are now more likely to be promoted because of what they know (expertise) rather than who they know (referent) or what personality they project (charisma). To the extent that this happens in the future, the more likely it will be that incompetence can be minimized.

Power undirected by high purpose spells calamity; and high purpose by itself is utterly useless if the power to put it into effect is lacking.

Theodore Roosevelt

However, a prudent manager today should recognize these various power bases and not rely on one or two at the exclusion of others. Of course, power due to expertise is a must, and power granted by the organization (rational/legal) is also very important. But a manager should also be concerned with acquiring to the extent possible, charismatic, reward, coercive, and referent power. Reliance on two narrow a pillar of power makes it easier to be toppled.

How Should a Manager Use the Bases of Power?

The use of power is essentially political. For power to be effective it must be exercised. The *threat* of power may work in the short term, but in the long term it must be demonstrated, else how will others know that the power actually exists? It's the same "paper tiger" accusation made by the People's Republic of China against the United States in the early sixties. The Chinese leadership accused the United States of having a powerful armed forces and nuclear arsenal but not the will or courage to use them. Unfortunately, this accusation probably provoked our involvement in Vietnam more than we originally intended.

Even today, the deterrence of our nuclear umbrella is questioned because it is believed by some that we would never conduct massive retaliation against the Soviet Union should it initiate a limited nuclear strike on a U.S. military installation or in Western Europe. Some argue that the strategy of Mutual Assured Destruction (MAD) should be replaced by one based on the ability to fight a limited nuclear war. The argument goes that we would more likely use nuclear weapons if they were targeted at a few strategic posts, depots, and ports rather than all large Soviet cities.

Since the use of power is essentially a political action, it involves the tools of politics: negotiation, bargaining, compromise, lobbying, forming coalitions, timing, posturing-bluffing, and enhancing personal visibility. In the last chapter we saw how forming coalitions can enhance power when dealing with others; but there are these other means of building a power base and of dealing with incompetence. Let's look at an example.

A HORSE TO WATER

Larry Cohen had just about had it with one of his subordinates, Darryl Wingate, data processing supervisor for the Jonitrol Division of SMR Corporation. Larry was divisional vice-president and chief operating officer, while Darryl supervised a staff of five key-punch operators and three computer programmers and reported directly to Larry. Darryl had previously worked as a member of this group. Larry had known Darryl for two years before appointing him to supervisor, and believed that he had strong managerial potential. He was now disappointed in Darryl's performance. During the past six months (the term of Darryl's service in the new position), Larry had yet to see Darryl exercise any initiative in solving data processing problems. When a problem came up, Darryl would immediately run to Larry for advice. He seemed hesitant to act on his own.

At first Larry attributed this behavior to Darryl's lack of confidence in the new job. But after two months, Larry believed the problem was more basic. Consequently, during a counseling interview, Larry told Darryl that he needed to "act more like a manager" and exercise his authority. He suggested that Darryl take more initiative to solve problems and that he did not need to clear everything through him. Larry offered to help if Darryl faced a particularly unique or complicated problem, but Darryl should handle the vast majority of problems and issues.

Darryl seemed to understand the situation and said he was still trying to get his feet on the ground but he would begin trying to handle more of the problems himself. During the third month, however, Larry saw no improvement and was at a loss to explain Darryl's lack of initiative and problem-solving ability. Although Darryl was black, Larry did not believe this was a factor. Two of the key-punch operators were black females, and race had never been an issue in the department.

Consequently, at the end of the third month Larry suggested that Darryl had to further develop his problem-solving skills. He recommended that Darryl enroll in a one-week seminar on Managerial Problem Solving which the local business college was holding. Darryl eagerly agreed to attend this seminar and said he thought it would help him.

It has been three months since Darryl attended the seminar, and while Larry noticed some initial improvement for a few weeks after Darryl returned, this improvement dropped off dramatically. Larry discussed Darryl's performance with him several times during the past month, but still saw no improvement. During these discussions, Larry tried to be gentle yet firm. He provided both specific suggestions and general guidance as to how Darryl should act. On one occasion, however, he had a mild loss of temper and told Darryl to "get back there and act like a manager should."

Larry did not know what to do. Darryl had been a co-worker of the group he was now supervising and Larry thought this might be part of the problem. But when he and Darryl discussed this issue on several occasions, Darryl said it was not a problem. Larry hated to give up on Darryl because of his firm commitment to EEO. But what could he do now? As he stated to another manager in the home office, when discussing Darryl's case, "I can lead a horse to water, but I'll be damned if I can make him drink."

Analysis

Larry faces a situation where a subordinate manager is performing incompetently. The cause of this poor performance is Darryl's inability to build a strong power base from which to act. That Darryl is a black, relatively new manager who once worked with the people he now supervises *is* an issue in the case, contrary to the impression Larry holds. Larry is partially at fault for not helping Darryl build an appropriate power base, lack of which undermines Darryl's competence and causes problems for Larry. Therefore, Larry must take some action.

Up to now he has tried two basic courses of action: to enhance Darryl's rational/legal power by telling him that he is the manager and should start acting like one, and to enhance Darryl's power of expertise by sending him to the one-week problem-solving seminar. Both steps apparently have had little effect, and indeed, may have been dysfunctional. Darryl's subordinates may perceive his being sent to school as a sign of lacking expertise and managerial competence.

Larry must therefore concentrate on helping Darryl build other power bases. Perhaps he can give Darryl more authority to reward and penalize subordinates or assign Darryl to a high-level corporate task force on EDP to enhance his referent power. Finally, maybe Larry can use a less obtrusive way to increase Darryl's competence in problem solving, like suggesting he read a few articles or a book on the subject.

Larry must also reinforce Darryl's supervising authority by encouraging him to make decisions and then backing him up on them. One sure way to undermine the authority of a subordinate is to second-guess him all the time. We don't know to what extent Larry and

Darryl agree on certain actions or to what extent Larry backs him up when he does finally make a decision. But Larry must convince Darryl's subordinates that Darryl has his full support and confidence. This is essential to building a strong base of rational/legal power.

Finally, Darryl's political skills in using power must also be enhanced. Many managers do not know the wise use of bargaining, negotiation, compromise, timing, and so on. Larry must help Darryl learn to use these tools without being abrasive or appearing shallow. Political skills can easily be overused by a manager, but when used in the right degree and in the proper way, they are essential to building a base of power.

Won't the Mice Play While the Cat's Away?

Some managers believe they have to be physically present on the job all the time in order to exercise power. They are afraid that if they are not present, the work will not get done. This is wrong. A competent manager makes his or her presence felt even when absent. There is no way a manager can completely rely on physical presence to maintain and enforce power. There are meetings, conventions, and conferences to attend; business trips to other cities are usually required; holidays and vacations are to be enjoyed. Anytime a manager believes physical presence on the job is necessary to make things go right, that manager is probably incompetent.

Managers who do not create the proper power presence when absent from the job have not created a supportive and demanding climate among their employees. They have not provided the proper leadership, coaching, counseling, and guidance that encourage employees to be self-motivated. The situation is similar to raising children. It's too late to try to control a child at age 16 if the parents have not done the proper job of rearing the child up to that time. Employees, like children, have to be nurtured, developed, and allowed to grow. This is a responsibility of every manager.

Some managers don't fulfill this responsibility, or attempt to fulfill it differently, as we see in this manager's statement:

Cream

I believe that the best employees will automatically rise to the top. Their performance will so distinguish them that they will be noticed and promoted in the firm. It is not necessary to "develop" employees in the normal sense of the word. Good employees develop themselves. Of course, a manager has to provide basic direction and guidance and has to monitor, follow up, and correct when necessary. A manager also has to set a good example. It's surprising how many employees learn by example and copy their boss. But a manager doesn't need to hold the employee's hand. He doesn't need to treat him or her like a child.

I believe in letting employees sink or swim on their own. They should be allowed to fail. If they fail too often, they should be fired. I watch my people pretty closely, and when they screw up I let them know it. Why keep it a secret? You're doing a person a favor when you point out his or her mistakes. A good manager keeps close tabs on employees so mistakes can be readily pointed out. Good employees don't mind this because they make so few mistakes. So what's wrong with watching employees closely? Good employees will do a good job anyway. Poor employees may find it uncomfortable, but they *need* to be watched closely to keep them from making mistakes that would really be harmful to the firm.

Analysis

I doubt that any of us would like to work for this manager. He is more concerned with pointing out the negative aspects of a person's work than the positive. You get the impression that he is looking over your shoulder just waiting for you to make a mistake so he can pounce on you.

While it is true that good employees will be visible in the organization, it does not mean they do not need additional opportunities for learning experiences to facilitate their growth and development. Managers can provide these experiences through special projects, job rotation, opportunities for off-the-job seminars and conferences, and through coaching and counseling activities. These experiences will make a good employee better and will improve the performance of marginal employees. Coaches do not stop coaching good players just because they are doing a good job. In fact, they often coach these players more and give less attention to poor players. They know they'll be counting on their best players to win games and they want to place their coaching efforts there.

The manager who believes that good employees will take care of themselves—that the cream will rise to the top—is overlooking a responsibility. Ignoring these employees while closely watching the marginal worker creates a negative power presence when the manager is away. For these managers, while the cat's away the mice will play.

Doesn't a Manager Have to Correct the Mistakes of Subordinates?

Of course a manager has the responsibility to correct subordinates' errors. But that is not the issue. The issue is *how* these mistakes are corrected. It's important to correct them in a tactful, positive, future-oriented manner, rather than in a negative, punitive, "should have" fashion. Consider the following two situations:

Situation 1

"Wanda, you lost the Higgins contract. I knew this would happen as soon as a woman was placed in this job. This women's lib thing has gone too far. Women just can't negotiate a sales contract like men. You didn't keep on him enough. You've got to be more aggressive. Plus, you need to get your facts straight and know what you're talking about. You've got to know more about the product than the customer does. I'm really disappointed in you, Wanda."

Situation 2

"Wanda, what happened to the Higgins contract?"
"I guess we lost it."

"It seems that way. What was the reason?"

"Well, I'm really not sure. I know he has been a good client in the past."

"We're going to have to work together to get that one back. Also we need to be sure we don't lose other important contracts."

"In your opinion, what can we do to get Higgins back?"

Notice the tone of the second situation compared with the first. It is a dialogue that connotes a supportive, positive, future-oriented mode of action. The first situation does not. In both, the manager is trying to correct performance. Chances are, in the first situation he will either alienate or frighten Wanda. This is not conducive to correcting behavior. The manager will likely have greater success in the second situation.

So it is necessary for managers to correct the mistakes of subordinates. But that isn't the issue. The issue is *how* those mistakes are corrected.

Doesn't a Superior Position Give a Manager a Lot of Power over Subordinates?

Yes, and with this power comes the responsibility not to abuse it. However, this power varies greatly by manager. Technically, each manager has *authority* by virtue of position. Usually, with authority comes power. Authority is usually power of position. But some managers have no other power base and rely exclusively on position. This is dangerous, because a manager must also build power bases on expertise, the ability to reward, and so on.

The problem arises when a manager who depends on the authority of position is absent for vacation, illness, or other reasons. This manager is the one who most fears that when the "cat's away the mice will play." Not there to exercise position power, the manager tries to create fear among subordinates. He or she may even go so far as to use informal spies. This is not conducive to a supportive relationship or climate. Furthermore, such action usually leads to an abuse of power. Hence the need to temper power of position with responsibility of position. Creating other bases of power besides reliance on position power alone can create power presence, when absent from the job, without developing fear in subordinates.

The potential power of a manager is awesome. If union or civil service protection does not exist, and if it does not involve race, sex, age, or religious discrimination, a manager can fire without having to prove due cause. Without going so far as termination, the manager can also make life miserable for subordinates by assigning them extra work within tight deadlines, not recommending them for promotion, or denying significant pay increases. Few managers exercise their full power of position; most of us don't want to be viewed as tyrants. But it is important to remember that an awesome amount of power is there for those who want and know how to use it.

Having power makes it easy for managers to play favorites. They are balanced on the horns of a dilemma. Rigidly enforcing every rule and procedure causes stagnation and red tape and will likely bring the organization to a halt. At the other extreme, indiscriminate flexibility results in no rules or procedures, for all practical purposes. Finding the proper place on this continuum without playing favorites is a real challenge for any manager, as we see in this example:

DOUBLE VISION

Beth could do no wrong, at least as far as Mark was concerned. Not only did she look good, she *did* good. She had risen quickly up the organization hierarchy and was now unit services supervisor in one of the largest districts served by the state's Human Services and Rehabilitation Department. As with any employee, there were parts of the job that Beth liked and parts she disliked. In particular, Beth hated to complete the weekly, monthly, and quarterly client-services-status reports required of all unit services supervisors. She would finish them, but they were frequently turned in late, often had several major errors, and usually looked sloppy. She often turned the entire job over to her assistant, who simply did not have the time or knowledge to do a complete report.

Beth was almost proud that she did such a poor job on the reports. She was fond of saying, "I work with clients and manage doers. I am not a super clerk pushing paper, nor do I intend to be." Mark accepted these statements and overlooked Beth's performance on the reports. But there's the rub, because other unit services supervisors are aware of Beth's behavior and Mark's response and are also beginning to delay reports.

The district cannot operate effectively without timely and accurate completion of the reports. These are given to the department secretary's office, as well as to the governor's office, key state legislative staff committees, and various agencies in the federal Department of Health and Human Services (HHS). Delays, especially at the federal level, can result in a temporary loss of federal funds on some state welfare programs. This can mean loss of checks to clients (often those on welfare or otherwise in need of assistance).

Mark is concerned that other unit supervisors in the district will also begin to delay their reports, but he hesitates to take action with Beth, who is a superior unit supervisor in Mark's opinion. She has a far better rapport with her subordinates than do the other supervisors. Mark also agrees with Beth's contention about paperwork, although he believes in the necessity of it more than Beth does. Although Mark has talked to Beth in the past about the late reports, he has not pushed the matter. He does not want to alienate her, but feels he should do something soon before the situation with the other unit supervisors deteriorates.

Analysis

Mark is treating Beth differently from the other unit supervisors. No doubt he is viewed by them as partial to Beth because he gives her a special exception on the reports. He is apparently unwilling to give the other unit supervisors the same exception because he feels Beth's superior qualities outweight her poor performance.

Failure to complete the reports accurately and on time can apparently have serious consequences for the district. It can even result in loss of funding which can affect the checks the clients receive. This is ironic, since Beth believes that service to clients is her first obligation, but she is unwilling or unable to complete her reports and thus ensure adequate funds to provide these services.

Consequently Mark has no other choice but to enforce the report-completion policy and procedure with Beth. Even though he risks alienating her, his failure to do this will cause serious problems for the district. He cannot expect other unit supervisors to meet report deadlines when they all know Beth is exempted from them. Furthermore, he cannot ask Beth's assistant to carry the full report load. If he does, not only is he allowing Beth to abrogate a major responsibility, but he will be asked by the other supervisors for similar staff assistants. Can he provide them? *Should* he provide them? Adding assistants because line managers fail to do their job is not an efficient way of operating and leads to excessive positions and layers in the organization.

So we see in this case that using managerial power to enforce rules, procedures, and policies requires some, but not too much, flexibility. Managers must exercise judgment when using power and must carefully consider the consequences of not only exercising power too firmly but also not exercising it enough. Careful consideration of the costs and benefits of being too firm or too lax can help a manager better use proper judgment to make a decision.

Summary

Power in the hands of an incompetent person can be very dangerous in an organization. Even in the hands of a competent manager power can easily corrupt. The potential power of any manager can be great because of the power inherent in a manager's position. This position power, or authority over subordinates, is potentially awesome. A manager can make a subordinate's work life miserable through task assignment, denial of promotion and salary increases, or insidious forms of job harassment. Fortunately, few managers fully exercise their authority over subordinates. They realize that they need subordinates to get the work done and so try to maintain harmonious, supportive, and constructive relationships.

Building positive relationships with subordinates is essential to create the proper power presence on the job. This is the power or influence a manager has even when not present at work. It is the power that encourages subordinates to fully perform their jobs, on their own, with minimal supervision.

Yet managers have the responsibility to guide, counsel, and

correct employees. If they do not, they are neglecting a fundamental responsibility of their job. Such guidance and correction, however, must be positive and future oriented rather than negative, punitive, and past oriented.

Using power to deal with poor performance is a key way to manage incompetence. Managers who do not recognize this and are not able to use power always responsibly will have difficulty managing incompetence.

9

Fighting and Beating Bureaucracy

One of the most significant causes of incompetence is bureaucracy. Incompetent people love bureaucracy because it gives them a safe, tangled web of security. If bureaucracy is nonexistent, incompetent people will create it. Within a good, strong bureaucracy, people don't have to make decisions or exercise judgment; all they have to do is to follow an existing rule or procedure.

We saw in the last chapter that rules and procedures are necessary for proper functioning of any organization. But excessive reliance on these is what characterizes bureaucratic behavior. What is required is flexibility based on sound managerial judgment.

Bureaucracy is nothing more than a hardening of an organization's arteries. Just as human arteries carry lifeblood to all parts of the body, so should good policy, procedures, and rules be communicated clearly and in such a manner as to provide guidance—but not inflexibility—to keep all parts of the organization healthy.

Understanding how to set up good policy, procedures, and rules while avoiding bureaucratic stagnation requires a good understanding of how best to structure and design an organization. Structure depicts both the way in which tasks are assigned and grouped in the organization and the network of authority that ensures the proper completion of those tasks. Design usually focuses on these issues: What tasks need to be done and who should do them? Who should ensure that the tasks are properly carried out? How many groups will be needed? What policies, procedures, and rules will enable people to better carry out their tasks? The structure of an organization is the "house" in which people live.

> Bureaucracy is a giant mechanism operated by pygmies.
> *Honoré de Balzac*

All organizations, even small ones, must have structure. The very purpose of an organization is to reach a goal or set of goals more efficiently and effectively than individuals acting alone. This means that mechanisms are needed for work specialization and to pull everything together—to provide a means of coordinating work effort so people are not at cross purposes with each other. Achieving this coordination without creating a rigid bureaucracy is a real challenge for every manager.

The structure of an organization provides four essential ingredients for operations:

1. Jobs are defined and specific tasks are assigned to each job. The total work of the organization is divided into tasks, which are assigned to various positions for performance by people holding those positions.
2. Unity of direction is provided and work efforts are coordinated.
3. Authority, responsibility, and accountability among the positions are specified.
4. Formal means of communication are established. These channels indicate to whom a person is to communicate as well as the topics covered.

Before we examine each of these factors, let's look at some traditional ways organizations have dealt with design and structure, many of which are found in today's discussions of modern organization design. Keep in mind that it is the misinterpretation of these historical principles that leads to many of our modern-day ills with bureaucracy.

How Have Organizations Traditionally Been Designed?

Let's look at two of the earlier approaches to design: the original concept of bureaucracy as best described by Max Weber, a German sociologist, and the functional/principle approach advocated by Henry Fayol, Chester Barnard, and other management scholars.

Weber's Bureaucracy

Although we now normally shudder at the word bureaucracy, our common everyday view of it is really inaccurate; Weber's bureaucracy was nothing more than an attempt to provide a logical, rational means to structure an organization.

Weber's model is based on the concept of rational/legal authority discussed in the last chapter. That is, the managers in an organization have formal authority delegated to them by the organization owners. In turn, these managers delegate authority to other managers. Authority is viewed as something flowing from the top of the organization (the owners or taxpayers) to the bottom (the workers). It gives managers the *right to command* the use of the organization's resources toward the owners' or citizens' best interests.

Weber developed this idea in the early 1900s when he saw that people in Germany were put in primarily government positions not so much because of their competence as managers but for other reasons. For example, nepotism was rampant and sons and friends of top managers were often placed in managerial positions because of the relationship these managers had with other managers or because of their political influence. Some were appointed to choice positions, even though they weren't always competent, because they had charismatic personalities.

Once these people got into managerial spots, they pretty much did as they pleased. They played favorites, created make-work jobs for friends, resisted rules and procedures or did not formulate them, and carried out only those tasks they wanted to carry out. They made the position's duties and power what they *personally* wanted them to be. After they left a position, the new appointee would remake it to his or her own likeness.

Weber believed this was terribly ineffective. He argued that there was one best way to set up an organization, and he labeled it *bureaucracy*. It was to be an impersonal means of organizing—that is, the design of the organization was *not* to be based on the fleeting whims and wishes of individual managers, but on sound concepts and principles. Basically Weber believed that:

1. Jobs should be logically specialized according to task and after a careful assessment of the work to be done.
2. Uniform policies, procedures, and rules should be developed which spell out the best way to perform tasks, regardless of who was doing them.
3. Each individual should be accountable to a superior for the effective discharge of assigned tasks.
4. The organization should be impersonal and stress formal relationships among people. It should be structured to maintain distance between members so that friendship groups—cliques—would not form and subvert the organization's structure or operations.
5. Managers should be selected because of their competence and qualifications, not because of nepotism or friendships. And they should learn the skills of management through experience and training.

Weber's concept of bureaucracy was fairly widely accepted. However, its emphasis on uniform procedures and rules and on an impersonal and formal hierarchy have subjected it to much criticism from both practitioners and academicians. The bureaucratic organization is often viewed as an unyielding institution that treats everyone the same, regardless of individual differences or unique needs. It is characterized as inflexible and unable to adapt to environmental change—in fact, of sealing itself off from the environment when change becomes too great. This leads to the popular view of bureaucratic organizations as oppressive cocoons that shield their members from change. Stability and uniformity become the highest values. Although this is a rather popular view, it is somewhat unfair.

Functional/Principle Approach

At about the same time that Weber's ideas of bureaucracy were becoming widespread, other writers were also examining organization design and structure. Fayol held that management was a process, and managers must perform certain functions, such as planning, organizing, coordinating, commanding, and controlling. The organization was to be structured around the performance of these functions.

In addition, Fayol, as well as Barnard, attempted to develop principles of organization that would define a sound structure. Some of these principles are:

1. Unity of Command—each subordinate should have only one immediate superior to whom he or she reports.
2. Scalar Chain—authority should be traceable down through the various positions in the organization. This chain of command should not be violated by by-passing an immediate superior.
3. Division of Work—specialization of labor will result in reduced waste, increased output, and easier job training.

The major objective of these earlier writers was to build a rational basis for designing and structuring organizations. We can summarize their intentions as follows:

1. The organization should be designed around the accomplishment of specific goals.
2. Work flow within the structure should be designed so that it will attain these goals.
3. Certain basic, logical concepts or principles should be followed to implement the most effective structure.
4. The performance of people within the structure should be evaluated objectively.
5. Personnel should be replaceable without having to restructure the organization.

These scholars made a significant contribution to the development of effective work groups and organizations. Attempts to follow their ideas are still widely made, while the ideas serve also as the basis for more recent developments, discussed later in the chapter. These individuals gave us ways to set up an organization that do not depend so much on the whims, wishes, and personal biases of individual managers, but on sound principles which they said should be followed regardless of the individual managers involved. But these principles also create the danger that a manager can hide behind the shield of bureaucracy.

What Design Methods Avoid Bureaucracy?

Before we turn to more modern concepts in organization design, let's take a look at two basic principles: the *activity approach* and the *general functional approach*. The activity approach looks at the specific work elements or activities that have to be performed by the organization and groups these into larger and larger units, going from the specific to more general groupings of activities and tasks. For this reason it is often called the *bottoms-up* approach to design.

The general functional approach is just the opposite. It looks at major functions and breaks them down into more specialized tasks. It goes from the general to the specific, and is often called the *top-down* approach to design. Let's look at each of these approaches in more detail.

Activity Approach

Assume you have recently been appointed head of a janitorial staff to clean a large building. Let's suppose you've never managed a group like this and that the job has to be done within two days. How would you go about getting it done? Would you split the staff up into groups and assign each group specific tasks? If so, how would you split them up and what would be your basis for determining and assigning the tasks? Would you set up group leaders for each group? How would you get the equipment and supplies you need and who would do this? How would you ensure that each group performed its assigned duties correctly so that the building was cleaned on time?

Or would you not split the group but let the entire group work on various steps in the cleaning process? What factors would you examine to determine whether it would be better to split the group or use it as an entire team?

If you decided to follow the activity approach, you would first identify the specific activities needed to get the job done. For example, you might identify the following: sweeping floors, washing windows, washing walls, mopping floors, moving desks, waxing floors, emptying trash cans, obtaining mops, buckets, brooms, sponges, and other equipment, obtaining water, wax, soap, and other materials, and inspecting the work to see that it was done properly. Notice that you haven't yet determined the order in which these activities will be done, but are simply concerned with determining which ones have to be performed.

You would then group these activities into more general tasks. For example, you might identify one task as *washing*. Another might be to *get the resources* (materials and equipment). Another might be *waxing*, and so on. Specific activities would be grouped around these central major tasks.

Let's assume that the building has three floors. You might wish to group the tasks according to floor. In other words, you could set up one group to clean all of the first floor, another for the second, and one for the third. You are grouping the tasks according to the *geographic* region to be covered. Or you could have all washers do the floors, walls, and windows on all three floors; all waxers wax all three floors; and so on.

Regardless of how you organize these activities, you would be grouping specific activities around larger and larger tasks and would set up your work groups on this basis. You would be going from the specific to the more general.

We can summarize the steps to follow in using the activity approach in this way:

1. Plan what is to be accomplished and how. The process of establishing a structure should relate to the objectives set in planning. In the example, our objective was to clean the building within two days.

2. Determine the activities required to accomplish the objectives. That is, identify the specific activities that have to be

performed. These were waxing, sweeping floors, washing windows, and others in our cleaning example.

3. Classify and group activities into larger tasks and functions so that work groups and units are created. In the example, we would group around major tasks like washing, sweeping, and others, and we would consider assigning people to each floor of the building.

4. Create a managerial position over each group of tasks. Each grouping—of activities into tasks and of tasks into major functions—requires a leadership position so that the people in each group work in a coordinated fashion. We would want group leaders to coordinate the cleaning of various parts of the building.

5. Delegate authority to the leader sufficient to perform the activities and tasks. Each leadership position we establish has to be provided authority—the right to command—in order to coordinate the work of others. This authority enables the leader to guide, inspect, direct, advise, and reassign the work of the people in his group. Without such authority, the leader will find it difficult to coordinate.

6. Provide overall coordination to tie all task groupings together. Someone or some mechanism has to be provided to ensure that all tasks are completed on time and that the objective is achieved. In the cleaning example, you would be the overall coordinating person. You might hold periodic meetings with your group leaders or perform periodic inspections to ensure that the work was going smoothly. You might also assume a troubleshooting role or assign it to one or two persons. You might even cross-train and reassign some people to perform other tasks should one group fall behind on its activities. Or perhaps you could create liaison positions, such as a person who works periodically in two or more groups, to ensure that cross communication occurs between groups.

General Functional Approach

The other way to structure an organization is to break down the major tasks into specific activities. In the cleaning example, if you chose this approach, you would first decide what major functions had to be performed in order for the building to be cleaned. You might identify the following: obtaining equipment and materials, washing, removing trash, waxing and polishing, and inspecting. You would then break each of these down into more specific tasks and duties:

1. Obtaining equipment—
    a. Obtaining brooms.
    b. Obtaining mops.
    c. Obtaining sponges.
    d. Obtaining buckets.
2. Obtaining materials—
    a. Obtaining wax.
    b. Obtaining soap.
    c. Obtaining water.
    d. Obtaining glass cleaner.
3. Washing—
    a. Washing walls.
    b. Washing floors (mopping).
    c. Washing windows.
    d. Wiping off desks.
4. Removing trash—
    a. Emptying trash cans into trash receptacles.
    b. Hauling off trash receptacles.
    c. Sweeping floor trash into piles.
    d. Removing trash from tables, chairs, and floors.
5. Waxing and polishing—
    a. Waxing floors.
    b. Waxing windows.
    c. Polishing desks.
6. Inspecting—
    a. Inspecting floors.
    b. Inspecting windows and other things.

Not all of these activities would each constitute a position; a person in one position might be able to perform several duties.

The point is that you've looked at the major things to be done and broken them down into specific activities, which are grouped into appropriate tasks and then into appropriate work groups.

Let's summarize the functional approach like this:

1. Plan what needs to be done and how it should be done. Once again, as in the activity approach, we start out with our objective: What is it we want to accomplish?

2. Determine the major functions to be accomplished in order to achieve the objective.

3. Break these down into specific tasks to be performed.

4. Break the tasks down into specific activities to be carried out.

5. Create a managerial position over each grouping of activities (as you did with the activity approach).

6. Delegate authority to the manager sufficient to perform activities (as you did with the activity approach).

7. Provide coordination to tie activities together (as you did with the activity approach).

Notice that for each approach the first step and last three steps are the same. Objectives, managerial positions with authority, and an overall coordinating mechanism must be provided regardless of the approach taken. Figure 1 summarizes these two approaches.

Perhaps the more common of these is the top-down or functional approach. It is often easier to see first the major functions to be performed and then to break them down into increasingly more specialized tasks and activities. This is especially true of organizations experiencing *growth* as they increasingly split up functions and tasks into ever more specialized units. Conversely, organizations often follow the activity approach during periods of *retrenchment* as they have to cut back and consolidate units. Previously existing, separate units are collapsed around increasingly larger groupings of activities and tasks.

This discussion of the functional and activity approaches to organization design prepares us for an examination of two key concepts: *differentiation* and *integration*. These are evolved, respectively, from the activity and functional approaches to design.

Figure 1. The activity and functional approaches to organization design.

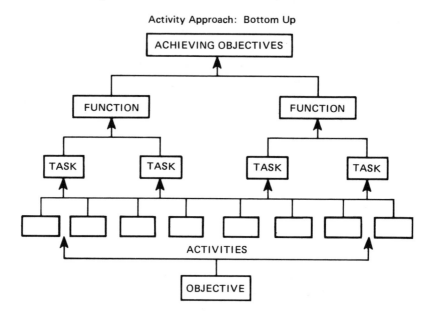

Activity Approach: Bottom Up

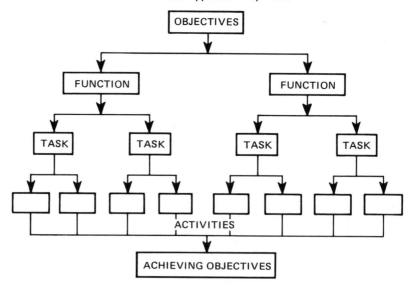

Functional Approach: Top Down

How Can Differentiation and Integration Help Build a Nonbureaucratic Organization?

Avoiding the ills of bureaucracy doesn't happen automatically. It takes conscious managerial effort. It's easy to try to make everything routine and to go by the book. It's more difficult to use policy and procedure so as to guide managerial judgment.

Two key elements in avoiding bureaucratic ills are properly differentiating and then integrating the work to be done.

Imagine an organization's total work to be a big square, as depicted in Figure 2(a). This includes all activities, tasks, and functions—an organization's overall work effort. For the tasks to be done right they must be broken up and assigned to people, as we discussed above. This dividing of the work is known as differentiation. It *specializes* work to be performed by organization members and groups.

Figure 2(a). The work to be done.

There are two basic types of differentiation—horizontal and vertical. Horizontal differentiation means breaking the work up into vertical slices of activities or tasks. This is represented by Figure 2(b). Here the *vertical* lines represent the fact that we have cut up the big block of work *horizontally*. We have constructed vertical slices of work by horizontally differentiating the work to be done. Horizontal differentiation is also known as *departmentation*. In other words we create departments or units responsible for the performance of a given set of tasks or activities.

Figure 2(b). Horizontal differentiation.

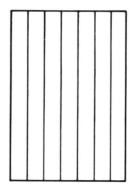

Vertical differentiation breaks up authority into various vertical levels by dividing the work as represented by the horizontal lines in Figure 2(c). We differentiate the vertical levels into authority groups. Each slice of authority within the organization represents the authority of a level of management over other levels of management. Vertical differentiation is also called the *scalar* process, which reflects the fact that scales or levels of management are created through vertical differentiation.

Figure 2(c). Vertical differentiation.

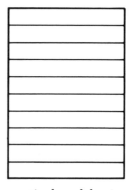

Before discussing vertical and horizontal differentiation in more detail, let's take a look at three often-confused concepts (confusion that leads to many bureaucratic problems). These are authority, accountability, and responsibility. *Authority* is the right to make decisions—regarding resource use, for example. *Ac-*

countability means a person is *answerable* to a higher authority level for the performance of assigned duties. *Responsibility* is a person's internally generated obligation to carry out these duties to the best of his or her abilities. It comes from within the person.

These concepts become very important when we look at the delegation process later in this chapter. Through confusion managers often do not delegate effectively. As explained more fully later, the authority to make decisions regarding duties and tasks is delegated. The person to whom authority is delegated is held accountable for effectively exercising that authority. The person should generate an internal obligation to carry out this delegated authority and perform to the best of his or her ability. That is, the person should act responsibly.

In designing vertical authority levels, these concepts become crucial, because with each level of authority we are creating accountability relationships and conditions that require responsibility. They also serve as a basis for delegation—a key method of avoiding bureaucracy. The following fictionalized newspaper article shows how these terms can become muddled and lead to confusion.

PIN THE TAIL ON THE DONKEY

"City Buys Everett Building Above Market Price"
by Sally Johnson, Staff Reporter

SALT LICK—The City of Salt Lick, a suburb of Metrotown, concluded the purchase of the Everett Building today. The signed purchase agreement stipulates that the city will pay $800,000 for the building located across from City Hall. Six weeks ago, the building was purchased by a group of investors for $500,000.

Last night at the city commission meeting, Ron Jones, a Salt Lick attorney, chastized the city for paying an inflated price for the building. Pointing out that even though the appraised value of the building and land was $750,000, he believed that the city could have obtained the building at a price substantially below what was paid, since it recently sold for half a million dollars.

Joe Dykes, purchasing manager for the city, disagreed. Responding to Jones, he said the city paid a fair market price and that the selling price six weeks ago was underinflated. When asked if he knew of the earlier, low selling price, he admitted that he didn't.

Emile Pucci, facilities manager for the city, also felt that the purchase price was fair and that the building would give the city needed office space for expansion. He too admitted he was not aware of the earlier lower sales price, however.

When Jones accused the city of poor, slipshod management in the purchase, City Manager Jack Haynes immediately defended the city's purchasing operations. He admitted that the building perhaps could have been purchased at a slightly lower price, but because of its location and the city's pressing need for office space, he felt a fair price was paid. He argued that neither the purchasing manager nor the facilities supervisor was responsible for the error and that he would take full accountability for the purchase. Mr. Haynes ended the discussion by saying, "There's no point in trying to pin the donkey's tail on somebody. What's done is done."

Analysis

There *is* a point in pinning the donkey's tail on somebody. While it is true that as city manager Haynes is ultimately accountable for the purchase, he does have people working for him to whom he has delegated certain tasks, for the proper performance of which these people need to be held accountable.

In this situation it's not clear whether the purchasing manager or the facilities manager had the authority to authorize the building purchase. It's also not clear if this authority existed with or without review by the city manager. But assessing the exact point of accountability is important. In addition to red-tape, rigidity, and impersonalization, bureaucracies are also famous for buck-passing. No one wants to admit to a decision. It takes conscious managerial effort to avoid this tendency.

Of course, Haynes could have said there was no point in assessing blame (pinning the tail on the donkey) to protect his people at a public meeting with the press present. In the privacy of his office the next day, he may very well take Dykes and Pucci to task over the purchase.

Horizontal Differentiation

Horizontal differentiation is the breaking up of functions and tasks into smaller units. Often it is based on the *organic* functions of business—production, marketing, purchasing, quality control, and finance—key functions every firm has to perform. When organizations differentiate along these lines, they are doing so on the basis of function.

There are other ways to differentiate horizontally: by geography, product, type of operation or process, customer, and project or program. When an organization creates differentiated units on the basis of the physical location of these units, it is differentiating on the basis of *geography*. Position titles tend to reflect this. This type of differentiation is often made in widely dispersed units, such as often found in sales divisions. Differentiation on the basis of *product* or *service* creates units based on product groupings, which is often done when the production and marketing of a product or service need to be closely coordinated.

Sometimes organizations differentiate according to the type of operation or process performed. This is common within a manufacturing operation, particularly where there is a definite beginning and end to the process. The whole process can then be placed within an organization unit, and a manager can be given the authority to coordinate the activities and tasks occurring in the operation or process.

Organizations find that differentiation on the basis of *customer* or *client* is appropriate when those who are served can be divided into several identifiable classes, each having substantially different needs. In order to ensure that the needs of each customer or client class are adequately served, units are created to properly coordinate the tasks and activities required to do this. We see such differentiation more and more in social service organizations like public health and welfare agencies. An effort is made to coordinate service delivery based on the different needs of each client group.

Commonly used in the aerospace and defense industries, *project* or *program* management differentiates resources as to project use. The work to be done is split up on the basis of the projects or programs to be completed. This approach works quite well when there are a definite beginning and ending to projects and when resources need to be shifted from one project to another as old projects are completed and new ones started. Actually, this approach is not that new, since construction firms with several crews have used a type of project management for many years.

What is new, however, is the use of project management along with *matrix management*. In the latter, the people are housed as to function (or some other basis of differentiation) but report to various project managers for the duration of a specific project. When it is completed, the people move back to their host unit. This gives the organization great flexibility to shift resources to changing projects and programs and is a great way to beat bureaucratic rigidity.

Actually, most firms use a combination of all these approaches. At one level they may be differentiated on the basis of product, at another on the basis of function, and at still another on the basis of geography. The advantage of this is that the organization can adopt the most appropriate differentiation for the work to be done.

However, there are a few guidelines that should be followed in the horizontal-differentiation process in order to reduce the ill effects of bureaucracy. First, the same basis of differentiation should be used within each level of an organization to provide equitable and understandable comparisons. For example, the sales manager should not have some of those who report directly to him or her differentiated on the basis of geographic region and some on the basis of function. Second, the method of differentiation should encourage multiple views and avoid the tunnel vision caused by overspecialization. The broadest base of differentiation should be chosen. This is one reason, for example, why differentiation on the basis of function is sometimes avoided. Everything becomes a marketing problem to the marketing manager or a production problem to the production manager. By differentiating on the basis of product, project, or program, overspecialization can be avoided, since the functions are viewed as an integrated activity in order to manufacture and market a given product or in order to effectively complete a given project.

Finally, the basis for differentiation should not be such that it creates short-term expertise (through specialization) at the expense of the long-term needs for broad-based managerial talent. A person who "grows up" in the organization working only in marketing or only with a particular product will not have the broad-based knowledge and skills needed to coordinate many activities should he or she get to the top. To the extent possible, the organization should be structured on several bases so that as people are promoted, they receive experience in various tasks and functions. This is an advantage to the project-management approach because the individual is given experience at coordinating a variety of tasks for a specific project, much as the president does for the firm as a whole.

Vertical Differentiation—The Scalar Process

This other type of differentiation is concerned with establishing authority levels in an organization. As we saw earlier, by differentiating the organization along the *vertical* dimension, we create levels of authority that represent the right to make certain decisions and to command resource use. In general, each authority level has less authority than the one above. This reflects the top-down notion of authority, which says ultimate authority rests with a board of directors, legislature, commission, or other elected body that represents owners, taxpayers, or members. These individuals delegate authority to top management, who in turn delegate it down through the organization through various authority levels.

One way to examine this vertical differentiation process is to look at the idea of *span of management*, which refers to the number of immediate subordinates reporting directly to a superior manager. This was originally viewed as a control concept and was often (and still is) called the span of control; the issue was how many subordinates a particular manager could control. Now, however, we view it also as an *integration* concept. The question becomes: How many subordinates can a particular manager coordinate and control?

It used to be thought that this span should be kept rather small. Five to seven immediate subordinates was often suggested as a proper number for a manager. More than this would make coordination and control too difficult. Fewer would not provide the manager with enough to do.

It is realized now that other factors affect the proper span of management—for example, the complexity of the task to be done and the level of management. As a person moves up the organization, the span of management should get smaller because the complexity of the work increases. Thus a pyramid-shaped organization evolves with wide spans of control at the bottom and narrow spans at the top.

Span of management also depends on the required accessibility of a manager. The more subordinates have to check with their superior, the narrower should be the span of control. This has merit, because increasing the span of control *arithmetically* increases the combinations of contacts between superior and subordinate *geometrically*. It was believed that at some point the manager would be overwhelmed by the resulting contacts and demands on his time.

Other factors determining the span of management include level of management, the skill of the manager and of the subordinate, the existence of clear policy to provide guidance, the amount of interdependency involved in the task to be done by the group, the existence of staff groups to help the manager, and the technology to be employed in performing the task. In general, the greater the skill and knowledge of the superior in dealing with subordinates and managing the task at hand, the wider can be the span of control. The manager has technical and human-interaction skills to deal with subordinates and can therefore coordinate and control a larger group. The greater the skill and knowledge of subordinates at their tasks, the wider the span of management, since they know their job thoroughly and don't need to run to their boss every two minutes to ask for advice or to check something out. They can control their own behavior better because they know what needs to be done and how to do it.

Still More Excuses for a Closed Mind

Has anyone else ever tried it?

Make a detailed report on your idea.

I don't see the connection.

It won't work in our shop.

What you are really saying is . . .

Maybe that will work in your department, but not in mine.

The executive committee will never go for it.

Don't you think we should look into it further before we act?

What do they do in other places?

What real success have you had with it?

It can't be done.

It's too much trouble to change.

It won't pay for itself.

I know a fellow who tried it.

It's impossible.

We've always done it this way.

What you mean is . . .

You don't have to say any more. I get the idea already (in mid-stream).

Who is important that has had success with it?

You haven't thought that out completely.

The clearer the policy in the organization, the wider the span of management can be. Clear policy provides guidelines for managerial and subordinate action. Should questions arise, subordinates can refer to the existing policy rather than constantly having to check with their superior. The greater the interdependency among and between subordinates, the superior, and other units in the organization, the narrower should be the span of management. If the task or work to be performed requires much interaction between subordinates and their superiors and other units, the more difficult it is to coordinate work to ensure that people aren't working at cross purposes. This extensive coordination requires a narrower span of control. The more the manager and his subordinates are assisted by staff agencies, the wider the span of management can be. Staff agencies can assist managers in performing many of their duties. For example, a personnel unit can assist in hiring, training, discipline, discharge, and promotion, thus making it easier for the manager to carry out his role with regard to these functions. An accounting or finance unit can assist the manager with the preparation of budgets and in keeping track of expenditures.

The technology involved in the performance of the task has a major impact on the span of management. It usually provides direction for the work flow. For example, on an assembly line, the work is laid out in a series of steps and is often machine-paced. The employees simply perform their routine tasks over and over; there is little need for direct control. This is common for production foremen and is the main reason why they have wide spans of management (often 20 or 30 immediate subordinates). So the more that control of work flow is determined by technology (the greater the effect of technology), the wider can be the span of management.

Although these are suggestions for determining proper span of control, we should caution that each factor ought *not* to be looked at in isolation. Rather, a manager should consider all elements separately and then determine their total effect on the proper span of management. Viewing these factors in isolation, or focusing on just one to the exclusion of others, may well give a manager a biased and incomplete view of the effect that all these factors have on the proper size for the span.

Tall and Flat Organizations

The size of the span of management relative to the number of authority levels of an organization results in the tallness or flatness of an organization. A *tall organization* is an organization with rather *narrow spans* of control relative to the number of levels of management. A *flat organization* has rather *wide spans* of control relative to the layers of management.

Tall organizations tend to provide for closer coordination and control of subordinates because of the narrower spans of control at each level. This often also results in *centralized decision making*—a key element in a bureaucracy. Decisions tend to be made in the upper management layers. Although there are many such layers, each tends to serve in a coordinating and controlling role more than in a decision-making role. They are there to enforce the rules, not make decisions. Tall organizations are thus very conducive to negative bureaucratic behavior.

Tall organizations also make upward and downward communication difficult, because a message has to pass through so many levels of management and is subject to great misinterpretation at each level. The number of layers also reduces the speed at which communication travels. The communication process, in fact, breaks down with upward communication because each layer of management tends to serve as a filtering screen and buffer for the information coming to it from lower levels.

In flat organizations there tends to be easier up-and-down communication, since the message is passed through fewer layers and so is subject to a reduced chance of misinterpretation. It also moves faster.

Furthermore, with wider spans of control superior managers tend to delegate more authority to subordinate managers because the superior finds it increasingly difficult to keep checking up on individual subordinates. Of course, this means that the subordinates must be willing and able to accept this authority—to exercise responsibility—and to be trained for their assigned tasks without frequent interaction with their superior. Studies show that there also tends to be greater job satisfaction for superior and subordinates alike in flat organizations (especially those of small to medium size) because of the improved ease of communication and greater delegation.

Buffering

A common problem with today's organization, be it tall or flat, is buffering. This occurs when managers are shielded from lower-level subordinates. In a tall organization this is commonplace because each level of management serves to shield the next higher level. But it also occurs in flat organizations through the use of the assistant-to staff position, as we see in this incident:

FAMILIARITY BREEDS CONTEMPT

"Julie, I'll be back in about an hour. I've got a meeting with Mr. Carlos. He wants to discuss a new job possibility for me. It sounds good. He may want me to be the new district manager. I'll see you."

With that, Dick Kidwell left the office on his way to Bill Carlos's office on the prestigious sixth floor. "Oh boy! Maybe I'll make the sixth floor at last," thought Dick as he rode up the elevator. "Let's see, Divisional V.P. Marketing. Yeah, here it is."

Dick entered the office.

"Hi, May. I'm here to see Mr. Carlos. I'm a bit early."

"Sure, have a seat, Mr. Kidwell. Mr. Carlos will be with you in a minute."

"Dick, my boy, glad to see you." Carlos's greeting startled Dick, pulling his attention from the current issue of *Business Week.* "I see you're catching up on a little reading. Well, you won't have too much time for that if you take this new job I have in mind for you. Come on in."

"Thank you," Dick replied.

"The trappings of power," Dick thought as he sat in a genuine leather chair and noticed the original paintings and teakwood desk.

"Dick, I'd like you to become my personal assistant," began Carlos. "I need someone who can handle this administrative detail that keeps bogging me down. Let me get to the point. Dick, you're a fine young man and I need someone like you to take over a lot of the routine stuff I have to handle."

"Why thank you, Mr. Carlos," Dick replied. "I appreciate your confidence in me. What does the job entail?"

"Oh, I don't know. Whatever needs to be done. Look here, for instance. Here's some memos from Jill, Gary, and June [Carlos's subordinates] which I just haven't had time to answer. I'd like you to answer them for me. Also, I get a lot of phone calls I just don't have time to return. You can do that for me. And there are other things—meetings, for example—which I can't attend," Carlos said.

"Well, I. . ."

"Look, Dick, I know that I hit you cold with this. Why don't you think about it for a day or two and get back to me, OK?" Carlos suggested.

Riding back to his office, Dick was amused at the thought of being Carlos's "Girl Friday." He thought Carlos had something else in mind for him, with a little more responsibility. He wasn't sure he wanted to be Carlos's "gofer." "It just goes to show," thought Dick. "Carlos is a typical bureaucrat—looking for ways to insulate himself from the rest of his work group. I'd be the buffer between Carlos and his subordinates. Why is it that so many managers seem to think they need an assistant to handle tasks that they should be handling themselves? I really think they want someone to lean on—someone to serve as a buffer between them and their work group. What a waste of money."

Analysis

Mr. Carlos may be playing the bureaucratic game or he may have a job with too many duties and functions. It is possible his job should be split into two positions. But if this is so, then that is what Mr. Carlos should recommend. His current suggestion is just to extend himself through an assistant, not to divide the work into two line positions.

The danger in following Mr. Carlos's recommendation is that it is a convenient way for an incompetent manager to create and use a bureaucracy to hide his failures. The key question is *not* how we can get Carlos an assistant to help him get his work done, but *why* Carlos is not getting the work done.

If Carlos gets an assistant, what is to prevent other managers at his level from asking for one? At what point do you stop adding assistants? Pretty soon each line manager is surrounded with assistants who buffer him from decision-making responsibilities. This should be avoided.

How Do Organizations Pull Together This Differentiated Activity Without Becoming Rigidly Bureaucratic?

We have been looking at various ways that organizations differentiate themselves both vertically and horizontally. But we must examine the other side of the coin—integration of activities. We said that organizations have a *synergistic effect* in getting work done; that is, the whole is greater than the sum of its parts. Individuals working together as a coordinated team can accomplish more than by working alone. This synergistic effect is achieved by integrating tasks and activities into a smoothly operating whole.

When you think of it, a big part of a manager's job is integrating activities. Planning is an integrating function, since goals are established and paths to achieve them are laid out. Organizing is an integrating activity, since proper amounts and types of resources are brought together at the proper time and placed under the proper authority to achieve goals. Directing is leadership applied to get people to work together in an effective, harmonious manner. Controlling is a means to ensure that resources are being properly used in following the paths and achieving the goals laid out. So integration is a major role in a manager's job. Let's look at how the design of an organization helps a manager achieve it.

Centralization and Decentralization

We saw in our discussion of flat and tall organizations that the structure of an organization can affect the extent to which decision making is centralized or decentralized and thus the amount of bureaucracy. In turn, this centralization and decentralization can affect the integration process. All other things being equal, the more centralized the decision-making process, the greater the degree of integration of activities. Centralization of decision making can put overall coordination of organization tasks and functions under one big umbrella.

However, all other things being equal is an important qualification. Centralized decision making can occur only when time is not a constraint. If lower-level units must respond quickly to an environmental demand or internal problem, centralized decision making will not work because it will take too long. Centralized decisions are also difficult in highly complex organizations, by which we mean organizations that are extremely differentiated both vertically and horizontally. Under these conditions there are so many layers of management and so many differentiated units that it is virtually impossible to make all decisions at the top. Imagine the difficulty for a production superintendent at a General Motors plant if every major decision he had to make had first to be cleared with the executive committee at GM!

Centralized decision making will not work in an unstable, unpredictable environment. Imagine having to contact top management to clear every decision because of constantly changing forces in the environment. If the environment is stable and predictable, however, top management can deal more easily with decisions that have to be made.

Decentralized decision making is inappropriate when time is a constraint, environments are unstable and shifting, and organizations are highly complex. It still can provide for integration if clear, general policy guidelines are established for subordinate managers to follow when making decisions, and if certain key decisions are reviewed and evaluated periodically by top management to determine their effectiveness.

There are other ways to achieve integration besides centralization. Decentralization under clear policy guidelines is one. Some others are the *fusion process,* the *linking-pin process, Management by Objectives* (MBO) and *matrix management.* Each is especially useful when centralization will not work and decentralization is required.

The fusion process refers to the bonds of the organization that hold people together. In order for people to join an organization, they must give up some things—like time, effort, and certain activities. They must adopt behaviors required by the organization. In short, to a certain extent they must conform to the expectations and norms of the organization. But in exchange for this sacrifice, the reward is a job—a job that provides security, money, and perhaps power, prestige, and other factors. People are willing to join organizations and give up certain things if they feel that the benefits of joining are greater than the costs. If everyone who is a member of the organization does this, there forms a common bond of expectations, norms, and behavior patterns. Integration of action is thus achieved. The organization acts as a great socializer, a leveler to bring about standards of behavior performance.

According to this theory, we can suggest that the more explicit the expectations and norms that an organization creates and communicates to its members, the more likely the organization will attract and hold members who "buy into" these norms and expectations, and the easier it will be to achieve integration.

The linking-pin process of achieving integration refers to each manager's being a linking pin in the organization because he serves as both superior and subordinate (with the exception of the chief executive officer). A manager is a member of two teams—a subordinate or follower with one, a superior or leader with the other. Furthermore, some managers can play a *liaison role* and link two teams horizontally. Not only are they members of two teams as subordinate and superior, but they are also a member of a third team as a liaison. The danger of liaison positions is that they may violate the Unity of Command Principle that each subordinate should have only one immediate superior to report to. However, if a liaison is held accountable to "A" position and still serves as a member of the "B" team, and if the tasks and functions for the liaison position are clearly spelled out, the chances of violating the Unity of Command Principle will be significantly reduced.

Management by Objectives can also be viewed as an integrating mechanism. When we establish clear purposes or issue clear goal statements for the organization and each of its units, set clear objectives, clear programs, clear standards, and effective measurement systems, we then make it easier to achieve integration of effort. People will know the goals of the organization and of their units and how the achievement of these goals will help the organization achieve its goals. They see how basic unit and organization goals dovetail. They see how major programs interrelate. When the MBO process is implemented in a participatory fashion so that everyone involved assists in writing organization and unit mission statements, objectives, and programs, there will be greater understanding of the organization's effort, which should make it easier to achieve effective integration.

We discussed matrix management when we reviewed the concept of project management. We need to point out, however, that this can also achieve integration. By assigning resources from host units to specific projects, unity of effort and coordination is created to complete the project. The project manager serves as a coordinator who directs the use of the various resources needed for the project.

The problems of integration are well illustrated in this example of a social service agency:

GETTING IT ALL TOGETHER

Advanced Services Systems, Inc. is a social service organization whose goal is to provide rehabilitative counseling services to clients in the Miami area. Much of the work of this new organization involves individual psychological counseling and personal problem solving, job counseling and placement services, marriage and family counseling services, and alcohol and drug rehabilitative services.

The organization staff is comprised of approximately 35 competent members in the fields of psychiatry, psychology, social work, and personnel placement as well as staff support in the form of secretaries and clerks. Most of the professionals have either Masters, Ph.D., or M.D. degrees. The organization's clients are individuals with various problems and tend to be fairly wealthy and to use private rehabilitation services over those provided by state or federal agencies.

The organization is currently structured as diagramed in Figure 3.

Recently the organization has experienced problems in coordinating its service offerings for client groups. Frequently, problems that a particular client has are multidimensional. That is, a particular client may have job-related problems because of an alcohol problem, and this also affects the client's family and marriage relationships.

Therefore, the organization, particularly its president, Mr. Jack Lewis, feels that a new structure is needed to better coordinate its service offerings.

Analysis

In this situation, horizontal differentiation based on the type of counseling offered is not serving the company well. The company is specialized by type of counseling needed, but many clients come to the firm often needing a variety of services. The firm is having difficulty providing these services in a coordinated manner. A case-management-oriented or unified-service-delivery approach is needed. But this may be difficult if the physicians, psychologists, and counselors are extremely specialized.

Figure 3. Advanced Services Systems, Inc.

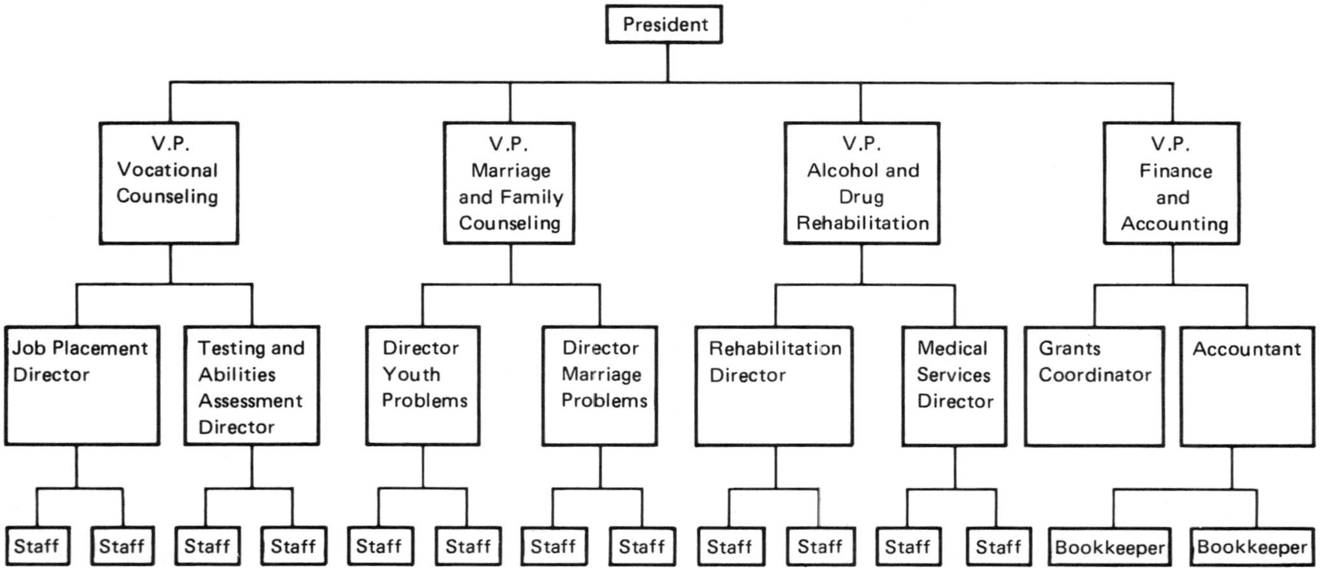

Since this specialization is probable, a generalized position, "case manager," should be created. This person would need knowledge of counseling and rehabilitation but also understanding of information flows, record keeping, and basic management functions. Each new client could be assigned to a case manager with the authority to monitor the client from the beginning to the end of the counseling or rehabilitation process. The case manager would refer the client to various specialists in the firm and would track the client's progress.

The case manager, therefore, serves much as a project manager might in a project matrix organization. By cutting across the various functional specialties of the staff, the case manager has the responsibility and authority to see that the client gets proper treatment.

Free-Form Organization

Do all organizations need integration? Yes, but some can achieve it through less structured means than we've discussed so far. We call these less structured organizations *free form*. Within a free-form organization there are minimum status and authority differentials between superiors and subordinates. Superiors might even be elected by subordinates and serve for a term of office. Or perhaps the superior position rotates and a different subordinate takes his turn as superior every two or three years. (This is often done with department chairmen at some prestigious and some not so prestigious universities.) The superior is considered to be first among equals and a team leader.

In the free-form organization, the skill and expertise of individuals create varying work groups that change over time. The organization's entire structure is built around specific projects for specific time periods, and changes as projects and time periods change. People work on projects to which they feel they can make the greatest contribution, in which they are interested, and for which they have the skills and knowledge. Free form differs from matrix in that there is no host unit.

Free form tends to work best in smaller organizations or in smaller units of large organizations where the skills and knowledge of the members are very high and where there is a high level of personal and professional responsibility so that members direct their own behavior. It can work best also where projects change over time and people move from project to project when they feel it necessary. Ph.D. research chemists for a pharmaceuticals firm, professors in a college or university, lawyers, highly skilled consultants, or workers at a research institute—each of these groups would be appropriate for free-form integration.

We should caution, however, that free-form integration does not mean *no* integration. It does mean that each group member assumes personal responsibility to ensure that integration takes place. And free-form organization does not mean no management or leadership. It does mean that the group members have significant input into the management process and that the manager manages with the consent of the managed.

Summary

Bureaucracies, with a life of their own, are hard to beat. But they must be attacked if we wish to fight incompetence. In this chapter we have looked at some of the major factors involved in designing organizations so as to avoid the ills of bureaucracy. Work groups can be placed within a hierarchy that allows freedom of discretion and decision making. Bureaucracy need not exist. In fact, most managers find it uncomfortable. But for incompetent people the bureaucracy is a life-saver since it allows them to hide their foibles from others.

It's unfortunate that Max Weber's bureaucracy has so evolved from its original rational/logical means for designing an organization to the present negative state of affairs. Organizations do need order, as well as rules, policies, and procedures. And these should be logically developed and communicated. But they should not be so rigid and slow to change that they hamper organization and managerial effectiveness. Nor should they so centralize decision making that lower-order subordinates become mere paper-pusher functionaries.

Differentiating and integrating organization activity in a way that avoids the ills of a bureaucracy is a genuine challenge for every manager. Achieving the proper size for the span of management is important. The fusion process, linking-pin process, MBO, matrix management, and the free-form organization are alternatives to centralized bureaucracies as roads to integration.

Bureaucracies behave as if they were closed systems that somehow screen out environmental influences. Too few variables are considered. Informal relationships and interactions are discouraged. Managers are forced to go by the book—and the book is usually quite thick. Instead, organizations need to take a more open approach, consider multivariable interaction, and examine and allow the relationships that form in organizations to speed things along. Unless the ills of bureaucracy are addressed directly and with vigor, it will be very difficult to recognize and reduce incompetence.

10

The Capacity
for Joy

Organization life can be dreary and monotonous. It can be full of stress, tension, frustration, and pressure. Or it can be fun, full of challenges, opportunities, rewards, and personal growth. Most jobs are a mixture of both desirable and undesirable attributes, though some jobs are more desirable than others.

It is very easy to get caught up in the daily work grind. We begin looking forward to weekends, holidays, and vacations. We count the years, even months until retirement. Work becomes a necessary bridge to get us from one pleasurable period—a weekend, for instance—to the next. It becomes an evil to be endured, not enjoyed. Even the best of jobs feel that way sometimes.

In this chapter we explore some ways to keep work from being drudgery. We can't like all aspects equally—that is virtually impossible. But we can do some things to minimize the unpleasant aspects of work and to maximize the pleasurable.

In particular, we are interested in the issue of incompetence as it relates to making work more enjoyable. Having to work with incompetent people is one of the more common and important reasons why people dislike their jobs. We hear complaints every day. A boss states, "If it weren't for Gary and Joe, I'd have a pretty good work team. It's just a small percentage of my employees who give me trouble." A subordinate says, "My job would be great if I didn't have to work for an S.O.B." Others at all levels in an organization will say, "My job would go smoothly if we could just get sales, accounting, personnel, production [you name it] to do their job properly." Although some of this talk is scapegoating, it is true that working with incompetent people is extremely frustrating.

We have taken the approach in this book that incompetence is not something to be ignored but to be managed. Dealing effectively with incompetence takes much time and effort initially, but the eventual payout is great. It's easy to throw up your hands and give up on incompetent people, but this temptation should be resisted. In the long run a person's job will be easier if incompetence is handled effectively, even when it first takes much time and effort. The point is, however, that you will never have time to stop and smell the flowers unless you first deal with incompetence.

Is Work Really to Be Enjoyed?

Yes, it is. Although some jobs are unpleasant, and all jobs have some unpleasant characteristics, in and of itself work is as natural as play. What is work? If a salesman closes a sale over lunch, is he working? If an executive discusses business on the golf course with fellow executives, are they working? Is a dinner party that is given to boost the morale of subordinates work? If I think of ideas for an article, book, or lecture while fishing, am I working? Most of us would agree that the above episodes are not work in the traditional sense, but elements of work are present. Generally, work is defined as carrying out the tasks and duties of a job, either for an employer or in self-employment, for financial remuneration. The implication is that such activities go on at a designated place of employment, usually an office, factory, classroom, hospital, or other location.

This definition of work, however, needs further clarification, since what is work for some people can be play for others. This is most notable in the sports and recreation industries. Professional golfers work at an activity at which most of us play. Charter boat captains perform the same work we do when we take friends out fishing. But they are paid for their efforts and we are not.

The issue of enjoying work is a relatively recent phenomenon. Under traditional Protestant and Catholic ethics, work was a form of punishment to be endured. Hard work was good for the soul and a way of pleasing God. It was to be enjoyed only in that it would bring us personal pleasure and satisfaction by pleasing God. Certainly, when these ideas dominated, most jobs of an agrarian and emerging industrial society were downright unpleasant. Walking ten or twelve hours a day behind a horse or mule that is strapped to a plow is not pleasurable for most people. Nor is working in a hot steel mill or dark, wet, coal mine 12 to 14 hours a day, 6 days a week, as at the turn of the twentieth century. Most jobs were hot and wet and required heavy physical effort for long hours. It was very difficult to enjoy any aspect of work.

Of course, things are different today. Machines have relieved humans of much drudgery. Workweeks are shorter. Working conditions and health and safety are much improved. Yet in many jobs today, mental stress has replaced the physical stress of the past. We see this not only on the face of the bored assembly-line worker, but also on the face of the harried executive running from one fire-fighting crisis to the next.

Some people actually thrive on job stress. They love to put out fires—it makes them feel important. If crises don't exist, they create them, believing this justifies their importance to the organization. Others actually enjoy routine, repetitive jobs that most of us would find boring. They don't experience the stress caused by boredom. Instead, they feel routine offers them stability, security, and a chance to think about other things (daydream) while working. They can forget their jobs when they go home.

But those who thrive on stress or who don't find repetitive jobs boring are exceptions. Most of us want to avoid these elements. And if we can't, then we want to redefine our job to reduce them. To some extent we are all hedonistic. We want pleasure—in our jobs, our home life, our social activities—because we equate pleasure with happiness and satisfaction.

If we take as a basic tenet that organizations should be places that efficiently and effectively produce goods and services as well as give us satisfaction, then we can accept the notion of finding pleasure in our jobs. In fact, if we can demonstrate that job satisfaction and productivity are closely related, then we can more readily accept the legitimacy of seeking happiness in our work.

Are job satisfaction and productivity closely related? Yes, they are. Not only do most of us intuitively support this idea, but the research also shows a close relationship. But here's the rub: It's not clear from the research whether job satisfaction causes productivity, or *vice versa*. If it is the former, then we would want to make employees happy so that they produce. On the other hand, if it is productive effort that results in feelings of satisfaction, then we should not be concerned with satisfying employees initially, but should first create the conditions that allow and encourage them to be productive, under the assumption that satisfaction will follow.

Satisfaction and productivity are interdependent. We're still not sure which causes the other, or whether there might not be a third, fourth, or fifth variable that affects both. But we do know the two are closely correlated. It can therefore be argued that seeking happiness in one's work is a legitimate goal to be pursued by individuals and encouraged by organizations.

If Job Satisfaction Is a Legitimate Goal, Why Are Many People Unhappy in Their Jobs?

There are many reasons why people are unable to achieve an appropriate level of job satisfaction. First, they may have jobs not too different from those found in an agrarian society or at the beginning of the Industrial Revolution. There are still many physically taxing undesirable jobs with low occupational prestige—dishwasher, roofer, trash collector, petroleum rig roustabout, hot asphalt pourer, glass furnace tender, and others come to mind. It is difficult for many people to enjoy these jobs, although some do. Most just tolerate them.

Second, people have jobs unsuited to their skills, abilities, and interests. It's difficult to enjoy a job if you do not know how to do it, can't do it, or find you are not interested in doing it. People often have to take a job because they need work and very little is available. Many people hold these jobs for just a short period of time, until something better comes along. This is true of many occupations in the restaurant industry (especially fast foods), in some clerical ranks, and in laborer positions, but it can occur in almost any occupation, with the probable exception of the professions. Sometimes personnel managers are guilty of poor placement, especially if there is a shortage in a particular job category. The "warm body" syndrome can prevail.

Third, some people will never achieve a high level of job satisfaction because they are workaholics who work long and hard but often do not really enjoy their job. They may work long hours because of poor home life or compulsive behavior, or to justify their importance to themselves and the organization. This isn't to say that all workaholics dislike their job; many enjoy their work. But others find it to be sheer drudgery as they put in one long week after another. As we've seen elsewhere in this book, these people are often incompetent, and their very long work hours are their way of trying to overcome their incompetence.

> The high prize of life, the crowning fortune of a man, is to be born with a bias to some pursuit, which finds him in employment and happiness.
>
> Ralph Waldo Emerson

Fourth, there are still those in society who do not believe work is to be enjoyed. Although this number is declining with each succeeding generation, many still view work as a penance to be endured. They believe this even when they hold a job that most of us would find satisfying.

Fifth, some people are searching for complete job happiness. Hopping from one job to the next, they are never satisfied. They are unwilling to accept a reasonable level of satisfaction, and instead, want perfect job happiness, which is virtually impossible. Every job has its bad points. People who believe they will eventually find the perfect job if they keep searching hard enough are deluding themselves.

Finally, there are those who have a good job but they don't enjoy it because of the organization in which they work. They may have an S.O.B. for a boss, live in a bureaucratic jungle, or be in a dying industry. These people will not be happy until they are able to find a similar job with another organization.

What Can I Do to Increase My Job Satisfaction?

What makes you happy? What activities do you enjoy doing? Are there jobs for which you qualify that promise these activities? If you do not qualify now, will training, education, and experience help?

People who find themselves in dissatisfying occupations don't have to tolerate them forever. It is possible to acquire new skills for different jobs. Often these people do not know what they really want, and have never genuinely and completely explored the job market to see what's available. They are victims early in life of poor career planning and guidance, and they selected a job because of expediency, family tradition, necessity, or availability. But once at these jobs, they are unwilling to change for something better, which involves risk. At least at the present job, we know what to expect; a new job holds many unknowns. Is it worth the risk? Many people think not, so they stay with what they have. This inertia is further strengthened by thoughts of the pension and security rights building up on the present job. So they go from one day to the next feeling trapped.

We are the masters of our own destiny. We do not have to tolerate a job we find intolerable. There are countless examples today of people who return to school for training and education in middle age to acquire new skills or knowledge in order to qualify for different occupations. The mid-career switch is becoming increasingly common and recognized by colleges, universities, and technical schools that have established night programs, weekend MBA programs, short courses, workshops, and accelerated undergraduate programs. Often this switch is complete. I know of one person who received a Ph.D. in music theory and later went back to school for technical training in computer programming. This person is now a computer programmer for a large state agency.

Others leave firms they have been with for years to accept better jobs with other companies. The person who starts and stays with the same company until retirement is today rare indeed.

And, of course, we are all familiar with the middle-aged military retiree who takes a job with a state or federal agency. These "double-dippers" provide government agencies with skilled manpower often at salaries lower than those paid in private industry, since they are collecting military retirement benefits which augment their government salary.

Most of us could maximize our level of job satisfaction if we took better advantage of the career planning and counseling process. Most of us have gone through this process in a most haphazard way. But it's not too late. We can benefit by finding answers to the following questions:

◆ Do you really understand your own strengths and weaknesses?
◆ Do you have a clear idea of your off-the-job and on-the-job interests?
◆ What specific goals do you want out of life?
◆ What job exists that allows you to reach these life goals?
◆ What specific goals do you want from your work?
◆ What characteristics would you look for in an ideal job?
◆ What necessary training, education, and experience would you need to acquire this ideal job?
◆ How realistic is it for you to acquire this necessary training, education, and experience?
◆ For what jobs do you qualify with your present training, education, and experience?
◆ How different is your present job from your ideal job?
◆ How different are the jobs for which you qualify from your ideal job?
◆ What can you do to close the gap (if any) between your present job or those for which you qualify and your ideal job?
◆ Do you have a career plan that sets out the jobs you want five, ten, fifteen, and twenty years from now?

These questions are not easy to answer, but if we find ourselves in unsatisfying jobs, we should try to answer these questions *before* we start looking for another job.

How Can I Locate a More Satisfying Job?

Never quit your present job before finding a new one. Your chances of finding a new job are lower when you're out of work than when you're looking while still working. Many employers see an out-of-work applicant as tainted. Looking for another job while you're employed, however, may cause problems with your present employer. There are two schools of thought about this. On the one hand are those who say you should be up-front and honest with your present employer, explaining that you are looking for a new job and why. You should also explain that this job search will not occur during your work hours, but that instead, you will use personal leave time, vacations, or other free time. This approach may help you secure a better job with your present company if it feels you are valuable and wishes to keep you. With some employers, however, this approach may hurt you; you could be immediately written off for future promotions, merit increases, or other rewards. Then if you do not find new employment, you're stuck with an employer who cares little about keeping you.

On the other hand are those who say you shouldn't tell your present employer that you are looking for a new job because if you don't find a new job, your present employer will not have written you off. But if your present employer learns about your search through the grapevine, it could cause you serious problems, especially if the employer believes you are looking during work hours or using organization resources (a typist for letter and resume, for example). However, during periods of retrenchment or a pending merger, some employers will make office space and secretarial services available to facilitate the transition to a new job for those employees likely to be laid off.

My own opinion is that you should inform your present company when you're looking for a new job. It is likely to find out eventually anyway, especially when some of your job leads call to check on a reference. If you are immediately written off, this will only confirm your desire to leave your present employment. Who wants to work for an employer that writes off its employees so quickly? If your present employer wishes to keep you, perhaps you'll get a better job in the organization. At least you'll know where you stand.

Here are some other job hunting tips:

◆ Obtain as much information as you can about potential employers—not only the usual information about salaries, benefits, and so on, but also about those you'll be working with. What are their strengths and weaknesses? Is the industry you'll be in growing? Where does your potential employer stand in the industry? A leader? Follower?

◆ Work through your contacts in other firms. Personal contact is vastly superior to blind mass mailings of your resume.

◆ Prepare an attractive, printed resume with a photo. Be sure a job objective is on the resume. Keep it short—three pages maximum. List the most important accomplishments first, not just job titles.

◆ Job letters should be personally typed and signed and sent to a specific person, not to an office or title. Mass mailings of a copied letter are generally a waste of time and money.

◆ Use an executive search firm if you're looking for an upper-middle or higher management job. More and more firms rely on these agencies to fill upper-level spots and almost always pay the placement fee.

◆ Use a job placement service run by a professional organization in your trade, industry, or profession. This will give you wide exposure to many potential employers at very low cost. Engineers, professors, medical personnel, accountants, editors, television and radio people, and many other groups regularly provide such services.

◆ Get active in trade and professional organizations and attend the conventions, seminars, and shows as a program participant or an officer. This offers high visibility. Use meetings and conventions to make initial contacts with potential employers. At a meeting or convention, you can make many contacts in a short period of time at relatively little cost.

◆ Ask potential employers what the negative aspects of the job and organization are. It's easy to find out the positive aspects, but every job also has a negative side that must be known before you accept it. A good employer will willingly tell you about it.

◆ Get an employment contract. It is becoming increasingly common today for upper-middle and top management to be hired on a contract basis—much as a coach or ballplayer is hired. Salary, fringes, and other conditions are specified for a given period of time, for instance, a year or two. If you are terminated prior to the contract's expiration, full remuneration is due.

◆ Don't take the first job you're offered, at least not right away. Always choose between two job offers as opposed to one job or no job. Postponing a decision may not always be desirable from an employer's perspective, but if the company wants you bad enough it will wait a few weeks.

◆ Make sure the job you finally choose is consistent with your career plans. You may have to take a less desirable position temporarily, but you should ensure that the job you view as permanent reinforces your career plan.

◆ Don't change jobs too often, but do change jobs occasionally. If you job-hop too often (say, more than three times in a ten-year-period), you'll be viewed as unstable and hard to satisfy. On the other hand, studies show that if you continue indefinitely with the same employer, your salary will not progress as fast as if you changed employers. Most companies will pay more to attract new talent than to keep existing talent.

◆ When choosing a job, consider the desires of your spouse and children. There are many examples of people who have a good job but a miserable life because their children and spouse are unhappy with frequent moves, geographic location, or the breadwinner's long absences from home due to travel. Also, today a person must be concerned with employment opportunities for the spouse, with either the same organization or a different one in the same area.

Does My Home Life Contribute to My Job Satisfaction?

Jobs are a central life focus for just about everyone in our society. We judge people by the job they hold. Think of what you ask people when you meet them for the first time, at a party, for instance. We ask what they "do" and stereotype them accordingly. Whether this is right or wrong is not the issue—it is a fact that we give great importance to a person's job in judging worth and prestige.

A person's job and home life are inexorably entwined. Happenings at work affect happenings at home, and *vice versa*. It is the rare person indeed who can leave office problems at the office and home problems at home. Consequently, job satisfaction and satisfaction with home life are very closely, but not necessarily *always*, related. Most of us can erect sturdy boundaries between the routine problems of home and those of the office, but it's more difficult to do so around major problems. Those who have gone through a divorce know the job disruptions it can cause.

Maintaining a balance between work life and home life is therefore essential to job satisfaction. It does no good to continually strive for the "better" job if the frequent geographic moves alienate children and spouse and destroy home life. How can a job be enjoyed if life at home is miserable? One reason why workaholics often dislike their work is because so much animosity is created in the workaholic's home life that feelings of dissatisfaction spill over to the job.

What Is the Proper Balance Between Work and Leisure?

As we've discussed elsewhere in this book, the executive or manager who regularly works much over 40 hours each week has a problem. Chances are that this person:

◆ Isn't delegating enough to subordinates.
◆ Isn't managing time properly.
◆ Spends too much time each day in idle discussion or long-winded meetings.
◆ Does not rely on enough staff work.
◆ Is counting lunches, dinners, and travel time as work time. (If these are counted, work time usually approaches 50–55 hours per week.)
◆ Has an incompetent superior and/or subordinates and is not changing this situation.

Each of these reasons for regularly excessive work hours can be and should be changed. We need our leisure time. In today's complex society, we need time away from the job to rest and recuperate. A large, successful grocery retail chain in Florida prides itself in its advertisements on its stores being closed on Sundays so employees can spend time with their families. The claim is made that on Monday the employees are refreshed and pleasant, so that shopping is a pleasure.

The justification for holidays and vacations lies with the claimed renewal and fresh approach that the employee afterward brings back to the job. (Often, however, the employee comes back in worse shape, especially if the period has been spent on a family cross-country camping trip.) Time away from the job places time at the job in clearer perspective.

Leisure time should not be wasted. Of course, one person's productive use of leisure is another person's folly. Is jogging good use of leisure time? Racquetball? Splitting wood? Gardening? Reading a good novel? Watching *Charlie's Angels*? Sleeping on the beach? Reading the daily newspaper? Playing "Monopoly" with the family? Riding a horse? Swimming? Generally, most of us believe that physical exercise, reading, and family activities requiring interaction are good uses of leisure time.

We usually deplore watching situation comedies and televised sports events, although a great many families do so. Yet watching a situation comedy can be altered from a passive to an active, enriching family experience. During the commercial breaks and at the end of the show, discuss the plot, the usual heavy emphasis on a sexual theme, and any moral the story presents. Speculate as to why the writers pursued the particular story line they did, and whether the show was successful or not. Critique the show and have each family member indicate how he or she might rewrite the ending. Have them evaluate the use of the time spent watching the show relative to other things they could be doing. Watching a typical television sit-com can be made into an interactive family learning experience. Most of us, however, just don't take the time and energy to do this.

Not every moment of leisure must have purpose. Sometimes it's fun just to loaf and do nothing. But for leisure to have its greatest benefit, complete idleness should be very infrequent. The active pursuit of enriching leisure time can improve mental health and off-the-job satisfaction, and thus add to on-the-job happiness.

How Can People Get What They Want
Out of Their Organizations?

We've heard and read about the "Me Decade" of the seventies. We've been told to grab power, look out for number one, find "it," and otherwise screw our neighbors and fellow workers. This brash assertiveness is certainly contrary to the love, cooperativeness, giving, and sharing espoused by the flower children of the sixties. We are all narcissistic to some extent, and we all have our rights, but to blow these out of proportion creates unrealistic expectations and can make people appear downright selfish.

Each of us expects a set of rewards from the organization that employs us. In return we give the organization time, effort, skill, loyalty, and so on. We form a *psychological* contract based on this exchange. Expecting reasonable rewards from the organization is proper. Working for increased rewards is also proper, especially if we are willing to give more time, effort, and other resources in return. Going after rewards by trying to earn them is much different from the narcissist who demands them as a matter of right. In other words, improved performance should bring greater rewards. They should not be a matter of right regardless of performance level. Across-the-board increases in rewards destroy the merit principle that should serve as the basis for any reward system.

Competent managers and employees are in a position to obtain what they desire from organization life. Incompetent people are not. Competent people can negotiate for higher salaries, promotions, perquisites, staff assistance, increased budgets, better office space, and redefined job duties, not in a selfish, high-handed fashion, but through a tactful, direct, low-key, and logical approach.

Here are some tips for obtaining what you want from the organization. First, know what you want and what you can reasonably expect to receive. Don't set your sights too low, or too high. Addressing the career-planning issues raised earlier in the chapter is therefore a necessary first step.

Second, know what the organization can offer. What are the policies and procedures for promotion, merit raises, fringes, and other benefits? How are these enforced? Are there exceptions?

How have other people been treated in the recent past on these issues? Do any union or civil service constraints and protections apply? Ignorance of the basic rules of the game will make it difficult to improve your share of the available rewards.

Third, negotiate from strength. Be sure your competence is visible, but don't toot your own horn. Let your actions and your colleagues speak for you. Don't ask for more immediately after a personal mistake or setback, or during a recession that is affecting your company.

Fourth, don't force an issue unless it is really important. Pushing for a promotion you don't really want, or a small merit raise increase just on principle, is not wise. Save your efforts for the important things. And work for them in a direct but tactful manner.

Fifth, don't threaten, intimidate, or personally attack another person to get what you want. Threatening to resign might get your resignation accepted. Don't threaten anything unless you fully intend to go through with it should your demand or request not be met. Losing our temper usually shows that we are not in control and will usually cost us much more than we could possibly gain from this behavior.

Sixth, build credibility before seeking additional rewards. You may be a competent employee, but if you are placed under a new manager or moved to a new division, you have to demonstrate this competence through a good track record. We all have to prove ourselves at each move. Lack of credibility causes many fresh MBAs to run into serious difficulty their first few months with a new employer. They are resting on their degree and haven't established credibility through performance before seeking additional rewards.

Seventh, know the actual paths to greater rewards. These might be very different from the stated paths. Look at those around you. What behavior is really rewarded? What has hard work and performance brought others? What behaviors are penalized? How do you make your performance known to others—for example, through performance review sessions, output logs, activity reports, or what else?

Eighth, find a good mentor or coach who will offer guidance

and speak up for you. This may be your immediate superior, but more often than not it is someone else at a higher level in the organization. Demonstrate your capabilities to this person through sound performance, perhaps by serving on a task force or committee with him or her. Ask for advice and listen. The mentor system is an excellent way to develop an informal advocate in the organization who can help you receive your due. Some organizations have even formalized the mentor process, especially for minorities and women who are usually excluded from the typical old boy network within the organization.

How Do I Handle Incompetent Employees Who Always Seem to Want More Than They Deserve?

First, be sure they are incompetent. Earlier we reviewed some ways of identifying incompetence. Once you are sure they are incompetent, don't be afraid to say no. But every no deserves a full explanation. Explain honestly why the person was passed up for promotion and what he or she can do to improve chances for the next one. It's easy to avoid this confrontation and to leave unsaid many things that should be said. But don't be tempted by this. The one theme that pervades this book is that incompetence must be forthrightly confronted, not ignored. Dealing with it openly when organization rewards are handed out is extremely important. An unwillingness to attack incompetence at that moment implies a failure to recognize the merit principle. It is also an avoidance of conflict for fear of hurting someone's feelings or because of uncertainty in using conflict management methods.

Management is not easy. It involves many unpleasant duties, one of which is dealing with incompetent subordinates, superiors, and peers. Counseling, disciplining, rewarding, and influencing are steps a manager must take when faced with incompetence. Tolerating and ignoring it only serve to give it implicit approval. In today's organizations, with increasing international competition in so many areas, managers must be highly concerned with improving organization effectiveness and efficiency. Incompetent performance is a drain on resources and just cannot be tolerated in today's competitive environment.

Summary

Enjoying organization life is important for improved productivity. Studies show that job satisfaction and productivity are closely related. Working with incompetent people in an organization makes it difficult to enjoy our jobs, and also to have high productivity. Effectively dealing with incompetence, then, has a two-pronged effect: it should increase productivity and make our jobs more enjoyable.

We all pay a penalty for incompetence. Is that penalty worth it? Can we do something about it? Is it not imperative that we do something about incompetence to ensure the continued existence of our productive system?

Epilogue

Theory and Assumptions for Understanding People at Work

We've made the assumption throughout this book that managers can understand and change people's behavior at work. We are not going to relax this assumption now, but we are going to temper it. Human behavior in organizations is complex and often difficult to understand. Yet all managers are required to work with people, and one mark of successful managers is that they are experts at understanding people.

Over the years a discipline has developed in business and public administration schools and colleges, called "organizational behavior." This field employs research principles and theory from psychology, social psychology, sociology, cultural anthropology, and institutional economics, as well as research done in ongoing organizations to formulate a body of knowledge that will help us better understand people at work. Organizational behavior applies this research and these ideas from a managerial perspective—that is, the field of study is concerned not only with what people at work do, but also with whom they do it, and how their behavior can be changed.

In trying to manage incompetence we must come to grips

with important behavioral complexities. The understanding of these is very much an inexact science. We have a difficult time not only in identifying relevant variables affecting a particular work situation but also in measuring these variables. In addition, although we are improving in both areas as research methods and statistics improve, it is difficult to determine which variables cause changes in others. But determining these independent (causing) and dependent (caused) variables is critical for managing incompetence. For unless we can determine cause-and-effect relationships, we cannot foretell with accuracy whether certain consequences will ensue when a manager takes a particular course of action. Nevertheless, enough concepts have been developed and enough research has been done to provide some general guidelines for managers in understanding human behavior at work and thereby correct incompetence.

What Is Theory?

Whether we realize it or not, most of us manage according to some implicit theory we hold about the real world. There are two different meanings of the word "theory." In one sense, theory can be a conjecture or guess about a proposed explanation of some event or issue. This is reflected in phrases like, "I believe (theorize) that managers are more intelligent than their subordinates," or "If one works hard enough, one will be promoted in most organizations." These statements reflect opinions that may or may not be true. In another sense, theory refers to a set of principles, propositions, or rules of action that have been tested and more or less verified by research or data analysis. The above conjectures could become two propositions in a theory or group of theories if they were tested in accordance with accepted research methods and were found to be generally supported.

In either case, theory, which tries to explain phenomena, increases the knowledge by which we operate not only as managers, but in our daily lives as well. It allows us to develop conclusions and opinions and attitudes. Unfortunately, most of us operate on the basis of opinions and attitudes that often do not rest on a valid, well-tested theory. Usually our theories are implicit—we are not aware of them. Often they have never been tested or verified, except maybe through our own experience, which may indeed be quite biased and atypical. But to live in our increasingly complex world we have to make certain assumptions about the phenomena around us. It would be nearly impossible for each of us to list on paper all the theories that guide our behavior and understanding, and then to run to the library and discover which ones have been verified by research.

Theory can be *descriptive, analytical,* or *predictive.* If it is descriptive it merely describes the relationships among existing variables. If it is analytical it answers the question: Why do these relationships exist? But the best theory is also predictive, allowing us to foretell the consequences of our actions *prior* to taking them. We can thus assess the likely outcome of actions in terms of success or failure before we take them. We can focus on just those steps that will maximize success and minimize failure. Descriptive theory is usually more easily developed than analytical or predictive theory, because in management and most social science areas, as mentioned earlier, we have problems determining cause-and-effect relationships.

How Is Theory Related to Management?

Managers need to know the explanations of various phenomena—that is, what is happening—not only in a descriptive sense, but also in analytical and predictive terms. They have to be able to predict the consequences of managerial actions before they are taken. Once again, just as in our daily personal lives, managers often operate on the basis of opinions and attitudes based on conclusions derived from ill-formed, often untested theories. A manager who believes a 10 percent wage increase for employees will result in a 10 percent increase in productivity, and who is surprised when it doesn't, reveals that his opinion was based on an unsound theory.

Since management is both an art and a science and is a relatively new discipline of study, there is no great body of predictive theory that has been developed and thoroughly tested. The vast majority of managers therefore rely on their own experience and judgment as the basis of their theories. They reason that if it has almost always worked for them in the past, it should work in the future. Provided that the variables affecting future conditions are identical to those in the past, reliance on past experience is a valid way of operating. Effective managers, however, can accurately analyze present and future conditions to determine if the same type, number, and intensity of variables that existed in the past exist *prior* to taking new action, action based on theory developed from their past experience.

In the example above, if in the past a 10 percent increase in pay always resulted in a 10 percent increase in productivity, but did not this time, then obviously the manager didn't analyze present factors properly. It may be that the employees are older and were physically unable to increase their output by exerting increased physical effort. Or perhaps on inflation rate of 10 percent over the previous year made the employees believe that a 10 percent pay raise required no additional effort, since it only put them where they were a year ago. Or perhaps many new, inexperienced employees had recently been hired and had not developed the skills for a 10 percent increase in productivity. These are but some of the many variables that could have changed but were not considered by the manager. This is what we mean when we say that management is a complex field and that any situation involves the interaction of many dynamic variables.

How Is Theory Developed?

In view of this complexity and multivariable effect, how can good theory ever be developed? The answer is through the generation of hypotheses. A *hypothesis* is the stated relationship between two variables. From our previous pay example, "If I increase the employees' pay 10 percent, then their productivity will increase 10 percent" is a hypothesis. Hypotheses are stated in an if-then manner when they are predictive in nature. They may or may not be "true"—that is, an accurate reflection of reality.

To determine whether a hypothesis is true, it must be tested. We can never conclusively prove that any hypothesis is true through testing, but we can show when it is *not* supported by data. If we develop a hypothesis, test it rigorously, and find it to be valid, and if this test is repeated many times and similar results are obtained, we still cannot say the hypothesis is true because in the very next test it could be shown to be unsupported by the research. That is, we can gather evidence that *supports* a hypothesis but does not actually *prove* it.[1]

To test hypotheses we must develop a stated relationship between two variables based upon what we believe to be true. In our previous example, we stated the relationship as follows: If I increase employees' pay by 10 percent, then their productivity will increase by 10 percent. To test this in our plant, we can select a representative sample of employees, measure their current productivity, give them a 10 percent wage increase, measure the extent to which their productivity increases, and then determine if the hypothesis is supported.[2] It would be best if we also monitored a control group of employees who did not get the raise, to see what happened to their productivity. If it also increased by 10 percent, then some other factor had increased the productivity of both groups; the wage increase apparently had little effect.

After the test we draw a concusion on the basis of our hypothesis and specify a course of action to follow in the future. Theory offers guidance for future managerial action.

Science is simply common sense at its best—that is, rigidly accurate in observation, and merciless to fallacy in logic.

Thomas H. Huxley

---

[1] In research and statistical terms, all we can do is reject a *null hypothesis*, which states that there is no relationship between two variables. Rejecting this supports the case that there *is* a relationship. For further explanation see any basic statistics text, such as Lawrence Lapin, *Statistics for Modern Business Decisions* (New York: Harcourt Brace Jovanovich, 1978).

[2] Hypotheses can be tested through direct observation of actual operations, simulated laboratory operations of phenomena (experiments), and survey analysis using questionnaires and interviews. For more explanation see Fred N. Kerlinger, *Foundations of Behavioral Research*, 2nd ed. (New York: Holt, Rinehart and Winston, Inc., 1975).

If we were to develop a number of related hypotheses on wage increases and productivity, test them, and find them to be valid, we would have a theory. The tested hypotheses would become propositions or *principles* that are accepted statements of fact regarding the relationships among variables. Many earlier management books were titled "Principles of Management" to connote that the book contained theory composed of accepted propositions and principles. In reality, however, these "principles" were often hypotheses that were either untested or poorly tested. Consequently, the word "principles" has been dropped from most management texts. Instead, terms like "introduction to," "analysis of," or "contemporary views of" now appear in the titles. Perhaps, as research progresses in the field of management, we will once again use the word "principles."

The untested and invalid nature of many so-called "principles" explains why many managers believe that the skills needed by an effective manager cannot be taught in college classes and from books. In their opinion, "real world" experience is the best teacher, and a person is either born with these skills or is not. Fortunately, this line of reasoning is fading as the body of management knowledge expands and becomes more sophisticated.

What Are Some Basic Premises for Studying Human Behavior?

Our discussion about managing incompetence has rested on implicit assumptions about human behavior at work. At this point let's make these assumptions explicit.

All Behavior Is Caused

Human behavior is caused. There are reasons why we behave as we do. Often these may not be apparent to others or even to ourselves. But they exist. We can explain behavior by identifying its causes. Since these causes are often implicit and not easily verbalized, and since any particular act is usually the result of several factors, determining the cause of behavior is often difficult. So we are sometimes tempted to give simplistic reasons for why people act as they do, or worse yet, to simply give up trying to explain their behavior. You've probably heard statements like, "Some people are just naturally born criminals," or "I don't know why he won't work hard. I guess he is just lazy." These reflect shallow thinking or an apparent futility at trying to explain behavior.

We should reject such simplistic approaches to understanding the cause of behavior, and instead adopt an inquiring mind that seeks answers. This is the only way we can correct incompetence.

Behavior Is Observable and Understandable

Behavior can be observed and understood, although our observations may be biased and our explanations incorrect or incomplete. The problem is to be objective observers of behavior by attempting to reduce any perceptual biases that color our observations.

Behavior occurs in observable transactions. A person does something or does not do something (a type of behavior), and something is done or is not done in return. A whole field of behavior analysis, called "transactional analysis" (TA), has developed and gives us a framework for viewing these transactions.

We sometimes make errors trying to understand behavior by describing attitudes that we think cause a particular act. We can't observe attitudes; they are a person's beliefs or opinions about specific ideas or objects. We can observe behavior, but this does not allow us to impute an attitude on which the behavior is based. For example, we may observe a person at a party who is not dancing and conclude that he doesn't like to dance. This may or may not be true; he may love to dance but not know the new steps, and is embarrassed to admit it and ask for instruction. The only way we can assess attitude is by trying to measure it, not by measuring behavior. We may do this through oral discussion or written questionnaires, and we may get an accurate measure. But we may not, because some people don't always truthfully express their attitudes when asked. Our dancer may say he likes to dance but is too tired to dance tonight. Is this true? It's difficult to tell.

This is not to say that attitudes are not important. They are, and an understanding of them will usually help us explain behavior. It is just that they are difficult to ascertain.

Most Behavior Is Goal-Directed

Most people behave in order to achieve goals, which once again may be difficult to determine. A person may not fully understand his or her personal goal, know why it is to be achieved, or be able to verbalize the goal to others, or even be *willing* to verbalize it. Yet the goal exists and the behavior is undertaken to achieve it.

Many specific acts of behavior are directed toward more than one goal. For example, I may join a country club not only to get exercise, but also because it offers me friendship and social status. Or I may buy a car not only so that I can get to and from work, but also because it gives me prestige and status among my neighbors, friends, and even complete strangers who see me driving it.

Since determining goals is problematic, and since behavior is often directed toward more than one goal, it is again tempting to make a shallow analysis of behavior. But since the cause of behavior is usually closely tied to a goal, we must attempt to understand the goals of others if we are to accurately explain their behavior. This is particularly true from a managerial perspective.

There are exceptions to goal-directed behavior; sometimes individuals are highly irrational. But most incompetent behavior observed on the job is not irrational. We just may not immediately see the goal premises on which the person is operating.

Behavioral Tendencies Can Be Predicted Within Limits

Although there are gaps in the science of human behavior analysis, we know enough so that we can make some general predictions about behavior. These are often expressed in terms of tendencies. That is, we may say a person has a tendency to behave in a certain way. Using probability analysis, we may be able to assign a probability, on the basis of previous research, that a certain percent of members in a group will behave a certain way in certain circumstances. As indicated earlier, the necessity to predict behavior is very important from a managerial standpoint.

Behavior Can Be Changed Within Limits

Not only can behavior be predicted to a certain extent, but within limits it also can be changed. This, too, is an important assumption for managers to make, since they try to guide, channel, and control human behavior. This implies that behavior can be changed when it deviates from a management-set norm or goal. Using principles of behavior modification, managers work to create conditions, often by offering rewards and inducements, to encourage people to behave in a desired manner. Certainly, we could not begin to manage incompetence if we did not believe in this assumption.

Summary

We have dealt with some of the complexities involved in understanding and managing human behavior at work. Most of the issues raised in this chapter serve as underlying assumptions pervading this book. It's important that we recognize these assumptions because they are key underpinnings for any action against incompetence.

Human behavior at work can be managed. Within limits, people can be influenced, guided, controlled, and directed. Deciding exactly what steps to take to change behavior is not always easy. We have difficulty in both management and the social sciences in determining the independent (causal) and the dependent (caused) variables. But determining cause-and-effect relationships is crucial if we are to describe, analyze, and predict behavior; and if we are to thwart incompetence or corrrect it once it occurs.

Believing you can do something about incompetence is the first step toward doing something about it. We've seen that the discipline of organizational behavior and management provides us with the necessary theory and assumptions to change human behavior so as to manage incompetence. Application of the principles and concepts of this book is necessary for all managers today. Managing incompetence is a difficult and continuing challenge for all of us.

Exercises

It's important that you have an opportunity to practice some of the concepts we've examined in this book. This section answers that need by presenting several exercises on diagnosing and handling incompetence in organizations. It is followed by a section of short cases for analysis.

Exercise 1   A Model for Diagnosing Organization Incompetence

Figure 4 presents a graphic representation of an organization from an input-output systems analysis. The resources, managerial decisions, and outputs of an organization are depicted. For each unit of the organization there are questions to diagnose the level of performance, and thus incompetence. By answering these questions you should get a good idea of where incompetence might exist in your organization.

Resource Availability in the Environment

1. Do we have good sources for employees?
2. Is our mix of hiring from the outside and promotion from within appropriate?
3. Do we have excessive dependency on a few suppliers?
4. Do we have good credit terms with suppliers?

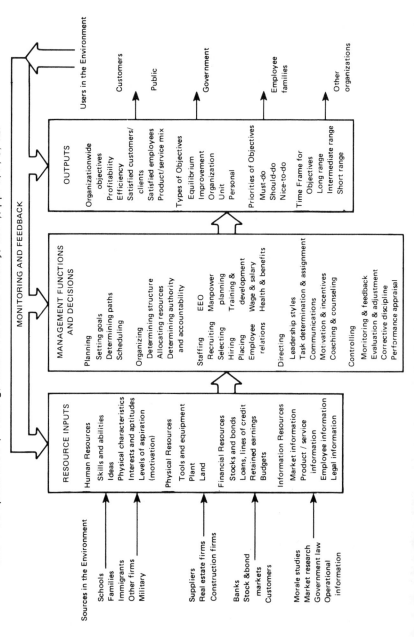

Figure 4. A model of the organization. Adapted from William P. Anthony, *Management Competencies and Incompetencies* (Reading, Mass.: Addison-Wesley, 1981), pp. 5, 7, 9, 12.

MONITORING AND FEEDBACK

Sources in the Environment

Schools
Families
Immigrants
Other firms
Military

Suppliers
Real estate firms
Construction firms

Banks
Stock &bond
markets
Customers

Morale studies
Market research
Government law
Operational
information

RESOURCE INPUTS

Human Resources
Skills and abilities
Ideas
Physical characteristics
Interests and aptitudes
Levels of aspiration
(motivation)

Physical Resources
Tools and equipment
Plant
Land

Financial Resources
Stocks and bonds
Loans, lines of credit
Retained earnings
Budgets

Information Resources
Market information
Product / service
information
Employee information
Legal information

MANAGEMENT FUNCTIONS AND DECISIONS

Planning
Setting goals
Determining paths
Scheduling

Organizing
Determining structure
Allocating resources
Determining authority
and accountability

Staffing   EEO
Recruiting   Manpower
Selecting   planning
Hiring   Training &
Placing   development
Employee   Wage & salary
relations   Health & benefits

Directing
Leadership styles
Task determination & assignment
Communications
Motivation & incentives
Coaching & counseling

Controlling
Monitoring & feedback
Evaluation & adjustment
Corrective discipline
Performance appraisal

OUTPUTS

Organizationwide
objectives
Profitability
Efficiency
Satisfied customers/
clients
Satisfied employees
Product/service mix

Types of Objectives
Equilibrium
Improvement
Organization
Unit
Personal

Priorities of Objectives
Must-do
Should-do
Nice-to-do

Time Frame for
Objectives
Long range
Intermediate range
Short range

Users in the Environment

Customers

Public

Government

Employee
families

Other
organizations

5. Do our suppliers supply us with the proper mix of goods and services at the time and place and of the quality we need?
6. Do we have good lines of credit?
7. Is our debt-to-equity ratio appropriate?
8. Can we raise money easily in bond and equity markets?
9. Are we making use of available free information about our market (e.g., trade and professional literature and government studies, for instance)?
10. Do we hire consultants as needed and do they give us good information?

Resource Inputs

1. Do our managers and employees have the proper mix of skills and abilities we need?
2. Do we encourage new ideas from our managers/employees?
3. Do our managers/employees have the proper physical characteristics to do the job?
4. Do we have a good racial, ethnic, and sex mixture of managers/employees?
5. Do our managers/employees have the proper interests and aptitudes to do their jobs?
6. Is the level of aspiration of our managers/employees high enough so that they are self-motivated?
7. Do our managers/employees have the proper tools and equipment to get the job done?
8. Do our managers and employees know expectations of performance?
9. Do we have capable purchasing agents who make good purchase decisions?
10. Are we energy efficient?
11. Do we have alternative sources of energy supply in case of shortages?
12. Is our transportation system efficient and effective at securing raw materials and semi-finished goods?
13. Is our plant and equipment outdated? (Is there a newer technology we should be using?)

14. Do we have enough of the proper type of land for future expansion?
15. Do we have idle plant, land, and equipment not generating a profit?
16. Are our unit budgets large enough to accomplish objectives?
17. Is there much waste in the way the budget is expended?
18. Are our budget and reporting procedures accurate and up to date?
19. Do we involve middle- and lower-level managers enough in budget determination?
20. Is our budget tied to objectives to be accomplished?
21. Are we using the right mix of stocks, bonds, loans, and retained earnings to finance growth?
22. Do we know enough about our customers and market?
23. Do we know our competition thoroughly?
24. Do we have a good human resource information system?
25. Does our legal staff keep us abreast of important legal developments?
26. Is our investment in new product research and development appropriate for future growth?
27. Do we know our market segments?

Management Functions and Decisions

1. Do we adequately forecast economic, demographic, technological, competitor, market, and social trends that could affect us?
2. Do we develop good goals on the basis of our forecasts?
3. Do we operationalize our goals and objectives by setting out clear paths for their achievement?
4. Are our goals measurable, specific, and realistic?
5. Are goals of various units integrated with one another and with overall organization goals?
6. Are our goals set in a participatory fashion, and thus internalized by managers and employees?
7. Do we have clear-cut, realistic schedules for goal accomplishment?

8. Have we assigned goal accomplishment to specific people and units for accountability purposes?
9. Do we update our goals and schedules at least quarterly?
10. Do our managers/employees manage time efficiently?
11. Is our structure flexible or bureaucratic?
12. Have we properly pinpointed authority and accountability at all levels?
13. Do we have too many management levels?
14. Are our managers surrounded by too many staff assistants?
15. Are resources properly allocated to units and departments?
16. Are we recruiting the right types of managers and employees?
17. Do we have proper, unbiased selection techniques and procedures?
18. Do we hire the best people available for the salary?
19. Are our people placed in jobs commensurate with their training, experience, skills, abilities, and interests?
20. Are we abiding by all EEO regulations?
21. Do we have an accurate and up-to-date manpower plan?
22. Are we really committed to training and development for every employee?
23. Does every manager and employee have an agreed-upon career plan with the organization?
24. Are we willing to terminate unsatisfactory employees when necessary?
25. Are our wages and salaries at all levels competitive with the market?
26. Do we have a current personnel-policy manual?
27. Is our health and benefits system competitive within our industry and labor market?
28. Do we have a strong employee relations program?
29. If a union is not present, what are we legally doing to prevent a union from forming?
30. If a union is present, do we have a strong, constructive, and beneficial bargaining relationship?
31. Do we give our managers enough authority to make important decisions?
32. Do our managers practice an appropriate leadership style with their subordinates?

33. What is the quality of upward communication in our organization?
34. Is cross communication among departments good?
35. Are our memos, letters, and reports clear, concise, and to the point?
36. Are our meetings short and do they encourage constructive dialogue?
37. Do we provide a good incentive package to motivate employees?
38. Is merit rather than seniority our primary basis for pay raises and promotions?
39. Do our managers willingly coach and counsel problem employees?
40. Do we have a system of referral to professionals for problem employees?
41. How well do our reports help us monitor organization and unit performance?
42. Do we have an objectively based performance-appraisal system?
43. Is performance appraisal viewed as a joke around here?
44. Are our disciplinary procedures positive and corrective in nature, or are they punitive and negative?
45. Are we consistent and fair in our use of discipline?
46. Do we encourage feedback from our employees?
47. Is our face-to-face communication open, honest, and candid?
48. Do we have a good Management Information System that gives managers relevant, accurate information in just the right amount of detail on a timely basis?

Outputs

1. How successful are we in achieving organizationwide objectives?
2. How successful are we in achieving unit objectives?
3. Is our product/service mix current and competitive?
4. Do we generate enough profit to finance growth and to pay competitive dividends?
5. How satisfied are our employees?

6. How productive are our employees?
7. Does each unit have improvement as well as equilibrium objectives?
8. Does each manager and professional employee have personal (professional improvement) as well as unit and organization objectives?
9. Have we set proper priorities on our objectives?
10. Do we follow these priorities?
11. Do we do enough long-range planning and forecasting to set good long-range objectives?
12. Are our short-range, intermediate-range, and long-range objectives smoothly integrated?
13. Do we usually achieve our objectives within the time frames set?

Users in the Environment

1. Are our customers generally satisfied with our product/service offerings?
2. How loyal are our customers?
3. Why do people *not* buy our products or services?
4. Is our market share appropriate?
5. Do we have a good public image?
6. Is our advertising and promotion program viable?
7. Do we have an efficient and effective system for distribution of our products/services?
8. Do we have good government relations?
9. Do we have programs for employee families?
10. Do we provide a competitive rate of return on investment to our stockholders/owners?
11. Do we have a good stockholder-relations program?
12. Is our stock value/price appreciating at a good rate?

Monitoring and Feedback

1. Do we regularly monitor output for quality?
2. Do we regularly survey customers to ascertain levels of satisfaction?

3. Do we have good market research efforts that serve as the basis for new product/service development?
4. Can we effect changes in inputs and managerial decisions on the basis of information we gather on outputs and users?

Exercise 2   Assessing Organization Incompetence

The purpose of this exercise is to determine to what extent you believe your organization is competent or incompetent. Using a 0–4 scale, circle the number which best reflects your opinion. To the extent possible, answer on the basis of your opinion of the entire organization. If this is too difficult for some items, just answer in terms of your unit and the units you come in regular contact with.

Key: (circle one for each statement)
    4 – Always   1 – Never
    3 – Usually   0 – Don't know
    2 – Sometimes

1. Our organization is generally regarded as a leader in our industry.   4 3 2 1 0

2. Around here, people are promoted according to *what* they know, not *who* they know.   4 3 2 1 0

3. If I had to do it over again, I would take a similar job with this organization.   4 3 2 1 0

4. People around here seem to know their job and do it well.   4 3 2 1 0

5. The top brass in this organization are people of vision and leadership.   4 3 2 1 0

6. Our organization is a product/service innovator.   4 3 2 1 0

7. From year to year, our organization has a strong financial base.   4 3 2 1 0

8. We recruit the best employees in the market for our managers.

4 3 2 1 0

9. It's easy to cut through the bureaucracy in this organization.

4 3 2 1 0

10. Our customers/clients hold our organization's products and services in high regard.

4 3 2 1 0

11. It's pretty easy to bring about change in this organization.

4 3 2 1 0

12. At each upward management level in this organization, the managers are increasingly more competent; the Peter Principle is not at work in our company.

4 3 2 1 0

13. The people around here look at a tough job as a challenge, not as a threat.

4 3 2 1 0

14. We are able to attract the best management and professional talent available because we pay top salaries and provide good working conditions.

4 3 2 1 0

15. Around here a person knows that, when productive, he or she will get ahead.

4 3 2 1 0

16. The merit principle, not seniority, is the guiding principle for salary increases for managers.

4 3 2 1 0

17. As I look around me, I see very little "deadwood."

4 3 2 1 0

18. When we do have problem employees we counsel them; if this fails we are able to terminate them rather easily.

4 3 2 1 0

19. Around here managers know that if they don't do their job, they'll be removed from their position.

4 3 2 1 0

20. We have good, hard measures of performance and effectiveness, such as units produced, costs reduced, or increased profits. 4 3 2 1 0

21. Our performance-appraisal system uses objective rather than subjective measures of performance. 4 3 2 1 0

22. Around here managers can look at a problem objectively, without letting their personal feelings and biases influence their decision. 4 3 2 1 0

23. Decision-making authority is pretty well dispersed in this organization; we do not need to get everything cleared by the top brass. 4 3 2 1 0

24. Around here managers are able to get their job done in 40–44 hours per week. 4 3 2 1 0

25. I would recommend a job in this organization to a close friend if he or she were qualified. 4 3 2 1 0

26. I hear very little rumor and hallway/office gossip in this organization. 4 3 2 1 0

27. I look forward to coming to work every morning. 4 3 2 1 0

28. Our organization is sincerely interested in developing its managers and employees. 4 3 2 1 0

29. Our managers and professionals are highly sought by other organizations for their job openings. 4 3 2 1 0

30. We have good, strong ethical and professional standards that people follow in our organization. 4 3 2 1 0

Now total all numbers you have circled. Use the following scoring guide. (If you have circled more than three zeros, this guide may be distorted. You may not be in a position to judge the extent of your organization's incompetence.)

105–120	Your organization tolerates very little, if any, incompetence.
90–104	Your organization tolerates some incompetence.
75–89	There are incompetent people scattered here and there in your organization.
60–74	There are quite a few incompetent people in your organization.
Below 60	Incompetence is the rule in your organization.

Exercise 3   Assessing Individual Incompetence

In this exercise you are asked to honestly rate yourself as to your competence/incompetence. This is difficult for most of us to do. However, an honest appraisal of our own strengths and weaknesses is what makes a good manager.

Key: (circle one for each statement)

4 – Always   1 – Never
3 – Usually   0 – Don't know
2 – Sometimes

1. I am able to meet important deadlines
   for reports, memos, and other matters.   4   3   2   1   0

2. If I recognize I don't know something, I
   admit it and try to find out.   4   3   2   1   0

3. I follow a conscientious program of
   personal/professional development, involving courses, workshops, and/or
   structured reading programs.   4   3   2   1   0

4. At the end of a day, I am satisfied with
   my work output.   4   3   2   1   0

5. I can get my job done in 40–44 hours per week.   4   3   2   1   0

6. People in my organization know they can count on me to get a difficult job done on time.   4   3   2   1   0

7. I am used as a trainer or mentor for new employees.   4   3   2   1   0

8. When we are interviewing prospective managerial or other employees in my unit/division, I am asked to participate.   4   3   2   1   0

9. I have received some of the highest salary increases in our firm over the last few years.   4   3   2   1   0

10. I have regularly been promoted to more responsible jobs.   4   3   2   1   0

11. People from other organizations ask me if I'd be interested in joining their firms even when I'm not in the job market.   4   3   2   1   0

12. If I quit my present job I know I could very easily find a new job at a comparable level in another firm.   4   3   2   1   0

13. I feel like I know a great deal more now than when I first joined this firm.   4   3   2   1   0

14. People in this organization ask me for advice on important issues.   4   3   2   1   0

15. The morale of the people in my unit is good.   4   3   2   1   0

16. I would rather work on a challenging problem than do daily, routine work.   4   3   2   1   0

17. I know our organization's current product/service offering and market pretty well.   4   3   2   1   0

18. I feel I could do as good a job if not better than my boss.   4   3   2   1   0

19. I meet and talk with important out-of-town customers/clients of our organization.   4   3   2   1   0

20. I am asked to represent our organization at important social and professional functions.   4   3   2   1   0

21. My unit's output exceeds that of similar units in our organization.   4   3   2   1   0

22. I make professional presentations at conventions and meetings.   4   3   2   1   0

23. I publish articles, books, and/or monographs in my field of specialty.   4   3   2   1   0

24. I am able to control my temper and approach a problem/crisis from a logical, rational basis.   4   3   2   1   0

25. I keep my memos, letters, and meetings short and to the point.   4   3   2   1   0

26. If our organization had a bad year I would feel somewhat personally responsible.   4   3   2   1   0

27. When I make a mistake, I admit it and take corrective action.   4   3   2   1   0

28. My peers generally regard me as competent.   4   3   2   1   0

29. I enjoy my work.   4   3   2   1   0

30. I enjoy working for my present organization.   4   3   2   1   0

Now total all circled numbers. Use the following scoring guide. If you have more than three zeros circled, you need to improve your knowledge of your strengths and weaknesses.

105–120   You are a competent manager/employee.
 90–104   You are competent but have some areas to watch.
  75–89   You have some major areas to improve.
  60–74   You are bordering on incompetence.
Below 60   You are incompetent.

Exercise 4   How to Identify a Problem

Assume you are a management consultant who has been invited by the administrator of a 750-bed municipal hospital in the Midwest to help "root out" incompetence at the hospital. The administrator has noticed problems in several areas of patient care, between the medical staff and nonmedical staff, and between the hospital and its governing board. While he felt that he had some idea as to what problems were involved, he wondered if his perception was accurate.

Therefore, he asked a group of 25 managerial employees from all levels of management (first-line supervision to those just below him) to meet with him for two hours one morning to discuss "issues of concern," as he termed it. He did not invite any nonmanagerial employees or any physicians, although he did strive to achieve wide representation from various areas of the hospital. Managers were present from purchasing and materials management, nursing, pharmacy, personnel and training, X ray, laboratory, maintenance, dietary, and other units.

After some preliminary remarks he asked people to write down the two most important problems or issues they currently faced on their jobs. He told them to do this on their own without benefit of group discussion, giving them 15 minutes. He then went around the room and asked each person to read his or her problems while he recorded them on a flip chart. (Not everyone responded with a problem or issue when called on.) As he recorded each problem he asked questions of clarification, and so on.

After all problems were recorded they were briefly discussed, and he asked the group what the hospital could do to solve these problems. After a considerable period of discussion, the group agreed that a management consultant should be hired to work with the hospital administrator and any others he or she might designate to develop solutions to the problems.

You are the consultant, and the list of problems the group developed follows. What do you do and why?

Some Factors to Consider

1. Administrator's method of identifying problems.
2. Priority of problems. (For instance, should number of times mentioned be used to indicate priority?)
3. Type of problems mentioned.
4. Lack of response from some people present.
5. Extent to which problems relate to the issue of incompetence.

Issues/Concerns/Problems Identified*

1. Understaffed because of low-quality help, low wages, low availability of qualified personnel. Related morale issues. (3)
2. Upper management not communicating all facts on reasons for priorities.
3. Upper management not communicating all issues early enough to ward off a crisis.
4. How to work effectively with employees who have bad attitudes and are uncooperative. (3)
5. Output and eagerness is low in long-time employees.
6. Increased volume of written communications.
7. Job pressures caused by increased workload and expansion with no additional employees. (2)
8. Role models needed.
9. How to overcome rush periods and slack periods—smoothing work. (3)
10. Communication between shifts for large volumes of patients—time shortage.

*Numbers in parenthesis indicate number of times mentioned.

11. Communication on patient size and other factors for pediatrics.
12. Use of standard nursing-care plans with existing shortage of staff—getting staff to accept change. (3) Examples: Unit dose, staffing for team nursing, others.
13. Supervisory role on management team to avoid stress and overload.
14. Budgeting time better.
15. Gaining respect, credibility, and confidence of supervisors and employees.
16. All aspects of communication. (2)
17. Use of strong attendants to lift patients.
18. Doctor communicating wih doctor as to patient care.
19. Meetings or classes cause work overload for others on the floor—related to understaffing. (2)
20. Personality conflicts among employees and also some patients.
21. Getting employees to help out with workload as needed. Example: Not my job. (2)
22. Employee fear of retribution if a mistake is made. Lack of self-confidence to carry out a job. (2)
23. Lack of upper-management support. Superiors not following chain of command with subordinates. (2)
24. More training for new employees.
25. More appraisal, praise, or pay for work done.
26. Management favoritism for some employees.
27. Managing for individual differences and yet being consistent.
28. Managers perform too much nonmanagerial work.
29. Getting feedback on requests and suggestions made to upper management. (3)
30. Personal job pride.
31. Getting staff to institute change and create new ideas.
32. Explaining quality of service to patients.

Exercise 5 Managing and Living With Change

Incompetent people usually have trouble adapting to change. They prefer the status quo because it provides them with a protective cocoon. They resist change because change means unlearning old habits and relearning new ones, and incompetent people have trouble learning anything.

Change usually brings challenges, new responsibilities, and opportunities for growth, whereas incompetent people prefer stability, routine, and security. While it is true that most of us want some stability and security, we also want the challenges and opportunities that changes brings us.

In the first exercise you are asked to rate yourself on your beliefs about change. In the second you are asked to rate your organization. The key aspect to note is whether your change quotient differs markedly from your rating of your organization's. If there is a major difference, chances are your will experience conflict brought about by a desire for more (or less) change than that provided by your organization. If there is similarity in the two scores, you are probably comfortable with the amount of change you find in your organization.

What's Your Change Quotient?

For each statement below indicate the extent of your agreement or disagreement on a 1–5 scale, with 5 = "strongly agree" and 1 = "strongly disagree." Circle the number that best represents your belief.

	Strongly Disagree		Neutral		Strongly Agree
1. If I had a choice, I would rather try a new restaurant than go to one I like.	1	2	3	4	5
2. Every year I take a vacation at a new place rather than go to the same place.	1	2	3	4	5
3. I usually try to vary my morning routine prior to going to work rather than follow the same schedule.	1	2	3	4	5

	Strongly Disagree		Neutral		Strongly Agree
4. My weekends are always different—I seldom do the same thing each weekend.	1	2	3	4	5
5. I try to vary my routine at work as much as I can.	1	2	3	4	5
6. I continually look for new challenges at work.	1	2	3	4	5
7. If I had my choice, I would like to switch jobs and residences at least every four or five years.	1	2	3	4	5
8. I enjoy redecorating my home and apartment and do it as often as my budget allows.	1	2	3	4	5
9. I always buy the latest clothing fashions (within budget) rather than buying something that will last for a long time.	1	2	3	4	5
10. If I had a choice for spending a $2,000 inheritance, I'd like to tour Europe rather than invest the money or purchase as item.	1	2	3	4	5
11. I try to trade my car as often as possible so I can have the latest model.	1	2	3	4	5
12. I get bored easily.	1	2	3	4	5
13. Variety is the spice of life.	1	2	3	4	5
14. I regularly try to fix (or have my spouse fix) at least one new meal a month that I've never had before.	1	2	3	4	5

	Strongly Disagree	Neutral			Strongly Agree

15. Vacations should be a time to take trips rather than catch up on chores around the house or apartment.   1   2   3   4   5

16. I enjoy parties where I don't know many people.   1   2   3   4   5

17. I enjoy taking on new assignments at work because of the challenge they usually present.   1   2   3   4   5

18. If I had a choice, I'd rather have a job with a lot of travel instead of one that requires me to be in the office all of the time.   1   2   3   4   5

19. I made it a point to learn what new things managers in other organizations are doing so that I can use them on my job.   1   2   3   4   5

20. I prefer a job that requires me to learn and do new things just about every day to one that just requires me to practice what I already know.   1   2   3   4   5

Add all numbers you have circled. Total _____

Key	80 and up	You enjoy a great deal of change in your personal life.
	60–79	You enjoy a moderate amount of change and do not find it uncomfortable.
	49–59	You prefer stability and do not enjoy much change in your personal life.

20–39 You are very happy with the status quo and are likely to strongly oppose much change in your life.

What's Your Organization's Change Quotient?

For each statement below indicate the extent of your agreement or disagreement on a 1–5 scale, with 5 = "strongly agree" and 1 = "strongly disagree." Circle the number that best represents your belief.

	Strongly Disagree		Neutral		Strongly Agree
1. My organization regularly updates its policies and procedures to keep them current.	1	2	3	4	5
2. My job description is current.	1	2	3	4	5
3. For higher-level positions, my organization hires from the outside more often than it promotes from within.	1	2	3	4	5
4. The managers in my organization are very change oriented.	1	2	3	4	5
5. My organization is always looking for new product/ service offerings to the public.	1	2	3	4	5
6. "Finding a better way to do it" characterizes the philosophy at my organization.	1	2	3	4	5
7. My organization spends a great deal of time and money in research and development work.	1	2	3	4	5

8. I'd characterize the top man-   1   2   3   4   5
   agement group at my organi-
   zation as change agents or
   catalysts.

9. My organization regularly   1   2   3   4   5
   uses outside consultants to do
   studies and usually follows
   their recommendations.

10. I have little trouble getting   1   2   3   4   5
    my ideas and suggestions for
    improvement accepted in my
    organization.

11. My boss moves pretty quickly   1   2   3   4   5
    on new ideas and programs.

12. I can actually characterize my   1   2   3   4   5
    boss as innovative and crea-
    tive.

13. I have little trouble in getting   1   2   3   4   5
    my subordinates to try new
    methods and ideas.

14. We have an employee sugges-   1   2   3   4   5
    tion system that really works
    at my organization.

15. My organization is generally   1   2   3   4   5
    viewed as being very progres-
    sive in our industry.

16. When we set goals in my or-   1   2   3   4   5
    ganization, it's pretty easy to
    revise and fine-tune them,
    even *after* they are set, as
    conditions change.

17. The structure of my organization is best characterized as flexible and adaptive; there is little, if any, bureaucratic red tape.

    1   2   3   4   5

18. The outside environment within which my organization exists is constantly changing.

    1   2   3   4   5

19. Most of the managers in my organization see change as a challenge rather than a threat.

    1   2   3   4   5

20. The budgets we use in my organization are rather flexible and allow us to change allocations (both amounts and categories) as conditions change.

    1   2   3   4   5

Add all numbers you have circled. Total _____

Key	80 and up	Your organization is very change oriented and not only easily adjusts to new conditions, but encourages innovation and new methods.
	60–79	Your organization is somewhat change oriented, but may have difficulty implementing significant change on a rapid basis.
	40–59	Your organization prefers stability to change.
	20–39	Your organization seeks to preserve the status quo at almost all costs.

Now compare your change quotient with that of your organization:

    a. Is there a substantial difference?

    b. If so, what do you plan to do about it?

Exercise 6   Cheer Up, Things Could Be Worse

Assume you are the manager of a medium-sized plant (600 employees), which produces latex products. Your plant is located in a medium-sized town (100,000 population) in a manufacturing area of northeastern Ohio. The plant is organized by the United Rubber Workers. Most of the jobs in your plant range from unskilled to semi-skilled. The latex rubber is shipped to the plant in bulk by railcar and is compounded into a liquid. From this liquid, various latex products are produced, like gloves, balloons, and rubber bands. Most are produced for other firms who sell them under their own brands.

It's Monday. You have not had a good morning. A power outage during the night caused you to oversleep 45 minutes. While having a cup of coffee before leaving home, you spilled some on your shirt and were not able to find another shirt that matched your other clothes. You finally put something together and arrived at work 30 minutes late. Since someone had parked in your normal spot, you had to find a place some distance from your office. A light rain was falling and freezing on the pavement as you walked to the office. In your haste, you fell and bruised your elbow.

As you approach your office door, you see John Hollander, one of your best foremen, nervously pacing back and forth. Before you even have the door completely open, John exclaims, "I think we are going to have an OSHA inspection today or tomorrow. My wife has a friend at the Holiday Inn and two people from Washington checked in Sunday evening. This friend heard them discussing . . . ."

The phone rings. You wonder why your secretary has not answered it. You look out at her desk and see she is not there. You answer the phone. Bob Klutznik, the president of the union local, is on the phone requesting an emergency meeting as soon as possible to discuss a very important matter that has just come up. While talking with him you notice a handwritten note from Diane Renault, the plant industrial relations director, asking you to call her as soon as you arrive. As you pick up her note you see a message underneath it from Frank Fields, corporate V.P. for human resources, that was taken by your secretary late Friday afternoon asking you to call him at home over the weekend (you were out Friday afternoon) or at his office in Chicago first thing Monday morning.

You promise Klutznik to call him right back and resume your conversation with Hollander.

"John, do you know anything about any problems with Klutznik, Renault, or Fields?" you ask.

"No, I don't. All I'm concerned about is this OSHA inspection."

"Oh, I think we're OK there. Has Johnson taken care of those extension cords on the floor?"

"No, he hasn't. And we still have that leak and slippery wet spot over by 231."

"Tell me about the slippery spot! I fell on the ice this morning and my elbow is killing me."

"Maybe you ought to see the doctor. You could have fractured it."

"Yeah, I plan . . ."

Just then Marsha Flannigan comes through the door. "Excuse me for interrupting, but there's been some mix-up and those parts that were ordered for the J-machine won't be in for two weeks."

"Two weeks!" you exclaim. "We can't wait that long. Has Bob [purchasing manager] called them?"

"Not yet," says Marsha. "He wants me to check with you first."

The phone rings again. You answer it. Joe Reynolds, gate security guard, is calling to tell you that he has detained a disorderly employee who refused to show his identity badge or to have his lunch pail searched as he entered the premises. (Such searches on entering and leaving plant property are standard practice.) He wants to know what he should do with the employee. You tell him you'll call him back.

You wonder why you got up this morning. You think of your brother-in-law selling insurance in Florida. "I bet I could sell insurance as well as he does," you think to yourself.

With John and Marsha in your office waiting for answers, you note mentally the activities that have occurred.

1. Alarm went off late.
2. Spilled coffee on shirt.
3. Parking place taken—had to park far from office.
4. Slipped on ice and hurt elbow.
5. OSHA inspection—John Hollander:
   a. extension cords;
   b. slippery spot.
6. Secretary not at desk.
7. Union local president wants an emergency meeting.
8. Plant I.R. director wants you to call her.
9. Corporate V.P. for human resources wants you to call him at the home office.
10. Parts for J-machine delayed.
11. Security guard has recalcitrant employee.
12. Brother-in-law is selling insurance in Florida.

Directions

1. Rank these occurrences in order of importance for resolution, and indicate why you rank them as you do.
2. How might occurrences such as these be prevented in the future? Has incompetent performance "caused" any of these? If so, who has been incompetent and what needs to be done to correct the performance?

Exercise 7   Using Survey Feedback to Identify Incompetence

A technique called Survey Feedback has recently been developed by specialists in the field of Organization Development (O.D.) that can be used as an aid to identifying and removing incompetence. The technique involves systematically surveying managers at each level in the organization and feeding this information back to these managers and their superiors. The process often works from the bottom of the organization up to the top rather than top down. It therefore encourages upward communication and participation. The process also usually involves an outside consultant to design the survey, administer and tabulate the results, and act as group moderator when results are presented.

There is a standard survey developed by the Institute for Social Research at the University of Michigan that is available from University Associates at P.O. Box 8517, San Diego, California 92102. However, any organization can design its own survey instrument or contract with a consultant to do so.

Some organzations have their own division or department of development with people skilled in survey feedback and other O.D. techniques. Often these people can do a survey feedback study at lower costs than an outside consultant. However, internal O.D. people may not be as objective as an outside consultant or have the same breadth of experience.

Steps In the Survey Feedback Process

Here are the steps involved in conducting survey feedback:

1. Select the level of management and unit where you wish to start. If you are in a large organization you may wish to survey a representative sample of people at each level.
2. Select or design a survey instrument. Two are provided here: one for a large organization and one for a small organization.
3. Administer the questionnaire either by mail, in a group, or in a face-to-face, one-on-one interview.
4. Tabulate and summarize the results. Keep them anonymous.
5. Copy the results and distribute them to a meeting of all managers at the level surveyed.
6. Analyze the results with the managers in the meeting and work with the group to develop solutions, with timetables for resolving problems identified.
7. Survey the next upper level of management and follow steps 2–5 above.

8. Feed the results and solution timetable from the first level of management back to the second level.

9. Finally, analyze the results of the second level in light of the first level's analysis and solutions, and build solutions and timetables incorporating both first- and second-level problems.

10. Repeat for each succeeding level of management until the information is finally presented to the CEO in a synthesized form.

Forms for Use in Survey Feedback

As indicated previously, there is a standard instrument developed by the Survey Research Center at the University of Michigan. Nevertheless, here are two other forms you may wish to consider. The first is for a smaller organization (or organization unit) and is best administered on a face-to-face, one-on-one basis. The second is for larger organizations or units and is best administered by mail or in an assembled group.

Survey Feedback Instrument
(for smaller organizations)

1. What do you believe to be the three most important problems faced by your unit? Do you feel you can do anything to solve these problems?

2. What do you believe to be the three most important problems faced by your organization? Do you feel you can do anything to solve these problems?

3. If you were your unit's boss, which issues would you address first?

4. If you were the CEO, what issues would you address first?

5. What do you believe is the greatest *managerial* weakness of your unit and of your organization?

6. What other units in your organization cause your unit problems, and what is the nature of these problems?

7. What time pressures do you experience on your job?
8. What has been your greatest disappointment since joining the organization?
9. What has been your most significant accomplishment since joining the organization?
10. Other comments?

Survey Feedback Instrument (for larger organizations)

Do not sign your name to this questionnaire.

1. Rank in priority the five most important problems faced by your unit from the following list. (Number them 1, 2, 3, 4, and 5. If less than 5, number only those that you feel apply.)

_____ a. Lack of clear-cut goals.

_____ b. Poor performance-appraisal system.

_____ c. Poor communications.

_____ d. Too much employee turnover.

_____ e. Inability to cope with change.

_____ f. Outdated technology.

_____ g. Short of staff.

_____ h. Too many reports to complete.

_____ i. Inability to achieve goals.

_____ j. Budget is too limited.

_____ k. Poorly trained and motivated employees.

_____ l. General incompetence of managers.

_____ m. Other (please specify) _____

Do you feel you can help solve these problems? _____ Yes
_____ No _____ Maybe

2. Rank in priority the five most important problems faced by your entire organization from the following list. (Number them 1, 2, 3, 4, and 5. If less than five, number only those that you feel apply.)

_____ a. Poor community/industry image.

_____ b. Outdated product/service offering.

_____ c. Outdated technology.

_____ d. Lack of clear statement of organization mission and goals.

_____ e. Poor communication.

_____ f. Declining industry.

_____ g. Lack of direction from the top.

_____ h. Inadequate financial base.

_____ i. Poor relations with regulatory agencies.

_____ j. Poor customer/client relations.

_____ k. Poor stockholder relations.

_____ l. Poor profitability.

_____ m. Lack of growth; stagnation.

_____ n. Other (please specify) _____

Do you feel you can do anything about these problems? _____ Yes
_____ No _____ Maybe

3. If you were your unit's boss, which issue(s) listed in No. 1 above would you address first?
   Issue(s): _____, _____, _____

4. If you were the CEO, which issue(s) from No. 2 above would you address first?
   Issue(s): _____, _____, _____

5. Rank in order of priority the five most important management weaknesses in your unit and organization.

	Unit	*Organization*
____ a.	Poor planning.	a. ____
____ b.	Lack of clear goals.	b. ____
____ c.	Poor leadership.	c. ____
____ d.	Poor communications.	d. ____
____ e.	General incompetence.	e. ____
____ f.	Poor placement of managers.	f. ____
____ g.	Too little use of positive reinforcement.	g. ____
____ h.	Poor management of time.	h. ____
____ i.	Lack of vision.	i. ____
____ j.	Inability to deal with change.	j. ____
____ k.	Poor management controls.	k. ____
____ l.	Out of touch with lower-level employees.	l. ____
____ m.	Inability to coordinate activities across units.	m. ____
____ n.	Other (specify): _____	n. ____

6. What other organization units cause your unit the most problems?

a. _____

b. _____

c. _____

d. _____

7. Indicate the time pressures faced in your job (check all that apply).

_____ Can't get my work done in eight hours a day.

_____ Not enough advance notice on major projects.

_____ Can't complete reports on time.

_____ Meetings take up too much time.

_____ Emergencies always coming up.

_____ Not enough good staff to delegate to.

_____ Too much correspondence to answer in a timely manner.

_____ Too many daily interruptions.

_____ Can't return phone calls in a timely manner.

_____ Not enough time for personal/professional development and growth.

_____ Have to work at odd hours (nights, weekends, holidays).

_____ Other (please specify) _____

8. What has been your greatest disappointment since joining the organization?

   _____

9. What has been your most significant accomplishment since joining the organization?

   _____

10. Other comments?

Cases for Analysis

The cases presented in this section are based on real-life situations, but names and locations have been changed to protect confidentiality. In completing the cases, do not be concerned about finding the one best answer—several approaches are appropriate for each situation. Use the questions at the end of each case to guide your analysis. A solution guide is also presented after each case, but try to resolve the situation before reading the guide.

Case 1 The Sixties Man: A Case on Affirmative Action

Jim Johnson is the industrial relations director of Bartlett Metals, a small metal fabrication plant near downtown Atlanta. The plant employs about 500 people in the factory in unskilled, semi-skilled, and skilled positions. There are also about 100 additional individuals employed as managers, salespeople, and clerical and office workers.

Jim has just had a meeting with Bob Wright, a member of the Atlanta Area Equal Employment Opportunity Council, a voluntary community group dedicated to EEO. Bob has asked Jim to commit his company to an affirmative action plan to hire blacks and women at all skill levels of the company. Bob has explained to Jim that the federal government would reimburse Bartlett Metals for any extra costs involved in training these individuals, and also that every company should do its part in this voluntary affirmative action program so that employment opportunities for minorities are improved in Atlanta and throughout the nation. He has also indicated to Jim that voluntary action might help prevent a program being mandated by a federal court.

Jim realizes that there are currently 28 openings for new employees in the plant and that manpower forecasts indicate more openings in the future due to retirements, resignations, and increased production. However, most of these openings are in the semi-skilled to skilled positions—only one is managerial. The company currently employs 45 blacks—all in unskilled positions. Fifty women are employed in semi-skilled positions in the plant and as secretaries. There are no black or women managers.

Jim feels that the company should do something to help. The firm does have one small federal contract but could receive more. He feels the company is developing a social responsibility to the community and that this attitude should be encouraged. However, he is not sure how Mr. Bartlett, the company owner, would receive the idea. He has noticed that Mr. Bartlett often has a poor attitude toward minorities and women, and therefore may not be receptive to hiring more. Jim also has some reservations about the whole concept of affirmative action, since it could end up as discrimination in reverse. He wonders whether hiring these individuals will upset the males and whites currently employed in the plant, as well as those females and blacks at unskilled positions.

Yet Jim firmly believes that only if the private sector of the economy does its share will the pervading influence of government be checked and, at the same time, will true equal opportunity in employment be achieved so that poverty in the inner city is reduced. As a 1969 MBA graduate of a major business school, Jim considers himself a pragmatic progressive and believes business should do more to help the disadvantaged.

Questions

1. Is voluntary affirmative action a good idea? Why or why not?
2. How can affirmative action increase incompetence in organizations? Must it do so? If not, what can prevent this from happening with an affirmative action program?
3. What should Jim do now? Should he wait until affirmative

action is forced on the firm, or should he take action at this time?

Solution Guide

An affirmative action plan for a firm doing federal contract work is not necessary unless the firm has 25 or more employees and $50,000 or more in federal contracts. If a firm does not voluntarily develop such a plan, it may not receive a federal contract. A court-ordered affirmative action plan is not required for an employer unless discrimination has been proved in court.

The advantage of a voluntary program is that the firm can institute the type of affirmative action program it wants rather than one imposed from the outside. This usually reduces the time pressure for meeting hiring goals by class, and indeed, preserves the true nature of hiring goals as goals rather than court-imposed quotas. This can make it easier to hire qualified minorities and to set up special training programs.

Jim has a progressive attitude toward affirmative action but will face a real challenge in convincing Mr. Bartlett. He needs to sell Mr. Bartlett on the idea by using the approach that it is in the best interests of the company to voluntarily undertake such action.

Jim must document for Mr. Bartlett the profit possibilities with federal contracts and the possible dangers of a discrimination suit. Bartlett still may not go along with the approach, but then he must realize the firm could stand to lose additional federal contract work. If business is good in other markets, Bartlett Metals may decide to forgo this federal work. Should it decide to do this, an affirmative action plan will not be imposed, even though the firm will naturally be expected to meet other federal and state EEO laws and regulations.

In other words, just because a firm does not have federal contract work does not mean it can forget about EEO, even though it will probably not have to have an affirmative action plan. The advantage of instituting your own plan is to help avoid the "warm body" syndrome sometimes followed in order to meet court-imposed quotas. In this way a voluntary plan can prevent affirmative action from contributing to incompetence.

Case 2 You Just Can't Plan

Sally: Well, how did you enjoy the program on Management by Objectives at Bay State University, Bob?

Bob: It was great! We had a good time. Played some golf, had a few drinks . . .

Sally: Didn't you learn anything?

Bob: Yeah. Learned a good bit. But, you know, a few things kind of bother me.

Sally: Yeah, like what?

Bob: Well, for instance, some of the material that was discussed may not be strictly applicable to our business.

Sally: What, for instance?

Bob: Well, there are too many changes and too many unknowns in our business. The EDP field is very dynamic. There are so many things on the horizon—more software packages, microchip, and so on. Most of the giants in our industry are in so many different pieces of hardware. Couple this with wide economic fluctuations and the changes we experience in our market, and it's almost impossible to plan. You know, we've done some fair planning in the past, and boom, the bottom falls out of the economy. Or we get some new people on board who have all kinds of different ideas about what we should be doing, and our plans go out the window. I don't know, it just. . .

Sally: Well, didn't you all discuss these issues at the program?

Bob: Yeah, we did, but I'm not sure what we decided.

Questions

1. What seems to be Bob's major concerns with regard to planning in a rapidly changing field?
2. Are these valid concerns?
3. What role does forecasting and contingency planning play in the planning process?
4. What would you suggest to Bob that he do to enhance his planning process?
5. Does your experience indicate that your firm has the same problems with planning as does Bob's? What have you done in the past?

Solution Guide

It's easy to throw up one's hands and say it's impossible to plan if one's in a dynamic industry. Yet it is precisely a firm in this type of industry that needs planning most. To make it work, the firm must have excellent forecasting and contingency planning. It must accurately read future technological, demographic, social, market, and competitor trends and set up alternative plans to capitalize on these trends. This is by no means easy, but it is necessary for success in a changing environment.

The key, then, is to develop planning and forecasting procedures that allow managers time to plan. Use of planning staffs, industry, literature, and economic-forecasting models are necessary. Quarterly planning retreats can also help.

Planning takes effort. A plan should never be cast in concrete, but needs to be a living document and revised as necessary.

Case 3   What Am I Doing Here? A Case on Organization

Terry Wilson was recently hired as the full-time credit union manager for Dynamic Industries Corporation, a producer of hydraulic valves and pipe fittings for the petroleum industry. Over the last five years the firm's employment has increased from 1,200 to 2,000. The credit union membership has grown significantly, and the firm recently decided to go with a full-time manager to replace the part-time manager who had supervised the union for the past eight years. The board believed that the company would continue to grow and that credit union membership would likewise grow, so it was necessary to have a full-time manager.

Terry had four people reporting to him: a loan officer, a collection officer (who also handled some administrative work), a full-time bookkeeper/receptionist, and a secretary. Terry soon found that the decisions he tried to make were resisted by his subordinates. They would often make comments like "Jack [the previous part-time manager] never did it this way" or "Jack usually left us alone; now you're trying to do our work" or "Terry really doesn't seem to know what he's doing."

Terry saw the problem intensifying. He believed there was much overlap of functions and duties and that roles were not clearly defined, that he needed to sit down with all four of his subordinates and "reorganize" their duties and functions to eliminate wasteful duplication and inefficiency. He decided to call a meeting for 8:00 the next morning to straighten things out.

Questions

1. What seem to be the problems Terry is facing?
2. What are the problems with the present organization setup?
3. How would you organize these jobs differently? Who would be responsible for what?
4. Assuming that this credit union's growth will continue, what additional positions (with attendant duties) would you propose?
5. What should Terry say at the meeting next morning?

Solution Guide

Credit unions are rapidly growing institutions. Many are becoming full financial institutions with checking accounts (share-drafts), mortgage loans, life insurance, money market funds, and various certificates of deposit. Anytime an organization grows quickly, there is the chance it will outgrow its managers. This appears to be the case here. Clearly there is a need for more competent managers and employees.

The present employees appear to be comfortable with the status quo. Terry will need to reorganize—redefine duties and responsibilities and get new employees if the current ones cannot cope with the new structure. Indications are that this credit union will continue to grow rapidly because its field of membership is associated with a rapidly growing firm in the petroleum industry.

Case 4   But I Am Controlling

Jeff: Stan, we still seem to be having trouble with Janet. Haven't you talked with her?

Stan: Yes. I've talked with her a couple of times about her attitude. She. . .

Jeff: Well, I'm not sure it's just her attitude. She does seem to be rude to people sometimes, but she also hands out bad advice. On several occasions I myself heard her tell clients things that simply weren't true. Does she really know our operating procedures?

Stan: Well, I've explained them to her several times, but I'm not sure if she really does understand them. I've also noticed the faulty information she hands out. In fact, I've been able to listen to her on several occasions. You know my desk is close to hers. On those occasions where I heard her giving bad advice I went over and corrected her, even if it meant interrupting her with the client. She doesn't seem to be improving, though.

Jeff: Well, you've got to control her more closely, Stan. Maybe even sit in with her and the client to be sure she doesn't hand out false information. Another thing you could do would be to call some clients at home that

Janet has talked with to see what she told them. We've got to get some control over Janet or we'll just have to fire her.

Questions

1. What seems to be the major issue here?
2. Is this a "control" problem?
3. What do you think of Jeff's suggestion?
4. How would you react if you were Stan? If you were Janet?
5. How would you correct this situation?

Solution Guide

This is a control problem with a social welfare counselor who is providing inaccurate information to clients. The issue is how to get Janet to be accurate. Apparently the past discussions Stan has had with her have not helped. Termination seems likely, although both Stan and Jeff appear willing to give her another chance.

This case could very well involve poor placement—Janet may not have the skills and aptitude to be in a client-interface position, and no amount of proper knowledge of correct procedures will change this. Perhaps there is another position for Janet that does not involve client contact. Often a situation like this, where incompetent performance is occurring, is a result of poor selection and placement, which is more the fault of the organization than the employee. Therefore, the burden for correcting this problem may rest with the organization, not the employee, although Janet could request a transfer.

Case 5   A Case on Decision Making

Incompetent managers usually have trouble making decisions. They often postpone them, hoping they'll go away or that the problem will become so difficult that someone else will have to make the decision for them. In this hypothetical situation you are asked to make a difficult decision involving life and death. The results of your decision are not so important as the procedure you use and your justification for your decision. After you complete this analysis, you might want to give it to your boss to compare his or her decision with yours.

You are the captain of a small ship that is sinking 50 miles out in the Gulf of Mexico near Florida. There are 11 people on board, including yourself. There is only one life boat and no life preservers, and the life boat will hold a maximum of seven. Your job is to select the seven who will be saved from the following list. You have three minutes to decide.

1. A 70-year-old minister.
2. A pregnant woman.
3. Her husband.
4. An electrical engineer.
5. A secretary.
6. A famous writer.
7. A professional athlete.
8. A high school girl.
9. The lieutenant governor of Florida.
10. A university physics professor.
11. Yourself (the captain).

Solution Guide

1. Decision Method—you have several choices:
   a. Use a purely random selection (such as names out of a hat).
   b. Ask for volunteers to stay back. Under this method, the minister and the pregnant woman's husband may volunteer to remain.
   c. Let them fight it out and take the seven strongest.
   d. Let them vote for the seven (democracy).
   e. Use decision rules: for example, women and children first (assume a sex for some passengers) captain should always go down with his ship.

2. Assumptions—you need to make several assumptions, about:
   a. Weather and water conditions.
   b. Existence of sharks, shipping lanes, and the like, nearby.
   c. Equipment and power for life boat (like radio, motor, oars, food, water, and others).
   d. Flotsam from sinking ship (for instance, ice chests, cushions, pieces of wood).
   e. Position in Gulf relative to Florida coastline.
   f. Chances of survival of those on life boat *versus* those left back.
   g. Temperament of each person.
3. Decision Criteria—those usually considered in this case are:
   a. Strength and stamina of each person.
   b. Age of each person.
   c. Sex of each person.
   d. Occupational prestige or contribution to society of each person.
   e. Person's contribution while in life boat to help life boat stay afloat until rescue.
   f. Events that will occur after rescue (such as inquiry or investigation, lack of life vests, reason for sinking, and captain's judgment).
   g. Composition of entire group saved: will they conflict with or cooperate with each other on the life boat?
   h. Leadership of group on life boat.
4. Factors to consider for each person:
   a. Minister—
      1. Age works against him. We value youth in society.
      2. May volunteer to stay back.
      3. Most prepared to die?
      4. Could keep group calm on life boat and give them hope.
   b. Pregnant woman—
      1. Female.
      2. Probably young.
      3. Two lives more valuable than one.
      4. Could deliver on life boat—baby may be disruptive.
      5. Verification of pregnancy. What if only two months pregnant and is not showing?

c. Her husband—
   1. Male.
   2. Probably young.
   3. Value of keeping family together.
   4. May volunteer to stay back if wife and unborn child guaranteed a position on life boat.
d. Electrical engineer—
   1. Probably male.
   2. May have some practical electrical skills to fix or operate life boat radio if one exists.
   3. May be able to get a final message off the sinking boat's radio.
   4. Valuable occupation for society.
e. Secretary—
   1. Probably female.
   2. Relatively low occupational prestige compared with others.
   3. Could have small children back home.
   4. Ability to help organize things on life boat.
f. Famous writer—
   1. Probably male.
   2. Could keep up spirits of people on life boat by telling stories.
   3. Could help in inquiry when life boat rescued by relating facts, and the like.
   4. May be a "weirdo" and not fit in with others on life boat.
   5. Public recognition—headlines if he dies.
g. Professional athlete—
   1. Probably strong.
   2. Probably male.
   3. Public recognition—headlines if he dies.
h. High school girl—
   1. Young.
   2. Female.
   3. Life ahead of her.
   4. Could be hysterical on life boat.
i. Lieutenant governor of Florida—
   1. Male.

    2. Older.

    3. Only person with a specific identity (can name him).

    4. Public recognition—headlines if he dies.

    5. May volunteer to stay back.

    6. Politician, therefore expendable (post-Watergate syndrome).

j. University physics professor—

    1. Probably male.

    2. Older.

    3. Value to society.

    4. Practical application of mechanics to keep life boat afloat until rescued.

k. Captain—

    1. Known navigator.

    2. Should provide leadership and organization to life boat.

    3. Decision rule: go down with ship. Applicable here?

    4. Consequences to him or her if survivor at inquiry.

Usual Solution

In sessions with over 1,000 managers, professionals, and clerical employees, the people most commonly saved are:

1. Pregnant woman.
2. Her husband.
3. Writer.
4. Professional athlete.
5. High school girl.
6. Physics professor.
7. Yourself (captain).

Case 6 Why Not? A Case on Group Decision Making

The executive branch of government of a large southeastern state is considering the possibility of changing to a flextime schedule for state employees who work in the capital. The state employs approximately 60,000 people, 25,000 of whom work in the capital city, which has a total population of 130,000.

State population has grown rapidly over the past ten years, and state government employment has similarly expanded, resulting in an enormous traffic tie-up during the 7:00–8:00 A.M. and 5:00–6:00 P.M. time periods on each workday. The citizens of the capital city have resisted street-widening efforts and the building of expressways because they fear destroying the character of the city's older neighborhoods. Although the bus system has been expanded, it still falls far short of the needs of downtown commuters.

The governor's office, therefore, working through the state's Department of Administration, has decided to investigate the establishment of a flextime system for state employees. Under most flextime systems, employees are given a choice of the times to begin and end work, usually within a specified period. For example, employees might be told they have to start sometime between 7:00 and 9:30 A.M. and must leave sometime between 4:00 and 6:30 P.M. During this period they have to work eight hours with an hour off for lunch. (Currently, work hours for all employees are 8:00 A.M. to 5:00 P.M. with an hour off for lunch.)

The secretary (chief administrative offcer) of the Department of Administration has decided to form a task force made up of appropriate state employees to investigate the possibility of adopting a flextime system. He believes there is much merit to the proposal and sees it as a way to reduce the terrible traffic congestion occurring every morning and afternoon. He also sees it as politically expedient and likely to earn much praise and loyalty for the governor from state employees and the public as a whole.

The secretary has asked the state personnel director who reports directly to him to carry out the mechanics of establishing such a force. In talking with the personnel director, the secretary made the following comments:

> I really believe there is a lot of merit to the flextime system. It's a way to reduce traffic congestion and it will cost us hardly anything. Now, I want you to put together a task force that will make

things go. Get wide representation on it. Involve people from the major state agencies such as Transportation, Commerce, Human Services, and Agriculture. Get city government employees in on it.

But, above all, get *creative people.* I want people who aren't afraid of suggesting new ideas. I want people who are innovative. Check with the university in town and get some of their best people to work on this task force. I want people who aren't afraid to ask "Why not?" to any idea, no matter how screwy it might first sound.

Assume you are the personnel director charged with setting up the task force. What will you do?

Questions

1. What type of charge and objectives will you set out for the force?
2. How will you select members? What criteria will you use? From what units will they come? How large will the force be?
3. What are the major issues your group will have to address in order to develop its recommendations on flextime?
4. How will the committee operate? Will subcommittees be formed? If so, which ones and how large will they be? How often will they meet? What will they discuss? How often will the full task force meet? How long should each meeting be? By when should the final report be completed? How (in what form) will it be presented and to whom?
5. How will you ensure that the members come up with creative ideas?
6. How will you deal with problems that may arise in other areas of the state if those employees also demand flextime? Will you anticipate these now and involve people from other parts of the state on the committee?
7. What will your force recommend regarding the means by which departments and individual employees can be encouraged to adopt flextime should it be recommended? (How should this change be managed?)

Solution Guide

Committees are a good way to pool diverse ideas to come up with a good course of action. However, they can be misused and become a tool of incompetent people, who sometimes assign a decision to a committee in order to shift the burden of decision making. Sometimes the committee is stacked with incompetents so the manager can say, "I let you have your input, but the committee came up with such a ridiculous recommendation I couldn't follow it." In other words, the committee is sometimes used as a facade.

While these are potential limitations to committees, we have no evidence that either of these situations exists in the present case. Since the flextime work schedule involves virtually all capital state employees, all agencies must have input as to how such a schedule might affect their operations. Furthermore, since committees sometimes do lead to "group think" and watered-down compromise decisions, it's a good idea to bring in outside people, such as professors from the university, to suggest ideas.

The personnel director will probably want to select a large task force of 20–25 people with wide representation. H'll need to set up subcommittees of four to five people each, and give each subcommittee a goal and a deadline. Since the flextime decision is occurring in a political environment, the personnel director needs to be mindful of selling the task force's decision, not only on an economic basis, but on a political basis too. Other areas of the state with heavy concentrations of state employees might also want flextime. Should they be permitted to have it? Realizing this, the personnel director should get four or five politically powerful people on the task force—perhaps a cabinet secretary or two and someone high up on the governor's staff. He should also investigate if it is possible to get a high-level staff member from the Senate and House to serve.

A task force can be an excellent way to institute a change of this type, or it can be used as a charade to give the appearance of making a decision. Incompetent people often use a committee in this manner, and the Secretary of Administration needs to ensure that this does not happen here.

Case 7 The Now Generation: A Case on Attitudes Toward Change

"The problem with most young people employed by business today is that they want to change the world. The won't accept things as they are, but want to tear down all that the older generation has built up.

"I have been with this company for 32 years. I have gone from a department superintendent in a foundry, to plant manager, to regional manager, and finally to group vice-president for steel products. It has always been the same. Young people are constantly trying to change years of my work and that of my contemporaries in this organization.

"Now don't get me wrong. I think young people have much to contribute to our organization. They usually have fresh ideas. But they lack experience. Their ideas are often impractical. Even though they have a college degree—often an MBA—they haven't gone through the school of hard knocks like the rest of us old-timers have.

"Young people have a total misconception of change. You just can't begin changing policies, procedures, and operations after just six months on the job. You gotta become seasoned. People resist change around here. They don't want some 'wet-behind-the-ears kid' telling them they have to change something they have spent all their work life building.

"Why do so many kids today think you first have to destroy the existing state of affairs in order to change things? Can't you build without first destroying? I'll tell you, I'm very selective as to what kinds of authority I give these young kids and what kinds of work groups I place them in. I don't want them disrupting the operations of this unit and causing chaos."

Questions

1. How does this individual view change? What are some of the reasons for which he believes people resist change?
2. Why do you suppose he singles out youth as his target?

3. Do you agree that the present situation must first be dismantled in order for meaningful change to occur? Can a person "build without first destroying"?

4. Do you think that this person's attitude toward change is fairly widespread among older managers in organizations?

Solution Guide

We all feel somewhat threatened by change. People who have been with an organization for several years naturally resist change even more so when it is advocated by new entrants into the organization. After all, they've helped establish the present state of affairs, and suggesting change is an implicit criticism that the present situation is inadequate.

This does not mean that long-tenured employees are incompetent because they resist change. Nor does it mean that new entrants are incompetent because they suggest change that is perceived as unnecessary by older employees. This conflict between the "old guard" and the "new guard" is relatively common. Mediating this conflict between these two groups without alienating either is a real challenge for a manager.

Organizations need new ideas and new people to keep from stagnating and dying. Integrating these new ideas and people into the existing organization without creating high levels of conflict requires great skill. What complicates matters is that there will be incompetent people who resist any kind of change, and there will be new people suggesting change who are also incompetent. Sorting out incompetent from competent people is sometimes difficult when dealing with change because change is an ambiguous and difficult topic anyway. If most changes were clear-cut as to effects, it would be easier to classify people one way or another.

Case 8   Doing Nothing, Very Slowly

Many people have an image of government as a big group of bureaucrats, shuffling paper, getting in people's way, and not being very effective. In sum, doing nothing, very slowly. Government agencies and operations at all levels—federal, state, and local—have always been subject to criticism in our society. The following conversation among three managers in an executive development course is typical of the concerns of managers in private industry and government.

Bert: Let's face it. Government organizations are both inefficient *and* ineffective. They don't do the right things, and what they do get done, they do very inefficiently.

Ernie: Now wait a minute, I work for the government and I think my agency is pretty productive. Maybe it's not easy for an outsider to see this, but we get a lot done.

Sally: Yeah, I work for a local agency and I think we're productive too. Oh, there is some waste, but that's true also in business.

Bert: You two don't know what you're talking about. I'm the manager of a large firm here in town, and I can tell you that my firm is both efficient and effective. I can point to my income statement and show you the profit my firm makes. You don't have a profit so how do you know when you're efficient and effective? I know. When my profit goes up, I know it's because I've given people what they want or they wouldn't be buying my product. I also know that I've kept my expenses under control, and so I'm efficient.

Ernie: You're right about profit. We don't have that. But we do have a budget we have to stay within, and my agency's operations are monitored pretty closely by the state legislature. I think this helps to ensure our efficiency and effectiveness.

Bert: I don't think government organizations can be either effective or efficient. They're too different from busi-

ness organizations. I don't think management concepts apply in government organizations like they do
in business. First of all, government employees are
not productivity minded. All they want is security
and an easy job. Second, government agencies are just
too large and complex to be run effectively. Third,
managers behave differently in government. All they
do is practice CYA (cover your a—) rather than real
leadership. In fact, I don't see how anything we will
learn in this class can apply to either of the government agencies you two are from.

Questions

1. Are government organizations substantially different from
   business organizations? In what ways are they similar and different?
2. Do people in government have different ideas about what's
   expected of them, and do they perform differently compared
   with those in business organizations?
3. Does a typical government organization have a greater share of
   incompetent people compared with a typical business firm?

Solution Guide

There's no question that it's easier for an incompetent to hide in a
large bureaucratic government organization than in a business
firm. Of course, in a large bureaucratic business firm incompetents
can also hide, but not so easily. The criterion of profit usually
makes a firm look more closely at individual performance.

Survival in a government organization usually depends on
not making the fatal mistake. A noticeable political blunder that
receives wide publicity and is embarrassing for the top leaders of
the administration will often result in termination or demotion.
This is why so many government managers play CYA: they do not

want to go out on a limb for fear of making a costly error. Government agencies do not inspire risk taking and innovative decision making.

Government agencies have traditionally offered security as a primary reward. Managers in government have become conditioned to security and do not readily risk jeopardizing it. In addition, if they do go out on a limb and make an extraordinarily good decision, they usually derive little if any benefit. Despite recent changes in civil service laws at the national level and in some states, rewards for meritorious performance in government are still rare. So what incentive is there for these employees to excel?

Yet, despite these facts, government should not tolerate incompetence any more than business. After all, government employees expend taxpayer dollars and work in the public trust. The tremendous increase in the cost of government at all levels needs to be closely examined, and any waste caused by incompetence needs to be eliminated just as much as in the private sector.

Case 9   All That Stuff: A Case on Management Education

George Breakstone is a production superintendent at Gemini Plastics, Inc., a producer of various products for use in the home and industry. George, 43 years old, achieved his position through promotions up "through the ranks."

Jack Rollins works for George as day-shift foreman of the extrusion process. Jack is 28 and was promoted to his present job two years ago. Previously he was a machine operator.

Jack has just returned from a one-week management development course at Pine State University. Jack much enjoyed the Supervisory Management course and felt he learned a great deal, not only from the instructors, but from other managers from other companies. He saw much need for improvement in his own management style and believed that his boss, Mr. Breakstone, could also stand some improvement and should attend this program.

Jack approached Mr. Breakstone and the following conversation took place:

Jack: I really appreciate the opportunity I had last week to attend the Supervisory Management Program at Pine State University, Mr. Breakstone. Thanks for sending me.

Mr. B: I didn't send you, the Personnel Department did, but I'm glad you liked the program. I hope it helps you on the job.

Jack: Oh, I think it will, For one thing, I don't think we really understand our people. We are always focusing on raising production, improving our machines, quality control, and so on. It always seems like we are asking for more and more, but we don't consider the people involved.

Mr. B: Well, production is the name of the game. It is through production that we get profits and that's the whole purpose behind our efforts. We treat our people fairly—pay them a good wage, give them holidays, vacations, and other benefits—but we expect production in return.

Jack: I know that, Mr. Breakstone, but we could get even more production if we really tried to understand our people and to . . .

Mr. B: I know people. Most of them are here on these production lines because they're uneducated and have fairly low skills. They can't get work elsewhere. We're doing them a favor by employing them. I don't know what you learned about people at that program, but it all sounds like a bunch of crap to me. As far as I'm concerned, you and I are here to get out production. That's why we hire people. That's what they're here for. So you just focus on getting the work out and let the people take care of themselves. Forget all that stuff you learned last week.

Questions

1. What views about people do Breakstone's comments reflect?
2. What role does an understanding of people have in the production process?
3. Is Breakstone's attitude conducive to locating and eliminating incompetent performance?

Solution Guide

Some people believe you've got to be a hard-hearted S.O.B. to root out incompetence, under the assumption that it's only weak-kneed softies who put up with it. Of course, this is not necessarily so. Coming down hard on employees in an autocratic fashion and firing right and left can cause many problems. Morale will sink, employees will become alienated, turnover will increase, and it will be difficult to hire new people because of the firm's reputation.

Understanding people and treating them fairly but firmly is necessary to eliminate incompetence. One can be fair and not be weak; one can be calm and tactful without being a pushover; and one can allow exceptions without completely collapsing. Creating the proper power presence at work means understanding the people you work with and setting the proper climate to guide their actions. It does not mean ruling through fear and retribution. A climate of fear breeds distrust. A manager using this technique can get short-run compliance but at the expense of long-run commitment. He or she can also eliminate incompetence by termination, but will never really deal with the incompetence. Autocratic managers treat the symptom of incompetence without getting at its cause, for which a manager must understand human behavior at work Autocratic managers think they know behavior, but they don't, else why would they treat people as they do?

Case 10   Life at the Top: A Case on Executive Isolation

"Carl, don't you think you've had enough martinis for one evening?"

"No, I have to have one more silver bullet—I have had a *rotten* day," replied Carl Pitkin, production manager of the local Hicksa Car Works Plant, a leading manufacturer of railroad equipment. He and Larry Mendinni, a salesman with a hospital supply company, were at a neighborhood party on a recent Friday evening.

"Wow! You're not going to drink all that?" asked Larry.

"Yep, it's a double—just what I need," said Carl.

"What has you so upset?"

"Well, it's another one of those damn cost-reduction programs that the top brass has come up with. We've been asked to cut 25 percent of our non-union personnel."

"What about the union personnel?" asked Larry.

"Oh! The brass are afraid of the union and they don't want to do anything to upset them. What gets me are the layers of unnecessary fat the company has at the top. Wheels sitting around in their ivory-tower offices, drawing big salaries, flying around in expensive jet planes, driving fancy company limousines, memberships in fancy private clubs—I'm sure you get the picture. If we got rid of all the waste at the top, we could improve profits by 10 percent or more. More importantly, it would set the right example and the people down the line would be more receptive to the need for reducing expenses."

"Why does your CEO permit such waste?" asked Larry.

"Oh, he's too busy jetting all over the world, supposedly entertaining customers and political leaders. When he was president he used to mind the store, but now that he has been named chairman of the board and chief executive officer, he seems to be more concerned with his image than with managing the company."

"Why don't you talk to him and tell him that he's ruining the company?" asked Larry.

"No, I can't go directly to him. I'd get canned but quick. We are a big company and we have to stay in channels. There are at least ten levels of management between me and the CEO."

"Do you need all those levels? Why does your company have such a structure? Ours doesn't."

"Because of the span of control. It's the number of people that one person supposedly can properly supervise or direct. It reminds me of an old army story. In one division there were 50 levels of command. One day, Petros, who was at the bottom of the organization structure, spotted the enemy approaching the city wall. Petros, being a conscientious soldier, hurriedly ran and told his superior, who in turn told his superior, and so up the line the message went."

"Well, was the enemy repelled?"

Carl took a long, slow sip of his martini and replied, "No, by the time the message got to the general, it was too late—the enemy captured the city."

"Carl, you made that up, right?"

"Right. But it does seem to me that the company would do better with a structure where the lines of communications are shortened and authority decentralized so that problems could be handled more effectively. But business is not that simple, I guess. We have complicated problems and we need a complicated system. Besides, our CEO would not go for a flat structure."

"Why not?"

"Well, he would be a lot closer to the people at the bottom and he would look at this as a loss of prestige. It would hurt his ego. It would appear like a demotion to him."

"This is such a vital matter to the success of the company," said Larry, "and it seems to me that there must be some way to change the structure so as to give the people down the line more freedom of action. The added responsibility and authority would help them grow—also the problems would be solved when they are small and would not be permitted to grow to unmanageable proportions."

Carl took another long sip and said, "Larry, I don't know how you throw out all that information from the top of your head. Management is an extremely complicated art and requires a complicated system. Ours is a big company. It's not easy to bring about change. How do we get our CEO to do something about getting rid of the fat at the top? How do we decentralize authority? These are not easy questions to answer, but we really should be doing something. Our CEO and other people at the top have got to be more involved in our operations."

Questions

1. How can it be determined if there actually is too much fat at the top?
2. Should a CEO of a large company be oriented to the external environment or to internal corporate operations?
3. Assuming Carl Pitkin's analysis is correct in this case, how can necessary change be brought about?

Solution Guide

In today's environment, the CEO does play a greater role as interface agent with the external environment. Complicated and changing laws, changing markets, and multinational operations all require a greater response from the CEO. However, since the CEO is the one ultimately accountable under the board for corporate performance, he or she cannot ignore internal operations. Assigning a president as chief operations officer does not release the CEO from personal accountability.

Of course, this external role for the CEO does not justify fat at the higher levels. Every person added at these levels only adds to corporate overhead. These people are not engaged in the production of primary utility, as is the assembly-line worker. Their positions must ultimately be justified on the basis of the direct or indirect support they provide for the creation of primary utility by the organization.

It is necessary in today's complicated environment to have various staff positions at the corporate level. But it is very easy to let these positions proliferate almost beyond control. A conscientious effort must be made to keep the number of staff positions within reasonable bounds, and this is the CEO's responsibility. There are several things he can do. First, objectives for all staff positions should be set and clearly tied to corporate objectives. It's very easy to avoid setting staff objectives or to set fuzzy ones. "Our work is too hard to measure" is a common complaint from staff people, an excuse that should not be accepted. Ways of identifying and measuring output can be found. If they cannot, then serious consideration should be given to eliminating the staff position.

Second, once objectives are set, a cost-benefit analysis should be made to see if each staff position's performance is generating benefits greater than its costs. All costs should be considered here—financial, personnel, space, time, effort, and opportunity. Every staff position should at least cover its costs in terms of benefits directly or indirectly generated for the organization.

Third, efforts should be made where possible to integrate staff activities. Can two or three units or positions be combined into one? Can unit functions be redefined and streamlined? Are there better ways to perform staff work? Should more staff work be farmed out to outside consultants on a fee-for-service/project basis?

Staff positions can create unnecessary overhead for the organization and can isolate top management from internal operations. In other words, these positions can exacerbate the problem of incompetence. They therefore need to be seriously and conscientiously examined in every organization where they exist.

Case 11   One Manager's Lament

"When I first joined the company 25 years ago, the first-line supervisor was really someone. I know, because I was one. I had the authority to hire, fire, transfer, promote, and do other things. I was somebody. Now the first-line supervisors are just flunkies. Oh, they are still responsible for production, but they have no authority. Nobody, including the union, pays any attention to them.

"It all began ten years ago when the union came into the plant. The top brass felt that letting the supervisor discipline union members might lead to a work stoppage, which the company wanted to avoid at any cost. To prevent this, management established a policy that required a supervisor to seek advice from the personnel manager before taking action. This was not too bad, but in time the advice became direction, and—bango!—the personnel manager assumed the authority that the supervisor once had. Of course, the supervisor still had the responsibility, but without authority—a violation of basic management practice.

"As we became more involved with the union, EEO laws, OSHA, and so on, we should have done a better job training and developing the supervisor, so that he could better cope with the new responsibilities. Those who couldn't meet the added responsibilities should have been replaced. Instead, we provided "crutches." We forced the supervisor to follow the personnel manager's advice and establish another layer of management between the supervisor and the department head. Whereas we should have upgraded the first-line supervisor's job and found people who could handle it.

"Instead of identifying and correcting the problem, top management compounded it. It starts at the top. The president, who used to be the chef executive officer, gets the board of directors to establish the job of chairman of the board and chief executive officer. The president becomes the chief operating officer. This is pure nonsense. This nonsense then spreads down the line, and instead of the director of personnel, director of engineering, and comptroller reporting to the president, a new position is established, such as director of administrative services, or executive vice-president in charge of staff services, and the director of personnel,director of engineering, and comptroller no longer report to the president. This only muddies the water. We are talking about highly paid, highly capable people—people who require very little supervision. There is no reason why one top-management person can't supervise 20 or more such people. If I were the stockholders of our company, I would make these fat cats earn their salaries.

"When I joined the company 25 years ago we seemed to get

the job done with a lot fewer people. It's true that we have gotten bigger, but after adjusting for inflation our total sales have only increased by 50 percent, but our management personnel have almost doubled. This is true not only at the top-brass level but at the plant level too. For example, when I was a first-line supervisor, this is how the organization's structure looked. [See Figure 5.] Supervisors reported directly to the department heads, and there were usually three or four supervisors in each department, depending on the number of work shifts.

"Here's how it is today. [See Figure 6.] Depending on the number of work shifts, three or four assistant supervisors report to each supervisor.

"We need to eliminate the assistant supervisors and the three superintendent positions. When production increases, I would increase the number of qualified supervisors, but not the number of levels. Three levels is all I would use.

"The key is not the number of managers but their quality. Never add another manager to support a weak manager. The solution is to replace the weak manager with someone strong. By so doing we eliminate the problem of incompetence. Let's let our managers manage. If they can't hack it, let's get ones that can."

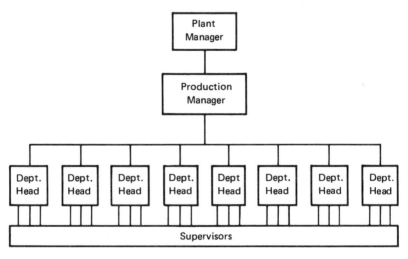

Figure 5. Old organization structure.

Questions

1. In your experience, has the role of the first-line supervisor been significantly eroded over the past few years?
2. Why is it that weak managers are often "shored up" with assistants?

Solution Guide

Management must take responsibility for eliminating incompetence. But so often management contributes to incompetence by refusing to clean its own house first. The manager quoted above recognizes this. Adding additional layers of managers and assistants to support weak managers compounds the problem of incompetence.

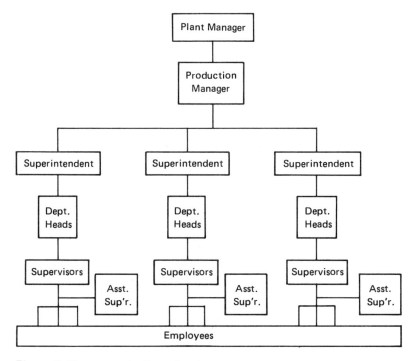

Figure 6. New organization structure.

The solution starts with the first-line supervisor. The authority and responsibility formerly allocated to this position needs to be restored. Today, because of the union, EEO and OSHA regulations, and corporate bureaucracy, the hands of the supervisor are often tied. More decision-making authority must be delegated to the first-line supervisor. Capable people who can accept these responsibilities need to be placed in these positions, trained, and developed so that they know the union contract and pertinent EEO and OSHA regulations and don't have to run to the legal or personnel departments every two minutes. Salaries for first-line supervisors must be increased so that top people are attracted to the position. Often today, a first-line supervisor will earn less than those working for him or her, because subordinates receive overtime pay while the supervisor is on salary.

Management's first step in managing incompetence is to get its own house in order and give the first-line supervisor the authority needed to get the job done.

Annotated
Bibliography

Adizes, Ichak. "Mismanagement Styles." *California Management Review*, Vol. 19, No. 2 (Winter 1976), pp. 5–20. The author contends that, to be effective, managers must perform four distinct roles: producer, administrator, entrepreneur, and integrator. If a manager performs one or more of these roles poorly, he or she can be labeled a mismanager. The author examines management styles in which the roles are unevenly balanced and asserts that when one of the roles is not performed, a certain style of mismanagement can be observed. A problem faced by organizations is that promotions often result from outstanding performance in one or two of the roles, but as these managers move up in the hierarchy, they are incapable of performing the additional roles required.

———. "Organizational Passages—Diagnosing and Treating Life-Cycle Problems of Organizations." *Organizational Dynamics*, Vol. 8, No. 1 (Summer 1979), pp. 3–25. This excellent article explains the problems of an organization as it goes through ten life-cycle stages: courtship, infancy, go-go, adolescence, prime, maturity, aristocracy, early bureaucracy, bureaucracy, and death. The article shows how organization problems of incompetence change as the organization grows, matures, and dies.

Anthony, William P. *Participative Management.* Reading, Mass.: Addison-Wesley, 1978. The author shows how to use participative techniques to bring out the best in employees and managers. Properly used, participation can be an effective method to identify and eliminate incompetence.

———. *Management Competencies and Incompetencies.* Reading, Mass.: Addison-Wesley, 1981. This book sets out the important knowledge and skills a manager should possess in order to be effective. It is important reading in order to avoid incompetence. Such skills as planning, leading, coaching, counseling, and conflict management are examined, and knowledge of the market, organization, and employees is explored.

Appley, L. A. "Executives Who Will Score in the '80s." *Nation's Business*, Vol. 57, No. 6 (June 1969), pp. 80–83. This is an interview with Lawrence Appley, retired chairman and chief executive of the American Management Associations, in which he lists and elaborates on qualities he thinks will be required to be a successful manager in the 1980s. Even though somewhat dated, the interview is still useful today.

Bartol, K. M., and Butterfield, D. A. "Sex Effects in Evaluating Leaders." *Journal of Applied Psychology*, Vol. 61, No. 4 (1976), pp. 446–454. The authors summarize a study conducted to detemine the relationship between sex role stereotypes and perceptions of appropriate managerial style. Consideration was perceived as a more effective style for a female, and a style that emphasized initiating structure was perceived as more appropriate for a male. A high emphasis on production was perceived as inappropriate regardless of the leader's sex.

Bassett, G. A. "The Qualification of a Manager." *California Management Review*, Vol. 12, No. 2 (Winter 1969), pp. 35–44. Bassett describes four polarities of managerial temperament. He notes two quantitative prerequisites to selecting capable managers: (1) a history of striving for personal betterment and a high level of energy and motivation for application to problems; and (2) a rich fund of experience and a variety of perspectives on life and business.

Bell, Gerald D. *The Achievers.* Chapel Hill, N.C.: Preston-Hill, 1973. This book examines six styles of personality and motivation for leadership: the commander, attacker, avoider, pleaser, performer, and achiever. Understanding effective leadership and various leadership styes is important for understanding incompetence.

Berry, D. "How Executives Account for Their Own Success." *Business Horizons*, Vol. 16, No. 5 (October 1973), pp. 31–42. The author's compilation of ten success attainment factors is based on previous studies and on his own survey to define success criteria and causal relationships more clearly.

Blake, R. R., and Mouton, J. S. *The Managerial Grid.* Houston: Gulf, 1964. Blake and Mouton have developed an extremely useful device for identifying distinct managerial styles. They call this tool the Managerial Grid. The two dimensions of the grid are concern for people, which is graphically represented by the vertical axis, and concern for production, which corresponds to the horizontal axis. A manager's style can be identified by measuring his concern for each of these two dimensions and plotting them on the grid. Five styles (task management, impoverished management, middle-of-the-road management, team management, and country club management) that fall at extreme points on the grid are identified and discussed.

Bobbitt, H. Randolph, Jr.; Breinholt, Robert H.; Doktor, Robert H.; and McNaul, James P. *Organizational Behavior.* 2d ed. Englewood Cliffs, N.J.: Prentice-Hall, 1978. The authors present a foundation for understanding human behavior at work from both an overall (macro) and a micro perspective. Theories and approaches for understanding, predicting, and changing human behavior are presented.

Borman, Walter C. "Consistency of Rating Accuracy and Rating Errors in the Judgment of Human Performance." *Organizational Behavior and Human Performance,* Vol. 20, No 2 (December 1977), pp. 238–252. This article points out the differences in rater judgments that can come about even when the same performance is being rated. Interjudge agreement among the experts was rather high, but there were some errors caused by the halo effect, being too lenient or severe, or using a restricted range for rating. It is important to recognize that these factors can cause different competence ratings for the same performance.

Cherrington, David. J. *The Work Ethic: Working Values and Values That Work.* New York: AMACOM, 1981. This book examines the work ethic of today's workers and suggests ways of developing proper work values, keeping them, and making them grow. Techniques are provided for defining negative work attitudes and changing them into positive ones. Career development, job enrichment, teaching job values, and worker satisfaction and productivity are all discussed.

Cooper, Cary L., ed. *Behavioral Problems in Organizations.* Englewood Cliffs, N.J.: Prentice-Hall, 1979. This is a collection of original contributions by leading people in their fields that explores a number of serious human behavior dilemmas at work. The authors examine such concepts as career development, personal work relationships, decision-making capability, quality of working life, and job satisfaction versus job stress. Each chapter highlights specific problem areas, offers a number of possible solutions, and evaluates present organization efforts to handle behavioral problems.

Dailey, Charles A., and Madsen, Ann M. *How to Evaluate People in Business: The Track Record Method of Making Correct Judgments.* New York: McGraw-Hill, 1980. This text suggests that observable performance should be used as the primary method to evaluate people in organizations. Both intermediate and long-term tangible results need to be reviewed in order to accurately assess an individual's true worth to the organization, and other, more subjective methods should be avoided.

Davis, Hiram S. *Productivity Accounting.* Philadelphia: The Wharton School, 1980. This reprint of the 1955 classic examines methods to define and measure worker productivity. The book can help in assessing areas of low productivity in the organization.

Davis, Keith. *Human Behavior at Work.* 6th ed. New York: McGraw-Hill, 1977. This best-seller presents the essentials of understanding human behavior at work in an easily readable style. Cases and many examples highlight important concepts.

Dunham, Randall B., and Hawk, Donald L. "The Four-Day/Forty-Hour Week: Who Wants It?" *Academy of Management Journal,* Vol. 20, No. 4 (December 1977), pp. 644–655. Attitudes toward 4-day/40-hour work schedules were studied for 1,041 mid-level exempt personnel who worked a 5-day/40-hour schedule. Results indicate that workers most likely to want a 4-day/40-hour week are young, with a low job level, low tenure, and low income. They have relatively low general satisfaction, low satisfaction with pay and the kind of work, and low company identification. Finally, their perception of the work group and the total organization climate is somewhat negative.

Ewing, David W. *Freedom Inside the Organization: Bringing Civil Liberties to the Workplace.* New York: McGraw-Hill, 1977. Written by the editor of the *Harvard Business Review,* this book is a must for executives. It points out how employee rights can be protected without giving in to entitlement claims and is important for understanding how to prevent these claims from serving as a mask for incompetence.

Fiedler, Fred E., and Chemers, Martin M. *Leadership and Effective Management.* Glenview, Ill.: Scott, Foresman and Co., 1974. The authors discuss some of the studies made of the relationship between leadership attributes and leadership status. The book shows what a leader must do to avoid incompetence.

Hall, Jay. "To Achieve or Not: The Manager's Choice." *California Management Review,* Vol. 18, No. 4 (Summer 1976), pp. 5–17. This article is based on a study of more than 16,000 managers, in 50 organizations of various sizes, over a five-year period. The author contends that a substantial relationship exists between managerial achievement and managerial practices. Factors such as a manager's motivational profile and attained level of interpersonal competence, which influence the manager's achievement, are directly under the control of the manager. Thus, according to the author, the level of achievement of managerial effectiveness is a matter of the manager's choice.

Hershey, Paul, and Blanchard, Kenneth H. "Life Cycle Theory of Leadership." *Training and Development Journal,* May 1969, pp. 26–34. The authors state the theory that maturity of subordinates should be considered in determining a leadership style. The authors' theory derives its title from the notion that as individuals reach psychological maturity, which is characteristic of later phases of the life cycle, they require less structure and less consideration from their superiors. For example, research and development scientists are usually more "psychologically mature" than assembly-line workers are. Therefore, they require less consideration and less structure. The authors also discuss how a manager can apply this theory to help subordinates "mature" and decrease the level of interaction and supervision necessary.

————. *Management of Organizational Behavior.* 3d ed. Englewood Cliffs, N.J.: Prentice-Hall, 1977. Motivation, behavior, and leadership are stressed in this book. Aids and understanding are provided for predicting, directing, changing, and controlling future employee behavior.

Inskeep, Gordon C. "What's Right—and Wrong—With Today's Young Managers." *Advanced Management Journal,* Vol. 41, No. 2 (Spring 1976), pp. 57–64. The author has based his writing on a series of interviews with high-level executives of 30 U.S. business organizations on what makes a successful manager in today's business environment. A comparison is made of today's managers with managers in similar positions approximately 20 years ago. The author concludes by offering a list of generalized suggestions and recommendations on what a manager should do to be successful.

Ivancevich, John M., and McMahon, Timothy J. "A Study of Task-Goal Attributes, Higher Order Need Strength, and Performance." *Academy of Management Journal,* Vol. 20, No. 4 (December 1977), pp. 552–563. Explores how six task-goal attributes are related to various effort and quantitative performance measures. From a random sample of 161 skilled technicians, 141 of them completed questionnaires pertaining to goal setting and were rated on performance by their supervisors. The initial analyses found little consistent relationship between the task-goal attributes and performance measures. When higher order need strength was introduced as a moderator, the relations between task-goal attributes and performance measures became clearer. Respondents with strong higher order need strengths said that goal challenge, feedback, and goal clarity were related to effort toward quality, reduced unexcused absenteeism and service complaints, and improved safety.

Justis, Robert T. "Leadership Effectiveness: A Contingency Approach." *Academy of Management Journal,* Vol. 18, No. 1 (March 1975), pp. 160–166. This article examines the factors upon which successful and effective leadership are based. The author describes an experiment that involved 84 male undergraduate students at Indiana University. His hypothesis is that two independent variables—reward dependence and leader competence—have both direct and interaction effects on a follower's behavior and therefore on leadership effectiveness.

Katz, R. L. "Skills of an Effective Administrator." *Harvard Business Review,* Vol. 52, No. 5 (September–October 1974), pp. 90–102. This article was first published in *Harvard Business Review* in 1955, when many companies were trying to identify the personality traits of the ideal executive. Katz tried to take what he considered a more reasonable approach—what observable skills does an effective executive demonstrate?

Kotter, John P.; Faux, Victor A.; and McArthur, Charles. *Self-Assessment and Career Development.* Englewood Cliffs, N.J.: Prentice-Hall, 1978. This book can help managers understand the career planning process from a personal viewpoint. It covers the selection of an initial career path, the development of a strategy for getting the desired job, and the balancing of career and nonwork activities in an overall lifestyle.

Lawless, David J. *Organizational Behavior: The Psychology of Effective Management.* 2d ed. Englewood Cliffs, N.J.: Prentice-Hall, 1979. The author emphasizes individual and small-group processes and shows how to conduct in-house experiments and apply theories to increase employee satisfaction and improve work performance. He examines individuals within the structural context in which they work, focusing especially on group dynamics.

Livingston, J. S. "Myth of the Well-Educated Manager." *Harvard Business Review,* Vol. 49, No. 1 (January–February 1971), pp. 79–89. Livingston is a professor of business administration at Harvard who postulates that what students learn about management in graduate school does not equip them to build successful careers in business.

Formal management training seeks to develop problem-solving and decision-making skills, or "respondent behavior," when what is really needed is *operant behavior.*" This can be developed only by doing what needs to be done.

Mackenzie, R. Alec. *The Time Trap: How to Get More Done in Less Time.* New York: AMACOM, 1972. This excellent short book deals with one of the biggest causes of incompetence: wasting time. It explains the importance of managing yourself, planning your work, getting organized, blocking interruptions, handling decisions, delegating, and working with subordinates.

McNulty, J. F. "Secrets of the Successful General Manager." *Nation's Business,* Vol. 54, No. 5 (May 1971), pp. 42–48. The author lists characteristics of successful general managers and describes development of potential general managers.

Mintzberg, Henry. *The Nature of Managerial Work.* Englewood Cliffs, N.J.: Prentice-Hall, 1980. This is a reissue of the 1973 edition of Mintzberg's popular work, which is based on interviews with many managers and examines the roles a manager plays. Emphasis is placed on the essential characteristics of managers' work—with whom they work, when, where, and for how long.

Morse, John J., and Wagner, Francis R. "Measuring the Processes of Managerial Effectiveness." *Academy of Management Journal,* Vol. 21, No. 1 (1978), pp. 23–35. The authors begin by examining three components of the management process: (1) the person—the characteristics and traits of individual managers; (2) the product—organizational results such as profit maximization and productivity; and (3) the process—the manager's on-the-job behavior and activities. They contend that previous attempts at constructing an instrument to measure managerial performance have focused on the person and the product while paying insufficient attention to the process, partly because it is still unclear what constitutes effective managerial behavior. They conclude that any measure of managerial effectiveness must identify and judge specific, observable behavior that leads to the accomplishment of the organization's goals.

Northrup, Herbert R.; Cowin, Ronald M.; and Vanden Plas, Lawrence G. *The Objective Selection of Supervisors.* Philadelphia: The Wharton School, 1978. This book examines industry's informal practices, the assessment center method, and Honeywell Corporation's performance standards system of selecting supervisors. The authors discuss the law and new uniform guidelines for employee selection procedures.

————, and Larson, John A. *The Impact of the AT&T–EEO Consent Decree*. Philadelphia: The Wharton School, 1979. This careful analysis utilizes both detailed statistics and field interviews of how the race and sex quotas required by the consent decree affect AT&T's labor force and operations. Implications are discussed both for the company and for national labor policy.

Peter, Laurence J., and Hull, Raymond. *The Peter Principle: Why Things Always Go Wrong*. New York: William Morrow & Co., 1969. This classic book explains how people rise to their level of incompetence in organizations. An understanding of this book is very helpful for identifying and correcting incompetence. It is especially important to note that organizations may be doing people a disservice by pressuring them to take jobs at higher levels when such promotions are not in the person's and organization's best interest.

Rawls, D. J., and Rawls, J. R. "The Latent Manager: Identifying Him." *California Management Review*, Vol. 13, No. 2 (Winter 1971), pp. 24–27. This is a study of a group of successful and a group of unsuccessful executives in the same company compared with a group of potentially successful and a group of potentially unsuccessful executives still in college.

Robbins, Stephen P. *Organizational Behavior: Concepts and Controversies*. Englewood Cliffs, N.J.: Prentice-Hall, 1979. Using a building block model of three levels of study—the individual, group, and organization structure—the author examines factors that influence employee productivity, absenteeism, turnover, and satisfaction. Special attention is devoted to current developments in areas of increasing importance, such as values, reward structures, power, conflict, and political forces in organizations.

Sayles, Leonard R. *Leadership: What Effective Managers Really Do and How They Do It*. New York: McGraw-Hill, 1979. The author examines the essential skills of managers and compares these skills to what managers actually do, with a strong focus on organization and systems. He points out why managers so often have difficulty in actually articulating what they really do and why they do it.

Schaub, Alfred R. "Managerial Facades." *Personnel Administrator*, Vol. 34 (Summer 1971), pp. 33–37. Blake and Mouton describe the managerial facade as deceptive behavior intended to act as a front or cover for the real approach or true intentions. Schaub examines this in light of the fact that some managers have a conscious and purposeful desire to control and manipulate people in their quest for personal status and power. Managers who are fearful and insecure in their management role often use facades as defenses against failure and loss of status. Since harm can result to both organizations and individuals through the use of these defensive devices, the author suggests replacing them with managerial and corporate integrity.

Shea, Gordon F. *The New Employee: Developing a Productive Human Resource.* Reading, Mass.: Addison-Wesley, 1981. Dealing effectively with the new employee is extremely important in order to prevent problems of incompetence from occurring later on. If organizations did more to orient new employees properly and integrate them into the organization, problems of incompetence would be substantially reduced.

Skinner, Wickerman, and Sasser, Earl W. "Managers with Impact: Versatile and Inconsistent." *Harvard Business Review,* Vol. 55, No. 6 (November–December 1977), pp. 140–148. The authors examine the relative success of two types of managers: those who are consistent in their approach to problem solving and those who analyze situations and vary their approach accordingly. In view of the variety of situations confronting managers, an inflexible or consistent approach to problem solving is usually less successful than a problem-oriented or flexible approach. Supporting information from the article was collected from 31 case studies of various industries and businesses at all levels of management.

Stead, Betty Ann. "Stereotypes, Statistics, and Some Surprises." *Forbes,* Vol. 113, No. 10 (May 15, 1974), pp. 118–124. This article is based on a *Forbes* survey of the characteristics of chief executive officers of 600 large, publicly held corporations.

_____. *Women in Management.* Englewood Cliffs, N.J.: Prentice-Hall, 1978. This book features 38 articles focusing on problems, solutions, and achievements of women in attaining responsible managerial positions.

Stogdill, Ralph M. *Handbook of Leadership.* New York: The Free Press, 1974. This book is an organized inventory of all the published research findings on leadership. It is a source book on who did the research, what results were obtained, and what conclusions can be drawn from the accumulated evidence. The book explores small-group processes, organization theory, and power.

Tannenbaum, R., and Schmidt, W. H. "How to Choose a Leadership Pattern." *Harvard Business Review,* Vol. 36, No. 2 (March–April 1958), pp. 95–101. This article utilizes a continuum of leadership behavior to illustrate the range of styles employed by different managers. The mix of formal authority and subordinate freedom which is characteristic of a manager's behavior determine his style. After a thorough discussion of this continuum, the authors examine the forces that determine which type of leadership a manager develops, such as forces within the manager, forces within the subordinates, and situational forces. Suggestions for establishing a style appropriate for the individual manager's personality, training, and situation conclude the article.

————. "Traits That Will Take You to the Top." *Nation's Business*, Vol. 60, No. 9 (September 1972), pp. 70–71. The authors survey successful businessmen's perceptions of good and bad traits that will either propel managers to the top or hold them down.

Weber, Max. *The Theory of Social and Economic Organizations.* Translated by A. M. Henderson and Talcott Parsons. New York: The Free Press, 1947. This is a translation of Weber's seminal work on bureaucracy. Weber sets out the required action and supporting theory needed to establish a bureaucratic organization.

Winstanley, Nathan B. "Performance Appraisals and Management Development: A Systems Approach." *Conference Board Record*, Vol. 13, No. 3 (March 1976), pp. 55–59. The author proposes a managerial performance-appraisal system to provide information for decisions affecting training, development, promotion, and salary administration in business organizations. The system described would be implemented in three phases: (1) improvement of conditions for accurate measurement, (2) application of the new instrument of measurement, and (3) multiple uses of the assessment obtained. The actual evalution process would be based on factors such as present job performance and the manager's talents (performance skill and motivation skill).

Index

Page numbers set in italic fall within case histories.